What Were They Thinking?

Really Bad Ideas throughout History

Bruce Felton

The Globe Pequot Press

GUILFORD, CONNECTICUT

Text and art design: Casey Shain
Art research: Sue Preneta
Images © 2003 www.clipart.com

Library of Congress Cataloging-in-Publication Data
Felton, Bruce.
  What were they thinking?: really bad ideas throughout history.
    p. cm.
  ISBN 0-7627-2667-9
    1. History—Miscellanea. 2. History—Humor. 3. History—Errors, inventions, etc. I. Title.

D10.F39 2003
902'.07—dc21   2003044923

Manufactured in the United States of America
First Edition/First Printing

What Were They Thinking?

Really Bad Ideas throughout History

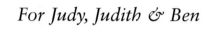

For Judy, Judith & Ben

Acknowledgments

This is a better book than it might otherwise have been thanks to the comments, contributions, and support of the following people: Madelyn Larsen, Josh Rosenberg, Mary Norris, Russell Hoffman, Peter Lange, Judith Felton, Ben Felton, Ed Kagen, and Mark Fowler. I am grateful to them all.

Contents

Introduction

What could Tommy Dorsey have been thinking in 1940 when he installed his orchestra in the Monkey House of the Philadelphia Zoo to perform a concert for the apes?

Could artist Rudy Giacomo have been serious when he proposed building a 39-mile manicotti around Manhattan Island?

Was the Nobel Prize Committee on drugs when they conferred the 1949 prize in Medicine on the man who perfected the lobotomy?

Such are the questions that arise whenever we contemplate a truly ghastly idea. Depending on their nature, scope, and impact, bad ideas amuse, horrify, and surprise us. But most striking is their power to bewilder: What could possibly have prompted Plennie Wingo to walk backwards from Santa Monica to Istanbul? Why in God's name would baseball great Ted Williams have agreed to let his son store his earthly remains in the high-tech equivalent of an Amana freezer?

Admittedly, *What Were They Thinking?* is short on answers. Within these pages, my aim has not been to probe the motives behind bad ideas, but simply to recount and, above all, revel in them.

First, of course, they had to be identified. No problem there: Bad ideas are *everywhere*—they're the tile grout of history, the crabgrass of civilization, poking up through every crack in our thinking. According to government statistics, they outnumber good ideas 600 to 1. Indeed, for every bad idea lovingly recorded in these pages, there are dozens, equally worthy, that simply had to be excluded. Biosphere, Tonya Harding, the designated-hitter rule, the color-coding of terrorist threat levels, telemarketing, the Crusades, the butterfly ballot, Prohibition, the attack on Fort Sumter, *Ishtar*, Adam's apple fixation, the 1975 Metric Conversion Act, the O. J. acquittal, genetically engineered foods, Attorney General John Ashcroft's naked-statue phobia, the hiring of the Hell's Angels as security guards at Altamont. . . . The harsh reality is that it's only encyclopedia editors who are immune from the tyranny of word counts and allowed to cover the waterfront; compendium writers are faced with Solomonic decisions at every turn.

Still, I've tried to cram several hundred harebrained schemes, fool notions, and misguided obsessions both grandiose and mundane into *What Were They Thinking?* In these pages you'll read about one man's effort to market a board game based on the Lebanese civil war . . . an Iowa State University professor's proposal to blow up the moon . . . and Senator Victor Biaka-Boda's ill-considered campaign trip to the Ivory Coast hinterlands. (Not only did he lose the election, his constituents ate him.)

Astute readers will note that, with apologies to Tolstoy, every unsound idea is unsound in its own way. At one extreme there are carefully premeditated lapses in common sense and good judgment, such as the public display of a human being in the Monkey House of the Bronx Zoo in 1904. At the other extreme are spur-of-the-moment, acting-on-impulse bad ideas, such as Floyd Malacek's attempt to jump Minnesota's 40-foot-wide Lacque Park River on a power lawn mower while thousands watched. (He missed by 35 feet.)

Another way to categorize bad ideas is by how long it takes for their impact to register. Some bad ideas look, sound, and smell bad right from the get-go—the grassroots push to make Sicily the forty-ninth American state, or Cecil Rhodes' lifelong campaign to make the entire world a British colony, for example. Others take their time flowering—anywhere from a few minutes to several years. At first glance Cleveland mayor Ralph J. Perk's decision to make a goodwill appearance at an industrial trade show seemed a perfectly legitimate idea—that is, until someone handed him a welding torch and he accidentally set his head on fire with it.

And sculptor Horatio Greenough was no doubt all smiles and self-congratulation when he envisioned a larger-than-life statue of George Washington, only to watch in dismay as the marble monstrosity sank through the floorboards of the U.S. Capitol.

Today you can see Greenough's magnum opus displayed prominently in—where else?—Washington, D.C., cradle of liberty, and incubator of some of the most gloriously bad ideas ever to spring forth from the human mind. It was here that the Bureau of the Mint approved the designs for the Susan B. Anthony dollar, America's most reviled and useless coin . . . intelligence operatives hatched a plan to make Hitler's mustache fall out by covertly seasoning his food with estrogen . . . and a future president admitted having smoked *cannabis sativa* but denied that he had ever inhaled.

What could they possibly have been thinking?

Bad Ideas in American Politics and Government

Wackos on the bench.

Two U.S. presidents appointed madmen to the Supreme Court.

When John Jay retired as chief justice in 1795, President George Washington named jurist John Rutledge to fill the spot. Although Rutledge had been acting strangely since his wife's death three years before, Washington apparently considered a touch of dementia insufficient reason to keep a man off the highest court in the land.

Rutledge didn't take long to bite the hand that appointed him. When the Jay Treaty was signed, giving preferential treatment to the North, the South Carolina–born Rutledge railed publicly against Washington in such abusive and insulting language that even his supporters were shocked.

Rutledge managed to serve a full term as chief justice before the Senate got around to voting him out on grounds of "intermittent insanity." As if to vindicate their judgment, Rutledge immediately attempted to drown himself. On his death in 1800, one associate said, "His mind was frequently too much deranged as to be in a great measure deprived of his sense."

Pennsylvania attorney Henry Baldwin was appointed to the court by his crony, President Andrew Jackson, in 1829. A workaholic long before the word was coined, he would go weeks with little sleep or food, surviving on a steady diet of small black Mexican cigars. According to H. L. Carson in his *History of the Supreme Court of the United States*, Baldwin bickered incessantly with his fellow justices, loved playing malicious practical jokes, and "was occasionally violent and ungovernable in his conduct on the bench." A compulsive speculator, he went seriously into debt, growing para-noid and reclusive and alienating his closest associates. When he died in 1844, the few friends of his left had to take up a collection to bury him.

Honk if you love radiation sickness, birth defects, and the end of civilization as we know it.

The Nevada state legislature authorized a new license plate in 2002 depict-ing a mushroom cloud from an atomic explosion. The design, awarded first prize in a competition sponsored by the Nevada Test Site Historical Foundation, symbolized the 928 nuclear-weapons tests conducted in the Nevada desert from 1945 through 1992. "It was meant to honor former workers at the test site and the role it played in winning the Cold War," said a foundation spokesman.

"I didn't inhale."

—*Presidential candidate Bill Clinton, on being asked if he smoked marijuana as a university student*

But the fallout was not altogether positive. "I find it extremely tasteless," said Denise Nelson, director of Support and Education for Radiation Victims. "Even Germany had enough con-science to not put a gas chamber on their license plates."

Ultimately the plate proved something of a bomb itself: In the aftermath of the September 11, 2001, terrorist attacks, the Nevada Department of Motor Vehicles rejected the concept, noting that "any reference on a license plate to weapons of mass destruction is inappropriate and would likely offend our citizens."

Thousands flee as mutant cheese attacks White House.

In 1835 an upstate New York dairy farmer named Thomas Meacham decided to show his support for President Andrew Jackson by sending him an immense wheel of cheese.

For more than a week, Meacham collected the milk produced by his 150 cows, turning it into 1,400 pounds of prime cheddar. He shaped it into a wheel 4 feet across and 2 feet thick, which he wrapped in muslin and girdled with a tricolor bunting featuring patriotic slogans and representations of each of the states.

The mammoth cholesterol bomb was carried to Washington on a flag-draped cart pulled by twenty-four horses. For the next two years, it aged quietly at room temperature in a White House vestibule. Then on February 22, 1837—ten days before Jackson was to depart the presidency—the cheese was brought out and served at a Washington's Birthday bash at the executive mansion.

Shops and businesses shut down for the day. Congressmen, cabinet members, ambassadors, and socialites showed up; so did thousands of ordinary citizens. "Mr. Van Buren was there to eat cheese," reported one Washington newspaper. "Mr. Webster was there to eat cheese; Mr. Woodbury, Colonel Benton, Mr. Dickerson—all were there to eat cheese . . . All you heard was cheese; all you smelled was cheese."

In fact there was cheese everywhere—staining the carpets, ground into the parquet floorboards, smeared on the walls, rubbed into the drapes. Guests left with crumbs of the stuff in their hair and in their pockets; it is said that the stink of overripe cheddar could be smelled for blocks. Inside the White House the odor didn't fade till well into the Van Buren Administration.

Deaf, no. Dumb, definitely.

As the noise from Ohio's Toledo Express Airport continued to exceed FAA standards and area residents' tolerance, Mayor Carty Finkbeiner suggested a novel solution in 1995: move in deaf people. "There may be people out there interested in living in a nice home if the noise factor was not going to be a problem," he said at a staff meeting.

"Thank you, Governor Evidence."

—*President Richard Nixon, addressing Washington State governor Daniel Evans in a speech during the Watergate hearings*

A lot of people thought they weren't hearing right. Advocates for the disabled jumped all over the mayor, labeling him biased and insensitive. A spokesman for Barrier Free Toledo said the proposal was comparable to "saying let the blind work at night because they can't see."

At a press conference a few days later, a weepy Mayor Finkbeiner apologized. "Nobody intended to be insensitive," he said. "My only words were that it was an interesting idea."

Fuzzy fruit. Fuzzier thinking.

DBCP is a potent insecticide that kills bugs that even *think* about bothering fruit that's been sprayed with it. Unfortunately, eating it, handling it, and, perhaps, even *reading* about it makes male humans sterile. Indeed, the Food and Drug Administration banned DBCP in 1977, whereupon many peach growers went bananas.

"If . . . sterility is the main concern, couldn't workers who were old enough that they no longer wanted children [manufacture DBCP] voluntarily?" said National Peach Council spokesman Robert K. Phillips. "Some might volunteer for such work posts as an alternative to planned surgery for a vasectomy . . . or as a means of getting around religious bans on birth control when they want no more children."

Israel on the Niagara.

If one early American Zionist had had his way, Israel would be located near Niagara Falls.

In 1820, Mordecai Manual Noah, editor of the *National Advocate,* tried to talk New York's state legislature into designating Grand Island, a piece of densely forested real estate north of Buffalo and the falls, as a "city of refuge" for Jews. The state nixed the idea, but five years later Noah got his friend Samuel Leggett to buy 2,444 acres of the island for the same purpose, and solicited investment from European Jews as well. Publicly Noah waxed eloquently about the importance of carving out a Jewish homeland on American soil. In private he drooled about raking in "an immense profit" from the plan.

The dedication of what Noah proclaimed "the Jewish State of Ararat" took place on September 15, 1825, at St. Paul's Episcopal Church in Buffalo. (It would have been held on Grand Island, but there weren't enough boats to ferry all the guests.) Having ordained himself "Governor and Judge of Israel," Noah dressed the part, appearing in a magisterial red robe trimmed with ermine. (It turned out to be a Richard III costume, borrowed from a local theater company.) The festivities were attended by public officials; local clergy; officers of various fraternal lodges, including the Masons and the Knights Templar; and the Seneca Indian chief Red Jacket.

In his dedicatory remarks, Noah decried polygamy, said flattering things about Native Americans (whom he believed were descended from the Tribes of Israel), and levied a tax of one Spanish dollar on every Jew in the world to defray the cost of getting the colony running. He never had the chutzpah to collect so much as a nickel, nor did a single Jew ever settle in his tree-covered wasteland. Politicians jumped on him "for swindling the wealthy Jews of Europe," and Noah quickly turned his attention to other pursuits. In 1833 all of Grand Island was bought for a song by a land developer, and in 1852 it was incorporated as a town. Of its 18,000 present-day inhabitants, barely a handful are Jews.

Ecology? Hogwash!

Logging companies applauded in 2002 when President George W. Bush appointed Allan Fitzsimmons to head the Interior Department's wildfire prevention program. But pygmy rats, sand skinks, and other endangered species started thinking about increasing their life insurance.

As head of Balanced Resource Solutions, a Woodbridge, Virginia, consulting firm, Fitzsimmons had authored a number of articles and monographs denying the existence of ecosystems and suggesting that there are worse things than letting endangered species die out. If every one of the 1,202 species on the Fish and Wildlife Service's endangered and threatened list "were to become extinct tomorrow," he said, "it would be . . . disconcerting, but would not constitute a crisis." Not surprisingly, his views made environmentalists nervous. "How can a man who doesn't understand ecological systems and community values for wildlife run a program that's supposed to protect forests and communities?" asked John McCarthy, a spokesman for the Idaho Conservation League.

How to stamp out woodchucks.

New Hampshire legislators once tried to wipe out the state's woodchuck population by offering a bounty for every woodchuck killed. They took back the offer when it threatened to wipe out the state treasury.

The bounty, which became law on September 11, 1883, was established on the strength of a report submitted by the New Hampshire Legislative Woodchuck Committee.

"[The woodchuck] is absolutely destitute of any interesting qualities," the report observed. "In some parts of the State it is found necessary to shovel a path through the woodchucks to reach the barns." Throughout New Hampshire, woodchucks were despised by farmers and townspeople alike as notorious despoilers of crops and clover fields. Anyone killing one and presenting the tail as proof to a town selectman was entitled to a payment of 10 cents.

In 1884, the bounty's first full year in operation, only 339 payments were made. But in 1885 the kill count sky-rocketed to 122,065, and state finance officials panicked. Treasurer Solon A. Carter called for the immediate repeal of the law, and on August 11 the legisla-ture obliged, although payments contin-ued to be made as late as 1888. Since then, the whacking of woodchucks in New Hampshire has been on a strictly not-for-profit basis.

"Hawaii has always been a very pivotal role in the Pacific. It is *in* the Pacific. It is a part of the United States that is an island that's right here."

—*Vice President Dan Quayle during a 1989 visit to Hawaii*

A "No" vote for Susan B. Anthony.

Only the most churlish antifeminist could object to minting a coin in honor of woman's rights pioneer Susan B. Anthony. But the silver dollar issued in her likeness is universally regarded as an abomination.

The Bureau of the Mint produced 857 million Anthony dollars in 1979, driven by egalitarian zeal and a conviction that the coin would save $50 million a year by eliminating the need to replace soiled and tattered paper notes. But silver dollars have never been popular in the United States, and the undersized "Susies," easily confused with quarters, were especially despised. They still crop up from time to time, but just try handing one to the checkout guy at the 7-Eleven; he'll look as if you've smacked him with a dead ferret.

It quickly became evident that the mint had a numismatic disaster on its hands. *The Washington Post* called the Anthony dollar "a federal white elephant"; columnist Jack Anderson pronounced it "a costly fiasco." A year after the coin's debut, production was halted, with 364 million Anthony dollars still in the Treasury Department vaults, never to see the light of day.

Even so the defunct coin retained its power to enrage and annoy for years to come. In 1984 residents of Skaneateles, New York, clashed with a local tour-boat line over its practice of allowing its buses to idle noisily in the town center until the tour was over and the patrons were ready to be picked up. In response the company rounded up as many Anthony dollars as it could find and used them to pay employees and make change. The coins were soon everywhere.

Retaliation wasn't the point, said tour operator Peter Wiles; he simply wanted to demonstrate "in an unobtrusive way" how much money he was bringing into the town. But to the people of Skaneateles, the coins were as unobtrusive as an infestation of crop-eating beetles and more unwelcome than a fleet of idling buses. They redoubled their efforts to shut Wiles down.

What—me, a spy??!

During the Cold War, it was no secret that the United States and the Soviet Union spied on each other. But when a U.S. high-altitude U-2 reconnaissance plane was shot down in May 1960 over Soviet territory and its pilot taken prisoner, Washington asserted that the U-2 was merely a fancy weather plane gone astray.

It was a lie, of course—and one the Americans should have known they could never hope to pull off. Interrogated by his captors, pilot Francis Gary Powers admitted he was a CIA spy and that he had been photographing military installations, not cumulus fractus clouds. Soviet premier Nikita Khrushchev hit the ceiling, blistering at America's "aggressive acts." With Washington's game exposed, Secretary of State Christian Herter conceded that the United States had been involved in "extensive aerial surveillance" over the Soviet Union, but only to deter "a surprise attack." That, too, was a lie.

Two weeks later, President Eisenhower publicly took "full responsibility for approving all the various programs undertaken by our government to secure and evaluate military intelligence."

Though his candor was refreshing, the damage had been done. Khrushchev broke up a four-power peace conference in Paris the day after it opened, calling the Americans "thief-like" and "cowardly," and withdrew his invitation to Eisenhower to visit the Soviet Union. Powers was convicted of espionage by a Soviet court and sentenced to ten years in prison. (He served two.) And U.S.–Soviet relations, already strained, suffered a devastating blow.

> **"I guess I should warn you: If I turn out to be particularly clear, you've probably misunderstood what I said."**
>
> —*Federal Reserve Board chairman Alan Greenspan*

Dirty money.

In a gross misreading of popular sensibilities, the U.S. Mint once circulated a coin bearing the likeness of a half-naked woman. The public objected so strenuously that the coin was withdrawn.

In 1916 the Treasury Department commissioned sculptor Hermon MacNeil to create a more contemporary look for the admittedly staid-looking "Liberty Head" quarter, which had been introduced in 1892. MacNeil's design featured a full frontal view of Miss Liberty in a diaphanous negligee, her right breast and right thigh completely exposed.

The uproar began as soon as the coin hit the streets. Thousands of outraged citizens wrote their congressmen and the Treasury Department to denounce the monetary lewdness. Anthony Comstock, self-appointed custodian of public morals and founder of the Society for the Suppression of Vice, was particularly vocal on the subject. There could be no possible argument, he said, for any form of currency that "showed the bared nipple and areola of an adult female."

"Mr. Lincoln is already beaten. He cannot be reelected."

—Horace Greeley (1864)

The following year Congress asked MacNeil to revise his design. But rather than explicitly address Miss Liberty's undress, the lawmaker requested that the coin be made more aesthetically appealing and easier to stack.

MacNeil obliged, also covering Liberty's breast and neck with a kind of chain-mail bra—an absurd anachronism—and chastely draping her thigh. Now properly attired, the Liberty quarter remained quietly in circulation until 1930.

Scrapping the Liberty Bell.

The Liberty Bell, which hangs in Philadelphia's Independence Hall, is among America's most hallowed relics. But that didn't stop the city from trying to sell it for scrap.

Cast in 1753 and installed in Philadelphia's Pennsylvania State House, the Liberty Bell became an instant legend when it tolled the signing of the Declaration of Independence in 1776. When the Revolution came to town, the bell was packed in mothballs and moved upstate to Allentown for safekeeping. It was brought back in 1781 and rung regularly to herald meetings and public ceremonies. But after the state legislature was relocated to Lancaster and the U.S. capital moved to Washington, the bell fell into disuse.

In 1828 the Philadelphia town fathers decided it was time to refurbish the State House, now known as Independence Hall. Along with plastering and rewallpapering, they decided to junk the Liberty Bell, now worn with age, and commissioned a Germantown, Pennsylvania, bell maker named John Wilbank to cast a replacement. He offered a $400 trade-in on the old bell, as if it were a used Buick. The city fathers jumped at the deal.

Luckily, Wilbank discovered it would cost more than that to remove and melt down the 2,000-pound bell. Instead, he gave it back to the city, which had the good sense, this time, to preserve it rather than throw it away.

The only time Michael Dukakis was ever mistaken for a heavyweight.

From a correction in the *Fitchburg-Leominster* (Massachusetts) *Sentinel and Enterprise*: "Due to a typing error, Gov. Dukakis was incorrectly identified in the third paragraph as Mike Tyson."

America's silliest coin.

If loose pennies jangling in your pocket drive you crazy, be thankful that Congress had the good sense to table a "midget-coin" bill brought before it in 1935. Inspired by Secretary of the Treasury Henry Morgenthau, the law would have required the minting of a new coin called the mill—worth exactly one-tenth of a cent. Not even the world's most closefisted tipper would have had much use for such a denomination.

Actually, the mill, "of which one thousand shall be equal to the federal dollar," had first been proposed by Congress nearly two centuries earlier. British lawmakers tried to push through a mill-bill of their own in the 1890s, with the denomination representing one thousandth of a pound. (Ten mills would equal one "victoria.") Luckily, neither the U.S. nor British government has ever actually minted a mill, although that didn't stop many American towns from levying taxes in mills well into the twentieth century.

Am I missing something?

Four less-than-inspiring state mottoes:

1. **Washington:** "By and by."
2. **New Mexico:** "It grows as it goes."
3. **Maryland:** "Manly deeds, womanly words."
4. **Michigan:** "If you seek a pleasant peninsula, look around you."

Seward's real folly.

As every grade-schooler knows, Secretary of State William Seward took a lot of heat for squandering $7 million on Alaska in 1867. But Seward's real folly occurred in 1861, when he tried to get the United States into a war with France and Spain for no other reason than to avert a Civil War back home.

In a memorandum addressed to President Lincoln on April 1, less than a month into the new administration, Seward pointed out that the nation "was yet without a policy, either domestic or foreign," and that it was the president's duty to draft one immediately. Seward's presumption in lecturing his boss on how to rule was outlandish, though hardly out of character. But his next idea must have made Lincoln think the letter was a bad April Fools' joke.

"FDR will be a one-term president."

—*Mark Sullivan, political commentator (1935)*

Spain and France, Seward noted, had lately been treating their colonies in the Americas rather shabbily, and while it wasn't really of U.S. concern, he urged that agents be sent "into Canada, Mexico and Central America to rouse a vigorous continental spirit of independence . . . against European intervention. And if satisfactory explanations are not received from Spain and France, [we] would convene Congress and declare war against them."

A war with Spain, Seward argued, would give the North and South a common enemy and keep the Union from disintegrating. Moreover, the United States would probably be able to seize a few European-owned islands in the bargain.

Lincoln answered the memo with more grace than it deserved, assuring the upstart secretary that he—Lincoln—was firmly in command. But he let Seward's bizarre plan to pick a fight with Spain and France pass without comment.

They've certainly sewn up the asshole vote.

Casting its vote for gender equality, the Woonsocket, Rhode Island, City Council unanimously approved an ordinance renaming manholes "personholes" in 1978.

Not surprisingly, a lot of people on both sides of the war for women's rights thought the lawmakers had gone overboard. Two weeks later the council changed the term back to manholes.

"We are sick and tired of the adverse publicity we were getting," council president Gaston Ayotte Jr. confessed. "All over the United States people were laughing at Woonsocket personholes." Ayotte said he had been particularly hurt by the gibes of a Washington columnist who had telephoned to interview him about "the personhole vote."

"He kind of made fun of me," Ayotte said.

Goat-Gland Brinkley for governor.

In the 1920s and 1930s, the voters of Kansas came frighteningly close to electing John Brinkley governor. A swindler, charlatan, and outspoken fascist, Brinkley had never served a day in any public office. What he had done was to make a fortune surgically implanting goat testicles into impotent men.

Though he billed himself as a doctor and tacked a string of degrees onto his signature, Brinkley's schooling consisted of little more than a brief stint in a meat-packing plant and a briefer one in the army (half of it spent under psychiatric observation). But it was all the qualification he needed to found the Brinkley Gland Hospital in Milford, Kansas.

Go ahead and laugh, but Brinkley found hard cash in limp libidos. Charging $750 to $1,500 per matched set of glands (the younger the goat, the higher the price), Brinkley attracted patients from all over the world. The Maharajah Thakou of Morvi made a special trip from India to be implanted; the publisher of the *Los Angeles Times* was so delighted with his new glands that he carried Brinkley's ads for free.

"Only Anglo-Saxons can govern themselves."

—*William Allen White, editor (1899)*

Brinkley thoughtfully used only Toggenberg goats; other breeds, he explained, "may give the patient a permanently goaty smell." At best the operation was a waste of money, time, and surgical thread; at worst it posed serious health risks to the recipient (not to mention the donor). But Brinkley miraculously dodged lawsuits while growing rich enough to purchase a fleet of limousines, three yachts, a private plane, a goat farm in Oklahoma, and radio station KFKB.

He used the station to promote his hospital and to read letters from ailing listeners. Sight unseen, he diagnosed everything from cancer to "elliptical epizootia," and prescribed one of fifty quack nostrums. Most were nothing more than diluted hydrochloric acid dyed blue. When the government shut him down, Brinkley bought a bigger station in Mexico.

By 1930 Brinkley's following rivaled that of FDR and Shirley Temple, and he ran for governor of Kansas three times. Incredibly, the voters turned out for him in droves, and on the third go-round, in 1932, he came within a hairsbreadth of defeating Alf Landon. Brinkley even polled thousands of write-in votes in neighboring Oklahoma, where he wasn't running for anything. A few more votes and the good people of Kansas would have elected themselves a governor who combined the talents of Huey Long, Jimmy Swaggart, and Dr. Mengele.

The fact is, Brinkley's politics were worse than his medicine. Though he never again ran for office, he generously bankrolled a number of homegrown fascist groups, including William Dudley Pelley's Silver Shirts—an Indiana clone of Hitler's Brown Shirts. He died in 1942, just after the Mexican government tore down his radio transmitter.

Badge of excellence.

The United States Consumer Product Safety Commission paid some $1,700 for 80,000 promotional buttons with the slogan "Think Toy Safety" in the 1970s. But the buttons turned out to be more of a menace than any toy ever concocted by the most socially irresponsible toy manufacturer. The metal tags had sharp, unrounded edges and metal tab fasteners that broke off easily and were a sure bet to be swallowed by orally aggressive children. Also, the buttons were coated with lead paint.

Much chagrined, the commission recalled the buttons with an eye to recycling them or just scuttling the lot.

A choice between hemlock and strychnine.

If you think the pickings were slim in the last presidential election—or in the one before that, or in the one before *that*—be glad you weren't around in 1872. The Democrats were in such pathetic disarray that they couldn't even manage to form their own ticket. Instead, they chose to back a Republican, shooting themselves squarely in the foot and paving the way for an election one wag described as a choice between "hemlock and strychnine."

The incumbent was Republican Ulysses S. Grant, whose first term had been marred by scandal and ineptitude. In May, a few months before the national nominating convention, the party's liberal wing broke off and went to Cincinnati to choose a candidate of their own. The man they picked was Horace Greeley, editor of the *New York Tribune*.

The Democrats were in even worse shape than the Republicans. At their convention the following month they couldn't come up with anyone to run. So, with an air of tired resignation, they ceded their support to Greeley, a life-long Republican who had once quipped, "All Democrats may not be rascals, but all rascals are Democrats."

Greeley was a great editor; as a candidate he was a joke. He gave the cartoonists a field day with his chin whiskers, nerdy clothes, and slouching gait; when he rambled on about the virtues of vegetarianism, prohibition, and utopia, he drew universal guffaws. He was also a firm believer in phrenology and went so far as to claim that railroad accidents might be prevented if engineers were hired according to the bumps on their head. Once a critic called him "a nincompoop without genius."

"Dewey is sure to be elected."

—Drew Pearson, columnist (1948)

"DEWEY DEFEATS TRUMAN"

—Chicago Tribune, November 4, 1948

Grant was no bargain either, but he was so sure of victory that he spent the summer relaxing by the sea, hardly bothering to campaign. Greeley ran hard, wearing himself into the ground and hating every minute of it. He told one associate he didn't know if he was running for the presidency or the penitentiary.

Not surprisingly, Grant clobbered Greeley, taking thirty states to the editor's six. Worse, when the editor tried to get his old *Tribune* job back, he was ridiculed on the front page and sent packing. His nerves shot, he died insane a month later. The Democrats didn't win a presidential election until 1884.

When Jefferson dissed the Federalists.

By 1796 Thomas Jefferson had had it with the Federalists, of whom President George Washington was the party leader. From where he sat, they were nothing but a gang of highborn elitists, pro-British, pro-business, and out of touch with ordinary people. Their only interest was in enlarging their own power base.

These were not especially radical sentiments. But they were incendiary, and Jefferson would have been wise to express them discreetly. He wasn't, and he wound up setting relations between his Republican party and the Federalists back years.

On April 24 Jefferson wrote a letter to Filippo Mazzei, an Italian merchant and friend from pre-independence days. In it he let his hair down about the "Anglican, monarchical and aristocratic" Federalists. Their antics, Jefferson wrote, "would give you a fever." Translation: They would make you sick.

Mazzei should have burned the letter. Instead, he leaked it to a Florence newspaper. A year later, in May 1797, the Mazzei letter, as it came to be called, appeared in Noah Webster's *New York Minerva*. Other papers picked up the story, and within days Jefferson had a full-blown scandal on his hands. Stung by Jefferson's comments, Washington stopped talking to him, and many other Federalists followed suit. It didn't help that Jefferson refused to discuss the matter publicly. The rift between the Federalists and Jefferson never healed, burdening him heavily during his presidency.

John and Tom's excellent adventure.

While serving as minister to France, Thomas Jefferson took two weeks off to visit his friend John Adams, who was the American envoy to Great Britain.

They visited Shakespeare's home at Stratford-on-Avon, where a chair that had belonged to the Bard caught their fancy. When the guards weren't looking, the two future presidents attacked the chair with pocket knives, carving off large slivers of wood to take as souvenirs.

A helluva town!

Crime, corruption, and urban decay had taken their toll on Hamilton, Ohio (pop. 65,000) when the City Council decided a bit of creative punctuation was all the town needed to perk things up. In 1986 the lawmakers voted to change the official spelling of Hamilton to Hamilton!

That's Hamilton! as in "Hamilton! is my kind of town," or "When in Hamilton! do as the Hamiltonians do." Official guidelines require that the exclamation point not be used with a question mark, lest an innocent query ("Where is Hamilton?") become an intended jibe ("Where is Hamilton!?").

The city spent more than $100,000 on a public relations campaign aimed at promoting the new name, boosting civic pride, and convincing businesses looking to relocate that "Hamilton! has it all." But not everyone got the point—or liked it.

In a *Hamilton Journal-News* opinion poll, forty-eight out of sixty-eight respondents said the ! was a crock of #@$?. According to longtime resident George Braegger, "it was not only a bad idea, it was stupid. The one who thought of it must be the one who suggested putting a fountain in the middle of our river." Another Hamiltonian, Ed Brown, said it was like grafting a shiny new Cadillac hood ornament onto a tired old Volkswagen. Ornament or no, "it's still a tired old Volkswagen," he said, "and it still stalls at every light."

Inconspicuously tucked between Dayton and Cincinnati, Hamilton! is the birthplace of William Dean Howells and the home of the National Women's Softball Tournament. It is also the nation's premier manufacturing center for coated paper, missile parts, food mixes, and safes. But no one has ever thought of it as Shangri-La, and even after the name modification, *American Demographic* magazine found Hamilton! to be among Ohio's most unlivable cities.

John Quincy Adams' New Deal.

John Quincy Adams had been president less than a year in 1825 when he delivered his first Annual Message to Congress. Adams, who dreamed of making America the center of western civilization, was abubble with plans for all sorts of government-backed programs. They included a national banking system; a federally endowed university; an observatory, overseen by a full-time astronomer; several weather stations; and a vast network of canals and turnpikes "multiplying and facilitating the communications and intercourse between distant regions." Russia, England, and France were light-years ahead of the United States in these areas, he told Congress. It was time for America to catch up.

But the country was not in a tax-and-spend mood, and Congress gagged on Adams' extravagant agenda. The legislators were especially turned off by his admonition that they not be "palsied by the will of our constituents." Never mind that the public might not think much of his ideas, Adams was saying: Push them through anyway.

"We have every mixture you can have. I have a black, I have a woman, two Jews, and a cripple."

—U.S. Secretary of the Interior James Watt, describing the makeup of an Interior Department advisory group

Fat chance. Congress summarily rejected Adams' schemes and went on to other business. Stamped as a fuzzy-brained idealist with no sense of what things cost, he lost all credibility with the lawmakers. And, in 1828, he lost his bid for reelection.

The worst federal law.

Even allowing for the spirit of the times in which it was drafted, the Fugitive Slave Act may have been the worst federal law ever passed.

It came about as part of the Compromise of 1850, a desperate and ultimately futile peace-making effort between North and South in the years before the Civil War. Although a comprehensive fugitive slave act had been on the books since 1793, this one gave law-enforcement officers in Northern states carte blanche to pursue and arrest accused runaway slaves and even to forcibly compel civilians to assist. Once captured, the suspect would be shipped south to his owner, without being permitted to defend himself or even to produce evidence that he wasn't a slave. For every slave successfully returned, the arresting officer was paid $10.

"Things are more like they are now than they have ever been."

—President Gerald Ford

Not a bad deal. But, as it turned out, only about 300 blacks were captured and returned between 1850 and the secession of the Southern states eleven years later. All the Fugitive Slave Act succeeded in doing was to exacerbate bad feelings between the South and the North.

Politics in America.

1. Cleveland mayor Ralph J. Perk accidentally set his hair on fire with a welding torch during the opening ceremonies of an industrial trade show in 1972. (After Michael Jackson's hair went up in flames during the filming of a Pepsi commercial in 1985, Pepsi consumption inexplicably increased among teenagers, senior citizens, and the Japanese.)

2. Reagan Brown, running for reelection as Texas state agricultural commissioner in 1982, thrust his hand into a large mound of dirt on live TV to

demonstrate the danger of fire ants. He was bitten so fiercely that he had to be rushed to the hospital. PS: He was defeated.

3. In an effort to elicit voter sympathy and win another term in office, Texas state representative Mike Martin arranged for his cousin to shoot him in the arm in 1981. Martin variously blamed the staged attack on devil worshipers and political foes. The cousin promptly went to the authorities and confessed the plot. Facing multiple charges, Martin disappeared. Law-enforcement officers traced him to his mother's house, where he was hiding in a stereo cabinet. "He always did want to be the Speaker," explained Texas-born columnist Molly Ivins. Martin later pleaded guilty to perjury and dropped out of the race.

"This is the worst disaster in California since I was elected."

—California governor Edmund Brown

The Mississippi state mineral.

In the early 1970s the Mississippi state senate wisely voted down legislation that would have designated the black widow the state spider, the earthworm the state worm, the wharf rat the state rat, and the vampire the state bat. However, a bill to make iron pyrite the official state mineral did pass. Pyrite is better known as fool's gold.

As a matter of fact, iron pyrite wouldn't be a bad candidate for national mineral since it was the first ore mined in the thirteen original American colonies. At the Jamestown settlement in Virginia, some gullible prospector discovered a bank of yellow dirt and, after that, as Captain John Smith lamented in his journal, "there was no thought, no discourse, no hope, and no work but to dig gold, wash gold, refine gold and load gold."

One Captain Newport carried a glittering cargo, optimistically valued in the millions, across the Atlantic and delivered it to the London Company. He waited eagerly while it was weighed and assayed—only to be told that it was totally worthless.

Why couldn't they have named the place "Springfield?"

U.S. towns whose residents can't be blamed for mumbling when asked where they're from:

1. Boring, MD
2. Bland, MO
3. Dull, OH
4. Flat, OH
5. Plain, WI
6. Ordinary, KY
7. Mousie, KY
8. Dowdy, AZ
9. Peculiar, MO
10. Difficult, TN
11. Petty, TX
12. Tightwad, MO
13. Low Point, IL
14. Pitts, AK
15. Hell, MI
16. Weakly, TN
17. T.B., MD
18. Pain, LA
19. Beans Station, TN
20. Gas City, IN
21. Crappo, MD
22. Flushing, NY
23. Wee Wee Hill, IN
24. Hump, ID
25. Climax, IA
26. Intercourse, PA
27. Lay, CO
28. Dick, IN
29. Ballsville, VA
30. Nipple Mountain, CO
31. Ova, KY
32. Kiester, MN
33. Cat House Creek, MT
34. Hooker, KY
35. Whorehouse Meadow, AZ (now Naughty Girl)
36. Poison, MT
37. Mount Misery, NJ
38. Swastika, NY
39. Ozone Park, NY

The straw poll that killed a magazine.

Beginning in 1924, *The Literary Digest* conducted a nationwide straw poll every presidential-election year and correctly predicted the winner each time. But when 1936 came around the magazine envisioned "a hotly contested election" between President Franklin D. Roosevelt and his Republican challenger, Kansas governor Alf Landon. Everyone—even grade-school dropouts and farm animals—expected Roosevelt to win, and win big; Landon, it was universally agreed, didn't have a prayer.

The *Digest* picked Landon.

What's more, it picked him to win by a hefty margin—370 electoral votes to Roosevelt's 161. Without a smattering of embarrassment or uncertainty, the magazine published its findings in its final issue before Election Day. Four days later the election turned out exactly the way everyone else in the world knew it would— a landslide for FDR, who won with 523 electoral votes to Landon's 8.

"My skin may be white.

But my heart is as black

as yours."

—*Mario Procaccino,*
New York City mayoral
hopeful, to a largely black
audience in the 1970s

In a postmortem in its next issue, the *Digest* archly insisted it had conducted its poll with uncompromising care and accuracy. Its survey of 2.5 million voters uncovered deep currents of discontent with FDR, pointing to the overwhelming likelihood that he would be ousted from power on Election Day.

What they didn't reveal was that the names of many of those 2.5 million were obtained through automobile registrations, and that much of the polling was done by telephone. This was in the depths of the Great Depression, when lots of people owned neither cars nor phones; the few who did were likely to be rich, white, and Republican.

Founded in 1890, the *Digest* had long been one of the nation's most venerated newsmagazines. But it quickly lost credibility and readers following the 1936 fiasco. By 1938 it was history.

How not to do time capsules.

1. In 1962 the Wilkinsburg (Pennsylvania) City Council appropriated funds to assemble and bury a time capsule, to be opened a quarter-century later on the occasion of the community's one hundredth anniversary. To protect the capsule from vandals, a select committee of councilmen drew up their plans behind closed doors and never told anyone where the capsule would be buried. Over the next twenty-five years, every member of the capsule committee died. Not one had ever thought to reveal the whereabouts of the buried canister. During 1987 centennial observances, a widely publicized "undigging" ceremony had to be canceled because no one knew where to dig.

> **"During my service in the United States Congress, I took the initiative in creating the Internet."**
>
> —*Vice President Al Gore*

2. For their twenty-year reunion, members of the Excelsior High School class of '63, near Los Angeles, gathered to unearth a time capsule buried the year they graduated. Actually "time baggie" is more like it. Rather than use a metal container, they had sealed the contents into a cheap plastic sack; when they located it, they saw that it had burst and all the items had disintegrated. "We weren't very bright," said one of the graduates. "But we saved three dollars by buying that bag."

3. A time capsule installed beneath the campus of Massachusetts Institute of

Technology in 1889 may never see the light of day. In the 1930s MIT built a cyclotron over it.

4. In 1999 the city of Orlando, Florida, demolished a century-old courthouse with the intention of extracting a time capsule lodged in the cornerstone and placing it in a museum. Unfortunately, the wreckers reburied the capsule in a landfill along with the rest of the debris.

5. When the twelve-ton marble cornerstone of the Washington Monument was laid on July 4, 1848, a time capsule was enclosed within it. Lined with zinc, the capsule was stocked with a representative assortment of documents and artifacts. More than 20,000 spectators were on hand for the ceremony; however, once construction began, no one made the effort to remember where the cornerstone had been placed. The capsule has never been located.

Two unspeakable practices involving the Social Security Act.

1. Denture wearers in Montana, Minnesota, and Illinois are required by law to have their Social Security numbers imprinted on their bridgework. "The markings shall be done during fabrication and shall be permanent, legible and cosmetically acceptable," states the Minnesota statutes. The laws are designed to make it easier for police officials to identify people who have been maimed beyond recognition in fatal accidents. They also spare nursing-home residents the embarrassment of inadvertently wearing each other's teeth.

2. In 1938, shortly after the Social Security Act was passed, a Lockport, New York, leather manufacturer inserted bogus Social Security cards in every wallet he sold. But instead of imprinting them with a bogus number, he used his secretary's—078–05–1120. To the manufacturer's

credit, he did stamp the word "specimen" on each card, which was printed entirely in red, but an astonishingly large number of customers still assumed that 078–05–1120 was the number assigned to them and filed claims accordingly. It took the Social Security Administration until the 1970s to straighten out the mess.

Bad Ideas in Politics and Government beyond U.S. Shores

Colonialist fatheads.

In the 1850s, the British seemed determined to make themselves as unpopular as possible in India. They summarily deposed village leaders, seized lands, and enacted laws that were grossly disrespectful to local customs.

But India's colonial overlords outdid themselves in 1857 when they issued a new version of the Enfield rifle to 223,000 native troops, or sepoys. To load the rifle properly, one had to bite off the ends of the cartridges, which were daubed with pig and beef fat and thus dietetically off-limits to Muslims and Hindus.

Accounting for three-quarters of Britain's fighting force on the subcontinent, the sepoys were renowned for their allegiance to the Crown. But with a single economical act of stupidity, the colonialists managed to alienate not one, but both of the religious groups that made up the sepoys.

Throughout India, regiment after regiment refused to load their rifles and were expelled from service. Anti-British sentiment spread quickly, fed by rumors that the Brits had polluted sacred waters with the powdered carcasses of pigs and cows. At Meerut, on May 9, 1857, sepoys stood at attention in the hot sun while eighty-five of their comrades who had balked at the command to bite, load, and fire were put in shackles and hauled off to prison. The next day the troops stormed the jail, freeing the prisoners and killing several British officers. They then headed for Delhi, where they restored the deposed Bahadur Shah II to the throne. The Sepoy Mutiny, as it came to be known, was in full swing.

A full-blown Anglo-Indian war erupted across north India. The fighting was bloody and protracted: at Cawnpore, sepoys massacred 900 men, women, and children; the British came back at the insurrectionists hard. Eventually the Crown had to bring in reinforcements from overseas to quell the mutiny, but the fighting, which might never have happened but for Great Britain's fatheadedness, couldn't be declared over until June 1858.

Good thing for him Jay Leno isn't Indonesian.

A high-ranking Indonesian official raised hackles in 2002 when he ordered the excavation of a fifteenth-century archaeological site in Bogor, just outside Jakarta. He did it because a soothsayer told him to.

In his defense, Minister of Religious Affairs Said Agil Munawar reported that the seer had assured him there was more than enough treasure buried at the site to settle Indonesia's $155 billion foreign debt. Although he claimed to be acting with President Megawati Sukarnoputri's approval, the digging proceeded without the knowledge of either local officials or Indonesia's Archaeological Heritage Protection office. In fact, Munawar took pains to cover the 12-foot-long hole with cardboard to conceal it from curiosity seekers. In the end the diggers found nothing, and Munawar wound up as a joke on the front pages of every Indonesian newspaper.

Senator soup.

Victor Biaka-Boda, a celebrated lawyer who represented the Ivory Coast in the French Senate, returned home in January 1950 to campaign for reelection. To paraphrase the Brooklyn Dodgers, he should of stood in bed: Described by colleagues as "a small, thin, worried-looking man," he set out on a tour of his district and was never heard from again.

On January 28, Biaka-Boda's belongings and a pile of bones were found near the village of Bouafle. The leftovers were shipped to police labs in Paris for analysis; meanwhile, Ivory Coast police questioned tribes near Bouafle, who played dumb. Everyone knew that Biaka-Boda had ended his days in a tureen, but until the facts were in, a successor could not be named, and his constituents would have to forgo representation. As the *New York Times* delicately put it, "You cannot have your senator and eat him too."

It took the French Overseas Ministry another two years before they officially acknowledged that Biaka-Boda had been eaten. Only then could the vacancy be filled.

Death by shoe horn.

Russia's RIA-Novosti news agency reported in 2002 that forty-three inmates of the Aktubinsk penal colony in Kazakhstan had attempted to disembowel themselves with shoe horns. The prisoners staged the mass suicidal gesture as a protest against harsh living conditions, including restrictions of movement and mandatory attendance at "socio-legal" lectures. Only one prisoner suffered wounds serious enough to merit hospitalization.

Making the whole world British.

If Cecil Rhodes had had his way, everyone would be British.

Diamond baron, imperialist, and white supremacist, Rhodes is best known for the scholarships that bear his name, awarded to men and women throughout the world for study at Oxford University. Less known is the fact that the Rhodes Scholarships were created for the express purpose of putting the wayward United States back where it belonged, in the British Empire—and of giving Great Britain sway over pretty much everyplace else.

The very notion of American independence had never made sense to Rhodes. As far as he could see, all it did was muck up the New World with hordes of "low-class Irish and German emigrants" who weren't fit to run a feed store, much less a country. Nor were the Italians, Poles, Danes, Africans, Chinese, or other "despicable specimens" in any way fit to govern themselves. He would not rest until the Union Jack flew over every square inch of God's green earth.

> "The honorable member is a disgrace to the colors he is flying under."
>
> —Irish parliamentarian (1914)

To carry out his insane plan, Rhodes envisioned a "secret society," somewhat like the Freemasons, that would draw its members from among Britain's power elite. They would use their clout to publish newspaper editorials, lobby Parliament, and woo foreign leaders, all in the service of anglicizing the planet. He spent a lifetime refining the idea, obsessing about it and working it into successive drafts of his will.

But a few years before Rhodes died, he rewrote his will yet again. This time he directed that his money be used to underwrite annual scholarships for deserving white male students throughout the British Commonwealth and the United States of America.

The aim of the grants was the same as that of his secret society—to train legions of English-speaking young men to go out into the world and extend the British Empire from New Jersey to New Zealand. But after Rhodes' death in 1902, his trustees ignored his wishes and made academic excellence the sole criterion for receiving a Rhodes Scholarship. Even non-whites were considered—a thought that would have given Rhodes chest pains. And in 1975 women became eligible as well.

A refreshing show of candor.

Brazilian finance minister Rubens Ricupero assumed he was speaking off the record when he boasted to TV reporters in 1994 that he routinely lied about the state of the economy to make himself and the government look good. But the cameras, microphones, and video recorders caught every word of his remarkable performance, which was carried live across the country to viewers with satellite dishes. Millions more saw taped replays. Ricupero resigned in humiliation the next day

The statements were made during a break between two interview tapings in a Rio de Janeiro TV studio. Believing that the broadcast equipment had been turned off, Ricupero let down his guard and said, "I have no scruples. What is good, we take advantage of. What is bad, we hide." Asked why the government had lowered gasoline prices the week before, he explained, "Every once in a while, you have to create confusion. There's no doubt about it—this isn't a rational country." But the equipment had inadvertently been left on, and after fifteen minutes a technician so informed the minister. "Then they got it," he said, realizing that he had just dynamited his own career.

Ricupero held a farewell press conference the next day. He claimed he was the victim of "an electronic breakdown," and that his statements had been taken "out of context."

The stamp of vanity.

In 1859 Postmaster General Charles Connell of New Brunswick commissioned a new set of postage stamps to reflect the province's switch from pounds and shillings to dollars and cents. For the most part the artwork he chose for the series broke no new ground: the 10-cent stamp bore a portrait of Queen Victoria; the 17-cent issue depicted the Prince of Wales. A locomotive graced the 1-cent stamp, and a steamship the 12-cent. But the 5-cent stamp showed Connell himself.

The governor of New Brunswick didn't care a lick for the prank, and Connell was forced to resign. Before leaving, though, he cannily bought all 5,000 sheets of the stamp, which he reportedly tossed on a huge bonfire in his garden. He kept a few for himself, however, and others have since fallen into the hands of collectors. Known as "Connell's folly," the vanity stamp today is worth a good deal more than the stamp hastily printed to replace it, which bears the portrait of Queen Victoria. In London in 1963 a pair of Connells was sold for £1400.

Labrador for sale.

The eastern Canadian province of Newfoundland once tried to avert financial disaster by selling a large chunk of itself.

It happened in 1931. The Depression, aggravated by gross financial mis-management and political corruption, had brought what was then the Dominion of Newfoundland to the brink of bankruptcy. Poverty was wide-spread and its fishing industry was dying. As a way out of the mess, Newfoundland decided to sell Labrador, a 110,000-square-mile coastal tract rich in minerals and timber. The asking price was $100 million dollars, although ninety-nine-year leases were also advertised.

Newfoundland found no takers. While the Canadian government consid-ered the proposal, the severely depressed economy ruled out any such pur-chase. Two years later, with Newfoundland no closer to solvency, the British government appointed a six-member commission to run the island in place of its local leaders, deemed incompetent to rule. The commission remained in power until 1949, when Newfoundland became a province, financially restored and geographically intact.

Malaysia's loafing crisis.

You never know what mischief adolescents hanging out in shopping malls *might* be planning—but why wait to find out? Better to arrest them *before* they get into trouble.

That was the rationale behind preemptive sweeps launched by police in Johor Baru, Malaysia, in 1993. In one, 224 young people were taken into custody and hauled before a magistrate, who charged them with the crime of loafing.

Loafing quickly became one of Malaysia's hottest issues. According to the *Economist*, one politician called it "a phenomenon of such proportion it can no longer be ignored." In the mid-1990s, government leaders, educators, and clerics regularly railed against pubescent loafing, which, they insisted, would inevitably lead to drug abuse, alcoholism, and crime.

Worse, a nation of idlers doesn't stand much chance of becoming an economic superpower. In fact the national government chartered a committee to study the causes of loafing and possible cures; meanwhile, the minister of youth and sports, Annuar Musa, said that shopping malls should expel mall rats, or herd them into mini-theaters and force them to watch educational films.

Another national committee leader, Hashim Ismail, urged a more draconian approach—jail sentences for "hard-core loafers." But he admitted police might have a hard time distinguishing unregenerate sluggards from "tired shoppers who are merely having a rest," the *Economist* noted.

Stamp out freedom.

In March 1765, strapped for cash following the French and Indian War, the British Parliament passed the Stamp Act, requiring the American colonies to pay a tariff on all printed materials—newspapers, diplomas, insurance policies, trade licenses, and even playing cards. An official stamp affixed to each item indicated the amount to be paid; the British thought the colonies wouldn't mind.

They minded. While the thousand-and-one petty payments added up to a massive financial headache for the Americans, what really got their Irish up was Britain's presumption in levying taxes in the first place. That had always been the colonies' privilege.

Parliament could have cut its losses by acknowledging its folly and canceling the Stamp Act at once. Instead they made matters worse by dispatching agents to enforce it and threatening deadbeats with summary trials. Britain's bullheadedness succeeded only in alienating the very opinion leaders it most needed on its side—lawyers, printers, merchants, and landholders.

Anti–Stamp Act sentiment peaked that summer. Colonial statesmen railed against it on street corners; ban-the-act demonstrations sometimes turned violent. In the fall the colonies convened a Stamp Act Congress to demand immediate repeal of the law, but it wasn't until the following March that the British took the hint and rescinded it. By that time the damage was done: The colonists were ready for war.

To Horseface with love.

During a campaign stop at a country fair, British MP Geoffrey Dickens chatted with an admiring but unsightly woman. She later wrote him at his London offices, requesting an autographed photo. Next to her signature she added the word "Horseface."

Dickens was amused by her good-natured self-mockery and responded in kind. "To Horseface, with best wishes, Geoffrey Dickens," he wrote across his photo and sent it off to her.

Later, Dickens' assistant asked if he'd received the woman's letter. "I wrote 'Horseface' after her name so you'd know which one she was," he said.

Taj for sale.

India's British overlords once planned to demolish the Taj Mahal and ship its marble facades to England, to be auctioned off to interior decorators.

The Taj was built by the seventeenth-century Mogul emperor Shah Jihan as a mausoleum for his favorite wife, who had died in childbirth. A work of transcendent radiance and majesty, the Taj took 20,000 laborers eleven years to complete. But the British colonial rulers treated the Taj, and, for that matter, all things Indian with contempt, razing or vandalizing mosques, temples, and historic sites, covering over others with whitewash and brick. They even considered carving the names of Christian saints into the marble floor of the Jami Mosque.

Under British rule revelers partied drunkenly on the grounds of the Taj; souvenir hunters came with hammers and chisels to remove chunks of agate and carnelian from the Taj's cenotaphs. But the most shameless plunderer of all was Lord William Bentinck, governor general of Bengal. He saw big money to be made in razing Mogul shrines in Agra and Delhi and selling the pieces to wealthy British estate owners and tchotchke-freaks.

"No woman in my time will be prime minister or chancellor or foreign secretary— not the top jobs. Anyway, I wouldn't want to be prime minister. You have to give yourself 100 percent."

—*Margaret Thatcher (1969)*

Bentinck started with the Red Fort, in Delhi. Under his watchful eye, workmen chipped and blasted away several tons of marble from the fort's pavilions. These were crated and delivered to England.

Next came the Taj. Work crews were hired; wrecking equipment was moved onto the grounds. The men were about to begin when word arrived from England that the auction of Red Fort relics had flopped miserably and that all future orders for Indian marble were withdrawn. For that reason—and that reason only—Bentinck called off the demolition team and the Taj was spared.

Europe, keep out.

Of all the Russian czars, Nicholas II (reigned 1894–1917) may have been the most intensely nationalistic. He allowed only Russian to be spoken by his ministers, read only Russian authors, attended only performances of Russian music. Determined to keep the czardom off-limits to European thinking and culture, he once proposed erecting an electrified fence around Russia. Aides talked him out of it.

Do planes go better with Coke?

Evidently so, if Zaire ex-president Mobutu Sese Seko is any authority. After ordering a C-130 military transport plane from the United States in 1977, he notified the U.S. Defense Department that the deal was off unless the aircraft arrived filled with Coca-Cola.

A Pentagon official told reporters that he didn't "have a clue" as to why strongman Mobutu wanted the Coke, which would have added another $60,000 to the cost of the plane. The *New York Times* reported that it was "dubious" that the Cokes-for-cash deal would go through.

Big spender.

In the fourteenth century, Musa I held sway over the Mali Empire, among the most powerful and far-reaching Islamic kingdoms of its time. Musa was an enlightened leader who sought peace with his neighbors, fostered the arts, and built majestic structures, including the great mosque of Timbuktu.

He also liked to have a good time. In 1324 he led 60,000 followers on a pilgrimage to Mecca; a retinue of 500 slaves bearing solid gold scepters accompanied them. Along the way Musa stopped off in Cairo for a few months of revels and relaxation. He spent so much gold in the Egyptian capital that the value of gold dropped drastically and the national economy collapsed.

Musa and his followers continued traveling to Mecca and returned to Mali all but broke; it was years before Egypt recovered from the emperor's excesses.

The Plot to Kill Hitler's Mustache

Bad Ideas in War— and Peace

The Bay of Turkeys.

The Bay of Pigs invasion is widely considered John F. Kennedy's most humiliating blunder as president. True, it was a dumb idea. But it was Dwight D. Eisenhower's dumb idea. Kennedy only carried it out.

In May 1960, with Eisenhower already packing for retirement, the CIA shipped several hundred Cuban expatriates to a country club in Mexico. There and in Guatemala they were secretly trained—mostly by World War II veterans—for an amphibious assault on Cuba via the Bay of Pigs. Objective: To oust dictator Fidel Castro and restore democracy to Cuba.

The State Department backed the idea; so did the Joint Chiefs of Staff. When Kennedy succeeded Eisenhower the following year, it was the Joint Chiefs who sold him on going ahead with the plan. "How could I have been so far off base?" he later said to aide Theodore Sorensen. "How could I have been so stupid to let them go ahead?"

Of course Kennedy couldn't have known that the émigrés weren't adequately trained in guerrilla tactics, or that only a handful were professional soldiers. Many had never fired a gun before. Several were in their fifties and sixties.

The strike, scheduled to occur at night, was supposed to take Castro by surprise. But the day before, a Manhattan public-relations firm hired by the CIA issued press releases proclaiming that "the principal battle of the Cuban revolt will be fought in the next few hours."

Once the invasion was launched, it was hamstrung by flubs at every turn. Machine guns on the landing craft were aimed in the wrong direction. Diversionary troops kept swimming back to their boat instead of toward the beach. Landing boats broke their propellers on coral reefs their pilots were never told about. And needed air support never materialized.

With the expatriates vastly outnumbered by Castro's ground troops and overwhelmed by heavy artillery from ground and air, the offense was stopped dead in its tracks. The Cuban people, who were expected to join forces with the invaders, never lifted a finger. Virtually all the participants in the debacle were killed or taken prisoner.

The following year, most were released to U.S. custody in exchange for $53 million worth of medical supplies and baby food.

To be sure, the Bay of Pigs fiasco wasn't the first U.S.–based invasion of Cuba to blow up on the launchpad. Between 1849 and 1851 a Cuban expatriate named Narciso Lopez led fellow exiles on several ill-planned attacks on the island. He even tried to draft Robert E. Lee and Jefferson Davis as his commanders; both turned him down. In 1851 Lopez pushed off from New Orleans with a 420-man fighting force bound for Bahía Honda, Cuba. But Spanish forces were waiting for the invaders and easily killed or captured all of them. Fifty were marched to the town square and publicly executed. They included the nephew of the U.S. Attorney General and Lopez himself.

The plot to kill Hitler's mustache.

U.S. intelligence operatives tried to win World War II with hormones.

In the midst of the war, the Office of Strategic Services (OSS)—forerunner of the CIA—commissioned a wide-ranging study of Hitler's health and habits. Among other findings the report suggested that the führer wasn't as virile as he would have liked the world to believe. In fact he was "close to the male-female line," writes Stanley Lovell, wartime director of research and development for the OSS. "A push to the female side might make his mustache fall out and his voice become soprano." There was also a good chance he would grow breasts.

Naturally, a smooth-shaven, big-busted Hitler would quickly become a national laughingstock and be driven from power. (Imagine crowds of smirking Germans saluting each other in the street with a breathy "Heil, Hitlette!") To make it happen, the OSS bribed Hitler's personal gardener to inject large quantities of estrogen into carrots headed for the führer's table.

Inevitably, this absurd "destabilization program" failed. Lovell speculates that either Hitler's official tasters noticed something funny about the carrots or, more likely, the gardener was a double-crosser who kept the bribe and threw away the hormones.

PS: Historian George Santayana was right: Those who cannot remember the past are condemned to repeat it. Since the early 1960s the U.S. government has formulated—and ultimately discarded—more than 600 plans to assassinate, embarrass, or overthrow Fidel Castro. Many make the OSS conspiracy to feminize Hitler look mundane by comparison.

"If we have to start over again with another Adam and Eve, then I want them to be Americans and not Russians, and I want them to be on this continent and not in Europe."

—U.S. senator Richard Russell, explaining why he voted for the antiballistic missile.

Under the code name "Operation Mongoose," CIA operatives and Kennedy administration advisors outlined a bizarre array of lethal gifts to be presented to the Cuban dictator: A case of cigars injected with deadly botulins . . . a fountain pen that would pierce him with a concealed syringe . . . a wet suit whose breathing apparatus would force tuberculosis germs into Castro's lungs with every breath as he trolled for seashells . . . and, if the wet suit proved ineffective, a booby-trapped seashell planted on the ocean floor, set to explode as soon as Castro touched it. The CIA also attempted to defoliate Fidel Castro's face by covertly placing a potent depilatory cream in his boots. Absorbed into his bloodstream, the chemical was supposed to strip Castro of all facial hair and political power. As of this writing, Castro retains firm control of both his beard and the Cuban government.

Oh, what a loony war I.

A British merchant vessel captain named Robert Jenkins appeared before Parliament in 1739 holding a jar containing a severed ear—his own. Much agitated, he related how it had been lopped off and handed to him by saber-wielding Spanish brigands who raided his ship near Cuba. The only possible remedy for such an outrage against the Crown, he told the lawmakers, was to declare war on Spain.

And so they did—not that they needed much convincing. Competition between Spain and Great Britain for commercial shipping rights in the West Indies had been building for several years, and Parliament welcomed an excuse to start firing. But while the War of Jenkins' Ear waxed and waned for two years, neither side seemed to be able to work up much enthusiasm for it. It began petering out after a few inconclusive naval battles, heating up only after it was absorbed into the War of Austrian Succession.

The plot to torch New York.

Things were looking grim for the Confederacy in November 1864 when Col. Robert Martin hatched a surefire plan to sock it to the Union. He would burn New York City to the ground.

Martin recruited eight secret agents and supplied them with 402 bottles of a highly combustible substance known as Greek Fire. On the night of November 25, the operatives checked into various New York City hotels. In their rooms they built piles of bedclothes, newspapers, and rubbish, which they doused with the liquid and ignited. Then they fled the premises. Since the hotels, like most of New York's buildings, were made of wood, the flames could be counted on to spread quickly, charring the city to a crisp within hours.

Fires did break out. One blaze even reached the Barnum Museum, where an audience of 2,500 was listening to a lecture by Phineas T.; panic ensued, but no one was hurt. Back in the hotels, the flames didn't amount to much, mainly because the agents had forgotten to open the windows and let in the air. (Colonel Martin also suspected the chemist who had supplied the Greek Fire of watering down the brew, either to cut costs or sabotage the mission.) A few hook-and-ladder units were summoned, but most of the fires were easily doused by hotel guests in their nightclothes. By midnight the fires were out, and New York was still standing.

Most of the arsonists escaped to Canada; one of the slow-footed unfortunates to be captured was Capt. Robert Cobb Kennedy. He enjoyed the distinction of being the last Confederate soldier to be hanged by the Union during the Civil War.

Advice from the enemy.

During the Civil War battle of Munfordville, Kentucky, the Union commander stopped fighting to consult with the enemy on whether he should surrender.

Outnumbered six-to-one by Confederate forces, the commander, Col. John T. Wilder, knew the outlook was bleak, but he lacked the confidence to choose intelligently between fighting or surrendering. He was an Indiana industrialist, after all, not a career soldier, and what he needed was professional advice—even if it had to come from the enemy.

Wilder carried a white flag across the battle lines to the Confederate camp and approached Maj. Gen. Simon Bolivar Buckner, esteemed by Northerners and Southerners alike for his decency and fairness. Buckner demurred when Wilder asked him what to do. Instead, he referred him to General Bragg, who was less impartial and patient. To push Wilder toward capitulating, Bragg showed him around the Confederate position and invited him to count the cannon trained on the Union forces. Wilder stopped counting at forty-six. "I believe I'll surrender," he said.

Almost immediately Wilder turned over 4,167 prisoners to his Confederate consultants, along with 10 guns, 5,000 rifles, and other supplies. Said Buckner later, "I would not have deceived that man under those circumstances for anything."

When U.S. insurance companies helped the Nazis.

U.S. insurance firms unwittingly gave the Germans information that helped them locate and sink countless American merchant ships during the Second World War.

When war broke out in 1939, several shipping insurance companies saw no reason to alter the practice of cabling their European partners with the names, contents, and sailing routes of insured oceangoing vessels—even those carrying war supplies to Great Britain.

One such partner, headquartered in Zurich, routinely shared this information with an underwriter in Munich, who then relayed it to German Naval Intelligence. As a result, Nazi U-boats were guided straight to U.S. ships, causing vast losses of cargo, vessels, and lives.

After newspaper columnists Walter Winchell, Drew Pearson, and Robert S. Allen exposed the scandal, the U.S. Department of Justice moved to regulate the flow of information sent out by the insurance companies, who denied the charges vigorously. Nonetheless, they continued to reveal ship positions and other vital data, jeopardizing U.S. ships at sea, until 1943, when they were silenced by the Espionage Act.

Oh, what a loony war II.

France and Mexico once went to war over pastries.

In 1838 the owner of a French bakery in the Mexico City suburb of Tacubaya complained that drunken Mexican soldiers had gorged themselves on pastries and then stiffed him on the bill. In fact, army thugs had been abusing foreign expatriates in Mexico that way for years, and King Louis Philippe now demanded 600,000 pesos in reparations. The Mexican government sneered at the claim.

In response, French gunboats took positions in the Gulf of Mexico off Veracruz in February and issued an ultimatum to the Mexican government: pay or fight. Mexico refused to negotiate unless the boats were withdrawn, but France stayed put. Other diplomatic initiatives failed and, by October, the two countries were at war.

"In the prosecution of the present war, every man ought to be ready to give his last guinea to protect the remainder."

—Sir John Parnell, Chancellor of the Exchequer of Ireland, before the Irish House of Commons (1895)

Casualties were heavy and Gen. Antonio López de Santa Anna lost a leg in the fighting, ridiculed by Mexican journalists as "La Guerra de los Pasteles," or "The Pastry War." On the brink of surrendering, Mexico agreed to pay France the 600,000 pesos, only to be informed that the ante had been upped to 800,000 pesos—600,000 for the pastries and 200,000 for the cost of the blockade.

But France softened and, in March 1839, withdrew its troops in exchange for a 600,000-peso settlement, brokered by Great Britain. How much of that was paid to the Tacubaya baker remains a mystery.

Swinging after the bell.

After Lee surrendered to Grant at Appomattox on April 9, 1865, Jefferson Davis exhorted the South to keep up the good fight anyway. He was speaking metaphorically, of course, but one man took him at his word.

As commander of the CSS *Shenandoah,* Capt. James Iredell Waddell had been battling the Union's Pacific whaling fleet. Although he knew Lee had given up, he continued to fight, capturing thirty-eight ships, destroying $1.3 million worth of U.S. cargo, and capturing more than a thousand prisoners. He even planned an attack on San Francisco, with an eye toward organizing a new Confederate fighting force and separating California from the Union.

"Why can't the Arabs and Jews resolve their disagreements at the conference table like good Christians?"

—*Warren Austin, U.S. ambassador to the United Nations (1948)*

Tipped off at last by a British merchantman that the war really was over, Waddell decided against returning to the United States and certain hanging. Instead he set sail for England, via Cape Horn. Along the way the *Shenandoah* docked at Ascension Island, where King Ish-Y-Paw offered Waddell his daughter's hand in marriage. Finding the young woman unbearably ugly, the captain politely declined and pushed on to Liverpool. He was arrested there by British authorities on November 6, 1865.

Bringing back the Hapsburgs.

During World War II, the U.S. Army created a special "Austrian Battalion" with an unbelievable mission: restore the long-defunct Austro-Hungarian Empire and reinstall the Hapsburg monarchy as its rulers.

The idea came from the exiled Archduke Otto von Hapsburg, a U.S.

resident who offered to organize the battalion himself and guaranteed 5,000 volunteers. President Roosevelt jumped at the idea of resurrecting the House of Hapsburg, which, he felt, never should have been dismantled in the first place. He also felt it crucial to liberate Austria from the Nazis in order to show the world that it was *not* an integral part of the German Empire, but a sovereign nation invaded by Hitler.

The battalion was announced in November 1942 and headquartered at Camp Atterbury, Indiana. Officers were required to be American citizens of Austrian descent and speak fluent German. The recruits were a mix of refugees from war-ravaged Europe and native-born Americans of Austro-Hungarian extraction. Training included studies in the German language and the history of the House of Hapsburg.

The battalion was doomed from the outset. The exiled Yugoslavian and Czechoslovakian governments despised all monarchs in general and the Hapsburgs in particular, and they protested loudly to FDR. So did numerous European-American political groups in the United States. By May 1943, with only 199 of the 5,000 promised volunteers, the battalion—and Washington's campaign to bring back the Hapsburg monarchy—were scrapped.

Panamania.

Sometimes people do dumb things in the service of good ideas. A case in point: the Panama Canal.

Building the canal was indisputably a good idea. But before a single spadeful of dirt was turned, the U.S. government let itself be played for a sucker, provoked an unjustified war with Colombia, and played fast and loose with long-established geographic verities.

When the canal was still in the planning stages, its French and U.S. backers wavered between putting it in Nicaragua or Panama.

In the U.S. Senate, Nicaragua was the front-runner, and with good reason: Construction costs would be substantially reduced because of the proximity of Lake Nicaragua.

Then in 1900 Nicaragua released a series of colorful postage stamps that showed Mt. Momotombo, a long-dead volcano, spewing fire and ash. One lobbyist for Panama, a French businessman named Philippe Jean Bunau-Varilla, circulated the stamps throughout the U.S. Senate as proof that so untamed a country was no place to put a canal.

Without checking out Bunau-Varilla's bogus story, the lawmakers dropped Nicaragua from further consideration, voting four years later to build the canal in Panama.

"Hitler is a queer fellow who will never become chancellor. The best he can hope for is to head the Post Office Department."

—*German president Paul von Hindenburg (1931)*

However, Panama at the time was a province of Colombia—a fact that stood in the way of President Theodore Roosevelt's plan to build a canal there. Panama would first have to be freed of Colombian rule.

That hardly presented a problem for the U.S. president. In collaboration with Bunau-Varilla, who stood to profit handsomely from the construction of the canal, Roosevelt incited Panama to revolt—and granted the rebels diplomatic recognition ninety minutes after they seized power. While shots were still being fired, Bunau-Varilla was drafting a declaration of independence and constitution for the new regime in room 1162 of New York's Waldorf-Astoria hotel; back home in Highland Falls, New York, his wife stitched the first Panamanian flag.

The United States sent warships to protect the new government against counterattack. Construction crews and dredging equipment arrived a few months later. And the cartographers declared that Panama, which had always been part of South America, was henceforth part of Central America—the southernmost section of North America. It was the first—and only—time a country had been moved from one continent to another.

Oh, what a loony war III.

When brigands from the Italian city-state of Modena raided neighboring Bologna in 1325 and absconded with the oak bucket from the town well, the Bolognese sent an army to retrieve it, setting off a twelve-year war in which thousands died.

Modena won and got to keep the bucket, which has resided ever since in the bell tower of the town's Ghirlandina cathedral. What little is known today about this silly conflict derives from the equally silly poem that commemorates it—Allesandro Tassoni's twelve-canto epic, *The Rape of the Bucket.*

The Burnside stratagem.

A West Pointer and a Mexican War veteran, Gen. Ambrose Everett Burnside certainly looked the part of a career officer. Handsome, well-dressed, and elegantly turned out, he set a new style for side-whiskers, which were called burnsides—and, later, sideburns—in his honor.

But it was during the Civil War, at the siege of Petersburg, that Burnside earned his place in history. Carrying out an inventive strategy, Burnside ordered his men to tunnel 510 feet under no-man's-land to the site of enemy headquarters. There, 6 feet underground, the soldiers planted four tons of dynamite, which exploded with a deafening roar, opening an enormous hole in the ground. The Confederates were caught off guard, and for a moment the plan looked like a stroke of genius.

Then, acting with uncharacteristic alacrity, Burnside ordered his troops forward and down into the crater. It was an unbelievably chowderheaded tactic, aggravated by the fact that Burnside's two division commanders were drunk in the trenches. The leaderless Union soldiers tumbled down the steep sides of the pit and found it impossible to climb out again. Meanwhile, Confederate reinforcements surrounded the crater and easily picked off the Yankees trapped inside.

The casualty figures at "the Battle of the Crater," as the debacle came to be known, showed 4,000 Union dead to 1,000 Confederates slain. Grant called the action "a stupendous failure . . . a positive benefit to the enemy." And when Lincoln heard about the Battle of the Crater, he said, "Only Burnside could have managed such a coup, wringing one last spectacular defeat from the jaws of victory."

The mighty mouse.

The world's biggest tank was also the most laughable.

After the Nazis were roughed up along the Russian front in 1942, Hitler commissioned Dr. Frederick Porsche to design a new species of armored tank heavy and potent enough to put the Allies in their place. Two years later Porsche presented Hitler with a prototype of what he whimsically called "the Mouse." An elephantine 20 feet high and 50 feet long, it was far and away the largest and most intimidating tank ever created.

It may also have been the most versatile: The Mouse was equipped with a 1,200-horsepower engine, encased in 13½-inch-thick armor plating, and immersible to a depth of 26 feet, so that it could actually cross rivers. Here was a battle vehicle so fearsome that it could frighten the enemy into submission without firing a shot. Actually, it wasn't a tank at all, Porsche boasted, but a mobile fortress.

But the Mouse turned out to be as mobile as a Louis XVI étagère— and just as battleworthy. At 188 tons, it was so heavy that roads crumbled like peanut brittle under its weight during test trials, while its vibrations shattered windows and splintered the foundations of nearby buildings. On a hard surface with the wind at its back, it could manage a top speed of barely 12 miles per hour; on unpaved terrain it couldn't move at all. It simply sank into the ground.

Against the advice of many high-ranking German military advisers, Porsche built two prototypes of the mighty Mouse at a cost of millions. They were destroyed by the Germans before they saw a day of service.

Smut-bombers of the RAF.

The OSS plan to season Hitler's carrots with estrogen (see page 39) was not the agency's only attempt to destabilize the führer. Early in the war an OSS staff psychologist theorized that, despite Hitler's now well-known deviant tastes, he was in deep denial over the wide prevalence of pornography in Germany. Therefore, if a heady dose of Aryan lewdness were to be pushed in his face, he would suffer a mental breakdown and the leaderless Germans would lose the war.

The plan, then: arm a squadron of RAF fliers with several tons of the ripest smut available in Germany, and have them drop it on Hitler's home.

The plan was never carried out, largely because the RAF refused to risk life and limb carpet bombing Hitler with photographs of women copulating with Shetland ponies. The war, they said, would have to be won through less inventive means.

Oh, what a loony war IV.

Well into the nineteenth century, Korea clung fiercely to the idea of glueless stamps. When Japan attempted to introduce the pre-glued variety there in 1884, the Koreans revolted, setting the main post office in Seoul afire and littering the streets with the alien postage. Japan sent troops in to quell the disturbance and annexed Korea a few years later.

Britain's sno-cone battleship.

During World War II, the Allies considered building an aircraft carrier out of ice.

The idea was hatched in a British government think tank that screened proposals for new weapons and schemes to aid the war effort. Most of the ideas that came in were dismissed out of hand: tanks powered by perpetual motion machines, a rubber raft the size and shape of England that would float in the North Sea and confuse German pilots, etc. But one scheme, proposed by inventor Geoffrey Pyke, intrigued the Britons enough for them to go into preliminary development. They called the initiative Project Habakkuk.

Named for an obscure Hebrew prophet ("Behold, for I will work a work in your days which ye will not believe, though it be told you"), Project Habakkuk involved slicing off a two-million-ton iceberg from the North Polar cap, blasting and bulldozing it into the shape of an aircraft carrier, and towing it into the North Atlantic. Besides being unsinkable, the ship would also supposedly be bombproof: Should it be hit with enemy fire, crew members would simply fill the holes with water, which would quickly freeze back into a level and usable landing strip.

To keep the carrier from melting, the ice would be infused with a generous dose of wood pulp. In fact, Lord Mountbatten, chief of Combined Operations, formally proposed the project to Winston Churchill while the prime minister was soaking in a hot bath. Mountbatten dropped a chunk of the specially treated ice in the tub, and both watched in awe as it resisted melting. Sir Winston was convinced.

In 1943 several small prototypes were built and tried out on lakes in Alberta and British Columbia, where they stood up well under heavy shellfire and bombing missions by Canadian geese. But there was no practical way to heat or motorize the ships or make them habitable for crew members, nor could they be used in warmer climes. When it was also discovered that building an ice ship cost at least as much as a frost-free one, the idea was scrapped.

Subnormal intelligence.

During World War I, British military engineers came up with something completely different in gunboats—a submarine massive enough to double as a battleship. They called their new family of steam-powered vessels the K-class submarines. That's K, as in Klod.

Because they were so big—338 feet long on average—the K-boats were klunky and kumbersome. K-1 sank like a stone off the coast of Denmark after colliding with K-4, which ran aground. K-2 burst into flames on its initial outing. K-3 could not pull out of its first dive and plunged to the bottom, with the Prince of Wales aboard. It was rescued and, on a subsequent trial, rammed by K-6; both boats sank to the bottom and became temporarily mired in the seabed.

K-5 foundered in the Bay of Biscay and sank. K-7 and K-17 crashed into each other. Leaks hampered K-14's first attempt to leave port; later, during North Sea trials, it was rammed and sunk by K-22—which had originally been dubbed K-13 until it toppled over in Loch Gare, Scotland, during early trials. The K-22 was later put out of commission after being run down by the aptly named cruiser, HMS *Inflexible*.

In the same exercise that destroyed K-22, K-17 went out of control and smashed into both HMS *Fearless* and K-7 before sinking. The captain of K-4 saw the whole thing from the

> **"Hurrah, boys, we've got them! We'll finish them up and then go home to our station."**
>
> —Gen. George Armstrong Custer, Little Big Horn (1876)

bridge and, to avert further mishap, killed the engines, shifted course, and promptly plowed into K-6, which nosedived to the ocean floor. K-15 sank in Portsmouth while it was still in the harbor.

Work on K-boats 18–21 began in earnest, but was wisely discontinued by the British War Ministry. By then K-boats had killed more than 250 sailors, all British. Later the keels of the unfinished K-boats were refitted for Britain's new-and-improved M-class of submarines. M-1 got in the way of a merchant ship in the English Channel. M-2 sprung a leak and sank.

Smelling bad.

Nuoc nam is a pungent fish-oil sauce popular in Vietnam as a rice additive. During the Vietnam War, Defense Department scientists developed a super-sensitive "Smell-O-Meter" aimed at sniffing out the odor of nuoc nam and air-dropped hundreds of the devices along the Ho Chi Minh Trail in hopes of tracking Vietcong troop movements.

Just as ingeniously, the Vietcong devised a strategy to neutralize the Smell-O-Meters: They hung buckets of urine on trees along the infiltration route, faking out the devices, which couldn't distinguish between nuoc nam and pee. Officially, the Pentagon discontinued use of the Smell-O-Meters because they had "a too-broad spectrum."

> **"My fellow Americans . . .**
>
> **I've signed legislation that**
>
> **will outlaw Russia forever.**
>
> **We begin bombing in five**
>
> **minutes."**
>
> —*President Ronald Reagan, joking before a 1984 radio broadcast and unaware that the microphone was on*

Visit America. See Sicily.

Sicilian nationalists once pressed the U.S. government to make Sicily the forty-ninth state.

Food was scarce and discontent widespread throughout that southern Italian island after World War II. Many Sicilians blamed the central government in Rome for their impoverished condition, and a grassroots secessionist movement quickly drew fervent support from landowners, peasants, mafiosi, and young idealists.

All wanted Sicily to break away from Italy and become part of the United States.

The guiding force behind the movement was the twenty-four-year-old guerrilla warrior Salvatore Giuliano. From a mountain redoubt outside Palermo, Giuliano led a ragtag army of 5,000 murderers, bandits, and terrorists bent on making life as uncomfortable as possible for Italy's ruling class. Gangster to some, folk hero to others, Giuliano wrote to President Truman in 1947, asking him to liberate Sicily and make it "the forty-ninth American star."

The Americanization of Sicily, Giuliano explained, would thwart Soviet expansionism in Europe, as well as end the island's subjugation by Rome. With the letter to Truman, Giuliano enclosed a flyer that had been widely circulated throughout Sicily. It featured a drawing of Giuliano cutting a chain that linked the island to Italy, while another man stood astride North America and chained Sicily to the United States.

Although Truman turned down the appeal, the separatist cause remained alive, only to be undermined in the end by infighting among its leaders. By the early 1950s, Sicily's surreal dream of American statehood was history.

Visit America. See Peru.

A small but growing party of annexationists in Peru is hoping to see its country affixed to the United States someday. The rewards of annexation, said Fernando Quispe, founder of the Constitutional Integrationist Movement, include the freedom "to taste different brands of soft drinks, paying no more than a dollar for each two-liter bottle." Even better, young Peruvian males "will immediately learn English for free and enjoy the opportunity to marry beautiful young American girls."

Let a smile be your umbrella, soldier.

And that's an order! Following a 1985 ruling, any man in the U.S. Army found carrying an umbrella while in uniform is subject to disciplinary action.

The Pentagon offered no official explanation for the edict, but one unofficial source told reporters that Army brass "felt the image of male officers walking around with umbrellas is somehow intrinsically unmilitary" and "an artificial affectation." Sissyish, too, presumably: Female Army personnel are still permitted the use of umbrellas. So are Air Force men.

Oh, what a loony war V.

The United States and Great Britain almost went to war over a dead pig.

San Juan Island, which lies in the Straits of Vancouver, was a tense spot in the 1850s. Both the United States and Great Britain claimed it, and residents found themselves drawn into the dispute. In 1859 a pig owned by Canadian farmer Charles John Griffin scampered onto a potato patch owned by his American neighbor, Lyman Cutlar, who shot the intruder on sight. Griffin filed a complaint with a British court, which ordered Cutlar to pay $100 in damages. Cutlar insisted he wasn't bound by British law and refused to part with a penny.

Tension spread. Washington and London exchanged angry notes. Neighbors stopped speaking to each other. It was brother against brother, hog farmer against hog farmer. And then the United States dispatched a fighting force to San Juan Island under the command of Gen. George Pickett to protect its interests. The Crown sent warships of its own.

For several weeks each side faced down the other. No shots were fired in the War of Griffin's Pig. But both nations maintained a military presence on San Juan Island for more than a dozen years.

Bad Ideas in Arts and Letters

Washington on the beach.

As a matter of course, sculptor Horatio Greenough inscribed all his works with the words "Horatio Greenough fecit"—"Horatio Greenough has done it." Not so his gargantuan statue of George Washington. On that one he wrote "faciebat," or "*tried* to do it."

Commissioned by Congress to produce the work in 1843, the Boston-born Greenough let his artistic vision run wild. Not many critics cared for the result; one exception was the writer Edward Everett, who praised the piece's "purity of taste, the loftiness of the conception, the truth of the character."

But Everett must have been on drugs when he wrote that. Greenough's *Washington* was truly a monstrosity.

For starters, it was so huge and heavy that it sank through the boards of the Capitol floor. So the statue was instead displayed outdoors. But no one knew about weatherization in those days, and the marble mammoth was ravaged nastily by the elements.

In its third niche, in the Smithsonian Institution, it sparked the anger of bluestockings who felt that the classically naked-to-the-waist representation of Washington was disgustingly lewd. Architect Charles Bullfinch said it would "give the idea of entering or leaving a bath." So the sculpture was removed again, and for years it was tucked away in a corner of the original Smithsonian "castle" building, hidden from public view.

Today you can view Greenough's folly in the Museum of History, where it is displayed prominently. With his naked pecs, Washington looks less like a statesman than a steroid freak showing off at Muscle Beach. Try not to laugh.

And what about all those Polish lightbulb jokes concealed in Chopin's Études?

A cellist with California's Eureka Orchestra refused to take part in a young people's performance of Prokofiev's *Peter and the Wolf*. The work was degrading to wolves and other endangered species, she claimed.

Feminist music critic Susan McClary decried the "phallic violence" and "assaultive pelvic pounding" of western classical music. In particular, Beethoven's Ninth Symphony is marked by the "throttling murderous rage of a rapist incapable of attaining release."

That's your idea of a best-seller? Books we never finished reading.

1. *Thank God I Have Cancer.* The Rev. Clifford Oden's compelling autobiography.
2. *The Joys of Jell-O.* The cookbook hit of 1964.
3. *Nutrition for Health.* By health-food expert Alice Chase, who died in 1974 of malnutrition.
4. *Is Another World Watching?* Science writer Gerald Heard's early-1950's so-so seller in which he suggested that UFOs indeed exist, piloted by extraterrestrial bees of superhuman intelligence.
5. *Dentologia: A Poem on the Diseases of the Teeth.* An epic in five cantos by the nineteenth-century dentist Solyman Brown.
6. *The Potatoes of Bolivia: Their Breeding Value and Evolutionary Relationships.* The definitive work on the subject, written by J. G.

Hawkes and J. P. Hjerting and published in 1989 by the Oxford University Press.

7. *Euthanasia or, The Aesthetics of Suicide.* By James Harden-Hickey. Four hundred spurious quotations from the world's great thinkers on why suicide is good for you. Crammed with tips on ending it all in style, including notes on eighty-eight different poisons and fifty-one instruments of death (including pinking shears).

8. *The History of the Concrete Roofing Tile: Its Origin and Development in Germany.* Author Charles Dobson offers that his single aim in writing this 1959 book is "to interest those who may like to learn something more about the origin and development of the concrete roofing tile than is generally known in England."

> **"Rembrandt is not to be compared in the painting of character with our extraordinarily gifted artist, Mr. Rippingdale."**
>
> —*John Hunt, nineteenth-century English art critic*

Down with Shakespeare!

Delia Bacon took nothing for granted. As a student at Connecticut's finest private schools in the 1840s, she had been taught that the author of Shakespeare's plays was, well, Shakespeare. Balderdash, she said. By the time she was in her mid-twenties, she was convinced that while Shakespeare the man indeed existed, he was an illiterate, slavering fool who could not possibly have penned a laundry list much less the thirty-seven plays commonly attributed to him.

Who, then? A committee of six, consisting of Sir Francis Bacon (no relation), Sir Philip Sydney, Lord Buckhurst, Lord Paget, the Earl of Oxford, and Sir Walter Raleigh, she argued.

When her obsession ripened like a burgeoning boil, the sickly Ms. Bacon took to lecturing and raging splenetically against the bard at every opportunity, prompted, some said, by a hatred of *all* men inspired by her disastrous romance with an elderly Protestant clergyman. As she explained it, the evil Sir Francis and company had slipped a deadly dose of radical politics into the plays by means of a secret code, and had then hired Ben Jonson to act as public relations shill and introduce the plays to a gullible public.

Furthermore—and of this she was *certain*—the key to the mysterious code lay buried with Shakespeare in Stratford, England. She traveled there in 1853 to pursue her theories in earnest, and she once managed to wheedle the vicar of the Stratford church into letting her pry open Shakespeare's tomb for a quick peek inside, only to lose her nerve in a fit of nausea.

"Shakespeare's name, you may depend on it, stands absurdly too high and will go down."

—Lord Byron (1814)

Finally, in 1857, she brought out *The Philosophy of the Plays of Shakespeare Unfolded*, 700 pages of sludgelike prose, ideas strewn wildly about and toppling onto each other like a child's playthings. The book was an overnight commercial failure and its author was widely hailed as a lunatic.

"Hawthorne [a sympathizer] in later years averred that he had met one man who read it through," notes *The Dictionary of American Biography*. "There is no record of another."

Ms. Bacon, who, by her brother's admission, "had been verging on insanity for six years," finally went around the bend soon after her book was published. She died in an insane asylum the following year.

Twenty-four reasons to choose Boca Raton over Borneo for your next vacation.

Phrases translated in the *English-Bazaar Malay Phrase Book* to "help English-speaking visitors . . . with their day-to-day needs" (Borneo Literature Bureau, 1966):

- Wait while I remove these leeches.
- I have been bitten by sand flies.
- There are too many rats.
- There are a lot of mosquitoes here.
- The cockroaches have eaten my shirt.
- Is this poisonous?
- What made that noise?
- Is Sibu Laut in a swamp?
- Is there a taboo on your house?
- Is the burning finished?
- Where can I defecate?
- Is that fish dangerous?
- This floor is not safe.
- The roof is leaking.
- There is no room in this boat.
- We must keep dry.
- I can't come for a time because the monsoon will soon start.
- She has a bad pain/snakebite/gunshot wound.
- Tear some clean cloth into strips.
- Keep him warm.
- Go quickly for help.
- This vomiting needs urgent treatment.
- I do not know what is wrong. You must take her to the clinic.
- Your eyes need treatment, or you will become blind.

The musical attorney.

Pay close attention, because we're only going through this once: Arias are for singing. Courtroom summations are for speaking.

Most lawyers and operatic virtuosos have little difficulty making that distinction. One notable exception was Florida attorney Steve Jerome. Representing Robert Infante, on trial in 1982 for kicking a neighbor's car with intent to dent, Jerome thought he could charm the jury into a not-guilty verdict by singing his closing argument.

For the melody, Jerome chose the aria "Vesti la giubba," from Leoncavallo's opera, *I Pagliacci*: "Innocent, or is this man guiiiiilty? He is not guiiiilty!" Jerome, a tenor, gave the performance of his life, his face reddening as he reached for the high notes. The jurors stared in disbelief and erupted in giggles. Then they came back with a guilty verdict.

Said the defendant about his counsel's ploy, "I don't think it helped."

Dali does Bonwit's.

In 1939, Bonwit Teller commissioned painter Salvador Dali to create a window display for its posh Fifth Avenue department store in New York City. It was possibly the worst marketing idea ever conceived by a major retailer.

Beginning work after the store closed on March 16, Dali fashioned a surrealist tableau depicting *Night* and *Day*. The centerpiece of *Day* was a female mannequin clad only in a tuft of feathers stepping into a fur-lined bathtub; three wax hands rising from the water held a vanity mirror. *Night* featured another mannequin asleep in a four-poster bed beneath a canopy that was actually a water buffalo holding a dead pigeon in its mouth. The bed was made up with black sheets and stuffed with glowing coals.

Dali completed his labors at dawn and returned to his hotel. When Bonwit's opened for business a few hours later, outraged shoppers complained that the display was risqué. Management obligingly draped the bather in a ball gown, replaced the sleeper with a standing mannequin, and made other improvements as well.

When Dali returned late that afternoon to admire his handiwork, he was shocked at the changes. He rampaged through the store shrieking imprecations in Spanish and French and startling the customers. A multilingual employee tried to calm him, but Dali only grew more exercised, griping that he had been "hired to do a work of art," and that he would not tolerate having his name "associated with typical window dressing." Surging past several store employees, he climbed into the window and tried to tip over the bathtub. In the effort he lost his balance and crashed through the plate-glass window, toppling onto Fifth Avenue in a hail of glass and water.

> **"[Byron's] versification is so destitute of sustained harmony . . . that I have always believed his verses would soon rank with forgotten things."**
>
> — *John Quincy Adams (1830)*

A passing police officer arrested the artist on a charge of malicious mischief. Dali drew a suspended sentence. Bonwit Teller spent a long time living down the fiasco.

For Dali, the Bonwit's debacle was all in a day's work. Several weeks before, he had executed a large mural for the New York World's Fair featuring a Dadaist reworking of Botticelli's *Venus*. In it the goddess' head had been replaced with that of a fish. When fair officials rejected the effort, Dali angrily and noisily resigned. Another time he appeared at a London art show dressed in a deep-sea diving suit. Lest anyone miss the point, he explained that the mission of art is to plumb the depths of the unconscious. When his air supply ran out, Dali was unable to remove the helmet. He almost suffocated before he could be rescued.

The only dictionary you'll ever need.

Following the publication of his Portuguese-French dictionary in 1836, José da Fonseca collaborated with an editor named Pedro Carolino on a Portuguese-English version. It was a bold effort, considering that neither man spoke a word of English.

The two hardly considered that an obstacle, however. They simply translated words from Portuguese into French, and then located the English equivalent in a French-English dictionary.

It was a creative modus operandi. It also produced a very strange dictionary. Published in 1862, *The New Guide of the Conversation in Portuguese and English* defines such diseases as "the vomitory," "a bald," and "an ugly." Hedgehogs and snails are listed as species of fish; other tasty "eatings" include "some wigs," "some marchpanes," and "an amelet." Among the English "idiotisms" it translates are, "He laughs at my nose," "I shall not tell you than two woods," and "Take that boy and whip him too much." The *Guide* also contains many of the more popular English aphorisms, such as "Who lhat be washed, too mann soaped, and the shirts put through the buck," and "The walls have hearsay."

A section entitled "Familiar Dialogues" advises readers exactly what to say in a variety of social situations—furniture shopping, for example:

Tradesman: Which highness want you its?

Customer: I want almost four feet six thumbs wide's, over seven of long.

Anglers will never grope for the right word when they pack a copy of Fonseca-Carolino along with their hooks and lures:

Angler A: That pond it seems me many multiplied of fishes. Let us amuse rather to the fishing.

Angler B: I do like it too much.

Angler A: Here, there is a wand and some hooks.

Angler B: Silence! There is a superb perch. Give me quick the rod. Ah! there it is. It is a lamprey.

Angler A: You mistake you. It is a frog!

Despite—or because of—such howlers, the *Guide* was a hot seller on both sides of the Atlantic and was reprinted many times. But Fonseca, a respected lexicographer, made certain to have his name deleted from the book after the first edition.

When will lawmakers ban batons and stop the senseless slaughter?

Leopold Stokowski never used a baton when he conducted and lived to be ninety-five. Evidently there was a connection.

Jean-Baptiste Lully, composer, director of the Paris Opera, and court conductor to Louis XIV, wouldn't dream of stepping before an orchestra with only his bare hands to lead the music; his preferred instrument was a heavy staff, which he pounded on the floor to keep time. While conducting a performance of his *Te Deum* in 1687, he pounded a bit too recklessly and bayonetted himself in the toe with the sharp end. Gangrene set in, and he died ten weeks later.

During a 1975 concert in Mexico City, Uruguayan conductor José Serebrier stabbed himself in the hand with his baton. While musicians and chorus members gasped, blood gushed from the wound, staining his white tuxedo shirt and spattering his shoes.

"The baton broke into pieces," the conductor later said. "One piece was sticking through my hand. Ironically, I never use a baton. But I decided to use one for this performance because I thought it would help me achieve greater musical control. That was a mistake."

The Plague II.

Since its 1941 Paris debut, Pablo Picasso's *Désir Attrapé par la Queue* (Desire Caught by the Tail) has seen only a handful of productions. That seems surprising, considering that its original performance drew on the talents of Albert Camus, Jean Paul Sartre, and Simone de Beauvoir, among others. The critics, however, are not clamoring for a revival.

Picasso's only theatrical effort addresses elemental themes—food, money, and sex—although the dialogue offers little explicit evidence of those concerns: "We sprinkle the rice powder of angels on the soiled bedsheets and turn the mattresses through blackberry bushes!" a character named Big Foot proclaims as the curtain rings down on the last act. "And with all power the pigeon flocks dash into the rifle bullets! And in all bombed houses, the keys turn twice around in the locks!"

In a 1967 production at the Festival of Free Expression in St. Tropez, France, the female lead, Tart, disrobed to the throbbing rhythms of a rock band while a chorus of go-go dancers boogalooed and slides of Picasso paintings flashed on the backdrop. Later she urinated on stage to the accompaniment of a symphony of disgusting noises projected over the loudspeaker. When the mayor of St. Tropez objected, director Jean-Jacques Lebel moved the play outside the city limits.

"We are not at liberty to emasculate a work of art in order to pander to bourgeois sentiment," he said.

Photographic shoot.

Conceptual artist Chris Burden arranged to have himself shot by a friend with a Winchester .22 while a third participant recorded the experience in a sequence of photographs. Burden's intention had been to be only grazed, but the marksman had an off day and Burden wound up in the hospital with a nasty gunshot wound in his left arm.

However, he did sell the pictures, along with several others, to a New York art dealer for $1,750.

Schumann's finger rack.

As a young man, composer Robert Schumann (1810–1856) showed enormous promise as a concert pianist. The only problem was the middle and fourth fingers of his right hand, which lacked suppleness and agility. To whip some discipline into the wayward digits, he invented a device that held them in place and stretched them while the others played freely.

Schumann's homemade finger rack turned out to be remarkably effective—so effective, in fact, that he wound up crippling his fingers. On doctor's orders, he marinated his hand regularly in a restorative bath of warm animal guts, but the injury was permanent, and Schumann never played seriously again.

Schumann, of course, went on to compose some of the greatest chamber and orchestral music of the romantic era, but his personal life was a series of calamities and disappointments. He suffered from syphilis, depression, and auditory hallucinations; things got so bad at one point that he jumped from a fourth-floor window. He survived but was forever phobic about living above the ground floor.

"Debussy's music is the dreariest kind of rubbish."

—New York Post *(1907)*

Schumann claimed that the ghosts of Mendelssohn and Schubert visited him at night to dictate melodies to him; other times he was convinced he was being chased by lions and hyenas. Later, plagued by an incessant ringing in his ears—he said it was a middle A—he hurled himself into the Rhine. Fishermen rescued him, but Schumann was never able to compose himself. He ended his days in an insane asylum at age forty-six.

Unavailable at fine bookstores everywhere. More books we never finished reading.

1. *Jokes Cracked by Lord Aberdeen.* Published in 1929 by Valentine Press. A companion volume might be *The Wit of Prince Philip* (Leslie Frewin, 1965).
2. *Who's Who in Cocker Spaniel Breeding.* A reference-shelf must.
3. *Weymouth, the English Naples.* Published in 1910 by Hood & Co. Indispensable for any traveler.
4. *Chanco: A Boy and His Pig in Peru.* Sutherland Stark's only book. Published in 1947.
5. *I Was Hitler's Maid.* The 1940 memoirs of Pauline Kohler.
6. *The Little Cyanide Cook Book.* By June DeSpain. A big hit at the 1977 Cancer Victory Convention in Washington, D.C.
7. *The Grant Poem, Containing Grant's Public Career and Private Life from the Cradle to the Grave.* By Adrian Hill. A 381-page biography of Ulysses Grant written entirely in verse. Published in 1886.
8. *Attitudes and Answers in the Controversy over Pay Toilets.* Published in 1975 by the Nik-O-Lok Company, of Indianapolis, Indiana, "the world's largest and oldest manufacturer of coin-operated locks and accessories for public rest rooms."
9. *Enjoy Your Chameleon.* Published by The Pet Library, Ltd. "A chameleon can be tethered on a light string to serve as a novel and attractive lapel ornament."

Guilt trip.

Novelist Thomas Wolfe was once injured jumping off a moving train as it pulled out of New York's Grand Central Station. Wolfe was on the way to spend a weekend at the Connecticut home of his editor, Maxwell Perkins, when he suddenly decided that he should be back in Brooklyn writing.

Music man.

G. G. Allin, lead singer of the Toilet Rockers (and also associated with such groups as the Texas Nazis, Cedar Street Sluts, Drug Whores, Sewer Scum, Afterbirth, and Murder Junkies), was arrested in 1991 for defecating on stage during a Milwaukee concert and hurling the results into the audience. His attorney, Peter Goldberg, cried censorship.

"We feel that Allin is a serious performer," he said, "and there's serious artistic value to what he does."

> **"It is probable that much, if not most, of Stravinsky's music will enjoy brief existence."**
>
> —*W. J. Henderson,*
> **New York Sun** *(1937)*

Famous biblical ca-cas.

A U.S. publisher came out with a modernized version of the Bible in 1971. In an overly zealous quest for clarity and relevance, the translators updated I Samuels 24:3—"Saul went into the cave to wash his feet"—to read, "Saul went into the cave to go to the bathroom." Their version was immediately dubbed "the Bathroom Bible," and the nickname has stuck ever since.

A boulevard named manicotti.

Artist Rudy Giacomo drafted plans to build a 39-mile-long manicotti around Manhattan Island.

Giacomo burst upon the international art scene in 1961 with an elaborate tableau of salami and eggs that covered 2 miles of beachfront real estate in southwest Africa. Later he erected a 17-foot-high tuna salad sandwich in front of his home in New York City; he called it "Spare the Mayo." However, plans for a 24-story middle-income apartment complex in Chicago built entirely from Ritz crackers and peanut butter never came off.

Neither did Giacomo's fabled Manicotti Project, although not for lack of planning. As the artist envisioned it, the 3.5-million-pound pasta special would be installed raw, then baked on the premises by a specially made 39-mile heating coil. Cheese would be pumped from offshore tankers at the rate of 2,000 gallons a minute; forty-two New York City fire trucks would be deployed along the route to hose away an estimated seven tons of excess cheese. A squadron of fifty-two crop dusters would drop 30,000 gallons of tomato sauce on the manicotti. Meanwhile 4,200 security guards, armed to the teeth with flyswatters, mouse traps, and service revolvers, would keep vermin and vandals away.

Finally, at a signal from the artist, the velvet ropes would be removed, and the public would be invited to eat the manicotti.

Maybe it was supposed to be for airmail letters.

No one knows why, but a mailbox was installed 9 feet above the ground in Ballymacra, Ireland, several years ago. It took three weeks for Irish postal authorities to get around to lowering the box; meanwhile, someone placed a stepladder nearby.

Yeats' sex-gland transplant.

William Butler Yeats suffered from impotence in his late sixties, and, as if that weren't enough of a cross to bear, he also felt creatively blocked. Then the poet read a brochure hailing the success of Dr. Erwin Steinach of Vienna in pepping up flaccid libidos using sex-gland transplants.

Yeats' personal physician had strong reservations about Steinach; indeed, one of Steinach's patients had dropped dead the day before he was to give a talk entitled "How I Was Made Twenty Years Younger" at London's Albert Hall. Undaunted, Yeats went to London in 1934 to undergo the procedure, which was more like a modern-day vasectomy than a bona fide gland transplant. Steinach claimed it would stimulate testosterone production and restore the poet's virility.

It did not. However Yeats did start writing again, and he even dallied in several extramarital affairs, although none could be consummated. When a friend of his asked why he'd had the surgery, Yeats was less than forthright.

"I used to fall asleep after lunch," he said.

> **"Quite a number of people categorize the German classical author Shakespeare as belonging to English literature because, quite accidentally born at Stratford-on-Avon, he was forced by the authorities of that country to write in English."**
>
> —Deuscher Weckruf und Beobachter, *a Nazi-American Bund publication (1940)*

The strange journey of Haydn's head.

Several years after the burial of composer Franz Joseph Haydn, his patrons allowed phrenologists to exhume the body and remove his head. It wasn't reunited with his body for more than two centuries.

Haydn, who died in 1809, was initially buried in Vienna. But he was reinterred in the Austrian town of Eisenstadt in 1820, having spent some of his most productive years there under the patronage of Prince Esterhazy. It was Esterhazy who yielded to requests from a phrenological society to disentomb the composer so that they could get a closer look at the bumps on his cranium.

Somehow Haydn's head fell into the hands of thieves, who held it for ransom. Esterhazy refused to deal with them, and the composer was reburied headless. The head next turned up in a glass display case in the main hall of the Gesellschaft der Musikfreunde in Vienna; later it graced the piano of an Austrian professor. Upon the professor's death, his widow lent it to the Vienna Pathological Museum.

The head found its way back to the Gesellschaft der Musikfreunde in 1895; meanwhile, his fans back in Eisenstadt negotiated for its return. But it wasn't until 1954 that the head finally came home. In a solemn ceremony on June 5, Haydn's head rejoined the rest of him in his burial crypt in the Bergkirche in Eisenstadt.

Where the hell is St. Ioseph, Mo.?

The publishers of the *St. Joseph Gazette* decided to get fancy in 1903 and reset the paper's nameplate in an Old-English typeface. They should have kept it simple. In 1980, reader Charles Bush wrote several letters to the editors, pointing out that the paper had been misspelling its own name for seventy-seven years as the *"St. Ioseph Gazette."* The embarrassed editors fixed the error on the December 9 edition.

How to get Americans to read.

Deeply troubled that Americans weren't reading enough, a Dallas disk jockey concocted a novel way of promoting literacy. He announced on the air that he had concealed $100 in small bills in books in the fiction section of the Fort Worth public library and invited listeners to find them.

Minutes later more than 500 people rampaged through the library in search of the hidden cash. By the time they could be stopped, they had hurled more than 3,500 books onto the floor, damaging many and leaving the building a shambles.

"People started climbing the bookshelves; then they started climbing on each other, and books became airborne," librarian Marsha Anderson reported. She was getting ready to leave work around 5:00 P.M. when hordes of treasure hunters burst into the library, shrieking, "Where's fiction? Where's fiction?" Dr. Jack C. Scott, a Texas Christian University psychologist, said, "It was massive hysteria . . . a kind of contagion in the air. It was completely unstructured and irrational."

Following the 1994 debacle, the radio station, KYNG-FM, apologized and offered to pay for clean-up expenses, as well as the cost of repairing and replacing damaged books. Unmollified, City Manager Robert Terrell sent a complaint to the Federal Communications Commission and said he was considering suing the station.

> **"*Rigoletto* is the weakest work of Verdi. It lacks melody. This opera has hardly any chance of being kept in the repertoire."**
>
> **—Gazette Musicale de Paris (1853)**

Henry Thoreau, arsonist.

Tree-hugger Henry David Thoreau once carelessly started a forest fire that turned 300 acres of virgin woodland to toast. Worse, he did nothing to stop the spread of the blaze, refusing point-blank to help local residents attempting to extinguish it.

It happened in 1844. Thoreau, twenty-six at the time, was camping with a friend near the Sudbury River, outside Concord, Massachusetts. When they built a fire in a tree stump to cook dinner, the flames flared out of control, engulfing much of Fair Haven Hill. While locals fought the blaze, Thoreau watched from the safety of a hilltop.

Some theorize that Thoreau, never an easy person to get along with, balked at helping because of a complex and long-standing feud with the people of Concord. They did not exactly find his resistance endearing, and tagged him "Thoreau the woodsburner" for the rest of his life.

Who Was Who at Harvard: Volume I.

In a frenzy of school spirit, Harvard chief librarian John Langdon Sibley began compiling a biographical encyclopedia of every person who attended the university from its founding in 1636. He never quite finished the task.

When Sibley died in 1885 after twenty-five years of painstaking research, he had gotten only as far as the Class of 1689. But he bequeathed $161,169 to the Massachusetts Historical Society to carry on the Sisyphean task.

The work continues even today. But Harvard keeps turning out new graduates at a rate of 3,000 a year and the biographers keep falling further and further behind. Of the more than 200,000 Harvard graduates, about 190,000 lack biographies.

The Brillo Brigade.

Seventy French high-school students descended on the Mayrieres caves, near Brunquiel in southwestern France, in 1992, armed with steel wool, strong soap, and coarse brushes. Their mission: to remove graffiti from ancient cave paintings.

But the kids, members of the Protestant youth group "Eclaireurs de France," had trouble telling where the graffiti ended and the artwork began, and wound up scrubbing away several 15,000-year-old bison paintings as well.

The leader of the misguided project faulted local officials for not officially designating the caves a national historic site and taking measures to protect them. But French cultural ministers and others put the blame squarely on the cave cleaners. Their actions, said René Gachet, cultural affairs director of the Tarn-et-Garonne department, were "absolutely stupid."

When the Rockefellers commissioned a portrait of Lenin.

In the 1930s, the Rockefeller family contracted the Mexican artist Diego Rivera to paint an enormous mural that would dominate the lobby of New York's Rockefeller Center. Although Rivera made no secret about his Marxist leanings, the Rockefellers hired him anyway, on the condition that he clear his preliminary sketches with them before proceeding. But as the magnificent work neared completion in 1938, Rivera appeared to have taken some artistic liberties, such as the inclusion of a bearded face that bore a distinct resemblance to Lenin. Yes, Rivera acknowledged, it *was* Lenin, watching in anger as American police thugs clubbed striking workers into submission. And that deformed little syphilitic girl in the corner? She symbolized the horrors of "life under capitalism."

Although more than $21,000 had already been invested in the mural, young

"But, oh, the pages of stupid and hopelessly vulgar music! The unspeakable cheapness of the chief tune . . . Do you believe that if this music had been written by Mr. John L. Tarbox, now living in Sandown, New Hampshire, any conductor here or in Europe could be persuaded to put it in rehearsal?"

—*Philip Hale on Beethoven's Ninth Symphony (1899)*

Nelson Rockefeller, in charge of the interior decorating, stormed into the lobby and summoned Rivera down from his scaffold. Rockefeller handed the artist a check for moneys due him, fired him on the spot, and ordered the mural covered up with tar paper. It was later chipped away piece by piece.

The language you can play on a French horn.

Solresol is but one of the 300-plus artificial languages devised over the past three centuries to bridge international communication barriers and unite mankind. The best known are Interglossia (a mix of Latin, Greek, and Chinese), Interlingua (based largely on the romance languages and used mostly among scientists), Monling (consisting entirely of monosyllabic words), and Esperanto, spoken today by as many as a million people. But the most bizarre, if also the most euphonious, is Solresol.

Solresol was invented by a French music teacher, Jean-François Sudre, in 1827. Written in musical notation, every word in its lexicon consisted of one or more of the seven notes of the diatonic scale—do, re, mi, fa, sol, la, and ti. As the stress was shifted from one syllable to the next, a single word could serve as a noun, adjective, verb, and adverb.

With its intricate grammar and extensive vocabulary, Solresol was not easy to master—yet it achieved an astonishing degree of popularity in

> "I'm sorry, Mr. Kipling, but you just don't know how to use the English language ... This isn't a kindergarten for amateur writers."
>
> —Editor of the San Francisco Examiner *in a rejection letter to Rudyard Kipling*

nineteenth-century Europe. Victor Hugo, John James Audubon, and Napoleon III were among its devotees, and formal instruction in the language was offered at Oxford, the Sorbonne, and the University of Padua. Chief among its appeals was that it could be hummed, whistled, sung, or played on a French horn.

Somehow, it's hard to imagine Kate Smith singing "God Bless America" in Hebrew.

After the American Revolution a movement was launched to replace English with Hebrew as the official language of the United States.

By 1776 English had acquired a bad name among the colonists simply because of its association with the monarchy. Several members of the young government advocated banning the language outright and replacing it with something else—Hebrew.

It made sense, sort of. Hebrew was held in high regard by the Americans, who viewed it as the mother of all tongues, the key to the Scriptures, and the foundation of a liberal education. They named their towns after those cited in the Bible, such as Salem and Bethlehem, and their children after biblical figures.

In 1759 Samuel Johnson, first president of what is now Columbia University, said that "as soon as a lad has learned . . . English well, it is much

"I'm a rock 'n' roll illiterate.

I was away during the

1970s in the Mideast.

I thought Fleetwood Mac

was a car."

—ABC anchor Peter Jennings, explaining why he mistakenly attributed the Fleetwood Mac hit "Don't Stop" to Jefferson Airplane

the best to begin a learned education with Hebrew." Other institutions of higher learning followed his lead. In the late 1700s Hebrew was a freshman course requirement at Yale, and it was stressed heavily at Harvard and other schools well into the nineteenth century.

Apossuls of Speling Reform.

Sir Isaac Pitman is best known as the father of modern shorthand. But in his own time he was as famous for the causes he championed—vegetarianism, temperance, and, strangest of all, spelling reform.

Although Pitman's shorthand manuals sold well, their author lived austerely, working sixteen hours a day and ploughing the profits back into his work. An outspoken proponent of spelling simplification, he believed all language should be written phonetically. By avoiding meat, wine, tobacco, and virtually everything else except for fruit and vegetables, he wrote in a letter to the *Times* of London, "I . . . gradiuali rekuvered mei dijestiv pouer, and hav never sins nown, bei eni pain, that I hav a stumak."

"Certainly, no man or woman of normal mental health would be attracted by the sadistic, obscene deformations of Cézanne, Modigliani, Matisse, Gauguin, and the other Fauves."

—John Hemming Fry (1934)

The simplified spelling movement continued well into this century. In 1906 President Theodore Roosevelt directed the U.S. Printing Office to adopt a simplified spelling system that had been created by two New York City university professors and underwritten by Andrew Carnegie. The idea drew widespread public scorn, and TR quickly withdrew it. In 1912 the Simplified Spelling Sosieti published *Nurseri Riemz and Simpl Poemz,* which included such favorites as "Litl Boi Bluu" and "Roc-a-bie Baibi." The book broke no saylz rekerdz.

In the 1930s the *Chicago Tribune* did its part for spelling reform by incorporating simplified versions of eighty words into its stylebook, including lether, trafic, frate, thoroly, and crum. For more than twenty years, only those spellings were permitted in *Tribune* copy; the practice was abandoned in 1955. "Teachers were having trouble with it," explained editor W. Donald Maxwell. "They'd tell a child a way to spell a word, and he'd bring in a *Tribune* to prove the teacher wrong." The return to conventional spelling didn't exactly jolt the paper's readership. According to an August 21 editorial, "Not one reader, as far as we are aware, noticed the change."

Kelp!

Book-designer Josie Hilton published a limited edition of Coleridge's *The Rime of the Ancient Mariner* printed entirely on seven types of kelp.

"This is my first attempt to produce a book printed on seaweed," she proudly told reporters.

Financial aid for the differently handed.

Juniata College, in Huntingdon, Pennsylvania, offers a special scholarship to left-handed students with financial need. The stipend was set up by left-handed alumni Frederick and Mary Francis Beckley, who were dropped from the college tennis team in 1919 because of their congenital deformity. Ambidextrous students are also eligible.

The Beckley gift is one of thousands of excruciatingly specialized scholarships made available each year through private endowments. According to David Cassidy, president of the National Scholarship Research Service, "There is a scholarship for everyone and every interest." For several years any Jewish orphan planning a career in the aeronautical sciences was eligible for a $3,000 scholarship from the University of California at Berkeley. Alas, that incentive no longer exists in that precise form; the same for a Seattle-based program designed to provide convicted prostitutes with a college education. However, these awards are still available:

1. **The Gertrude U. Deppen Scholarship,** given annually to a Bucknell University student who "shall not be a habitual user of tobacco, intoxicating liquor and narcotics and shall not participate in strenuous athletic contests." Only students from Mt. Carmel, Pennsylvania, are eligible. According to a Bucknell spokesman, Deppen scholars are barred from playing varsity football "but a little weekend golfing is OK."

2. **The International Boar Semen Scholarship,** a $500 stipend earmarked for the study of swine management at the undergraduate level. International Boar Semen is a division of Universal Pig Genes, Inc.

3. **The $500 NAAFA-NEC Scholarship,** awarded to obese college-bound high-school seniors by the New England Chapter of the National Association to Advance Fat Acceptance.

4. **The Zolp Scholarship,** available exclusively to Loyola University students named "Zolp."

Buttheads decry postage stamp.

A national smokers lobby angrily protested a 1994 stamp honoring the great blues guitarist Robert Johnson. The reason: The commemorative showed the musician minus his signature cigarette.

The stamp was based on a well-known photo of Johnson with a cigarette in his mouth. But the United States Postal Service requested that it be omitted "because they didn't want the stamps to be perceived as promoting cigarettes," according to a USPS spokesman. Indeed, an earlier issue honoring Edward R. Murrow was likewise smoke-free, despite the fact that the celebrated journalist was almost never seen in public or private without a cigarette.

Tom Humber, president of the National Smokers Alliance, decried the alteration in a letter to the Postmaster General. He called it "an affront to the more than fifty million Americans who smoke."

Byron, Olmedo, Rod McKuen — what's the difference? They're all poets, aren't they?

The City Council of Guayaquil, Ecuador, once voted to commission a statue of the great Ecuadorian poet Olmedo. Alas, the sculptor's estimate was far more than the city could afford. Fortunately the city fathers were able to swing a good deal on an almost-new statue of the English poet Lord Byron, who looked something like Olmedo. They erased Byron's name, chiseled in Olmedo's, and placed the statue in a plaza in the center of town.

Opera in the jungle.

Brazil's rubber barons were raking in more money than they knew what to do with in the late 1800s. So they decided to spend some of it building a lavish opera house in the middle of the jungle, 10 miles from the mouth of the Amazon.

They spared no expense, importing marble, cast iron, brass fittings, and lavish murals from Europe; the ballroom was assembled from 12,000 separate planks of polished Amazon mahogany. They situated their domed music palace in the town of Manaus on a bluff looking out over the Rio Negro and called it El Teatro Amazonas. It took twelve years to build and had 2,000 seats. Filling them was another story.

El Teatro opened on New Year's Eve, 1896, with a production of Ponchielli's *La Gioconda*. But Manaus was populated mostly by nouveau-riche Europeans and Brazilians with vile table manners and no taste for great music. So after opening night the grand edifice lay unused and untended, and it soon began to decay in the damp, overheated jungle climate. Termites gnawed at the woodwork. The crystal chandelier in the Grand Foyer fell from the ceiling; no one seemed to care. By the 1930s the rubber boom was over, the town of Manaus was beginning to look worn around the edges, and El Teatro Amazonas was a ruin.

In later years the town made a comeback, fueled by the arrival of oil and lumber interests. The opera house was refurbished, and the surrounding gardens restored to some of their original splendor. Even so, only recently have operas again been staged at El Teatro. For years it was used mainly as a rehearsal hall for local school glee clubs.

"Officer, Arrest That Projectionist!"

Bad Ideas in Popular Culture

The movie that never was.

In June 1932, the Communist International brought a cast of African Americans to Moscow to film what would be the first honest screen depiction of American racial inequality. Titled *Black and White*, the movie would rise above cheap Hollywood sentimentality to offer a frank look at the suppression of American blacks and their struggle for freedom.

But when the cast arrived in Moscow, according to *American Heritage* magazine, they discovered there was neither a screenplay nor a director. By the time they sailed home three months later, not a single frame had been shot.

Originally the Comintern planned to film *Black and White* with Russian actors in wigs and blackface. Realizing the absurdity of such an approach, they instead recruited twenty-two American blacks sympathetic to the cause of international communism—an assortment of young intellectuals, cabaret singers, and stage actors, as well as an insurance clerk, a salesman, and a farmworker. None had ever performed before a camera before. The poet Langston Hughes also went along as script doctor.

Sailing from New York the Americans disembarked in Berlin to learn that the Soviet consul knew nothing of the project and there were no visas for them. Eventually visas were secured, and the group continued on to Moscow to learn there was no script.

Ensconced in the Grand Hotel, they whiled away the days eating lavish meals of borscht and blini, dancing, and sight-seeing. Meanwhile the Soviets hired a director, an unknown German named Kurt Jughans, who spoke little Russian and less English and had never been to America. His sole contact with blacks—African blacks—had been through the filming of a documentary about African birds.

Miraculously after several weeks a script materialized and was handed to Hughes for his comments. The poet read it in his hotel room and laughed till tears came. He found it a "pathetic hodgepodge of good intentions and faulty facts," and utterly beyond salvaging, he told his Russian contacts.

Again the project was without a usable script. And again the Americans had nothing to do but party, overeat, and vacation on the Black Sea while they waited for the Soviets to get their act together. In September, three months after they had arrived, the project was abandoned and the Americans were sent home.

Back on U.S. soil, the actors railed publicly against the Soviets; journalist Henry Lee Moon spoke of the "betrayal of the twelve million Negroes of America and all the darker exploited colonial peoples of the world." Later some speculated that the U.S. State Department had sabotaged the project. But troupe member Frank Montero, who would later serve as assistant executive director of the National Urban League, had a simpler explanation: "It was never made because it was such a goddamn lousy movie."

He should have stuck with *Wuthering Heights.*

Cast members of Orson Welles' Mercury Theater were openly skeptical about his plans to air a radio adaptation of *The War of the Worlds* the night before Halloween, 1938. They thought H. G. Wells' tale of a Martian attack on planet

Earth too far-fetched to pull much of an audience. But Welles felt he could jazz up the story by moving the setting from England to the northeast United States and adding a heady dose of broadcast-age realism.

He was right.

The year 1938 wasn't a relaxed time in the United States. The Depression had yet to ease, and Europe was readying for war. Since early summer the words "we interrupt this broadcast . . ." had jarred radio listeners frequently. So it seemed only natural to Welles to capitalize on America's jitters by presenting *The War of the Worlds* as a series of realistic bulletins, interviews with scientists, official announcements, and on-the-spot news reports. The problem was that more than a million listeners across the nation thought the attack was real. There was panic everywhere.

In Indianapolis a woman raced into a church shrieking, "It's the end of the world—you might as well go home to die!" A Hillside, New Jersey, man ran into a police station and demanded a gas mask to protect himself against "the terrible people spraying liquid gas." Fifteen people were treated for shock in

"He must have made that before he died."

—*Yogi Berra, commenting on a Steve McQueen movie*

a Newark, New Jersey, hospital while reports of a gas-bomb attack spread through the city; ten squad cars and an ambulance were dispatched to one stricken neighborhood. Kansas City hospitals reported at least two broadcast-induced heart attacks.

The hysteria subsided by the following day, but widespread anger toward Welles lingered for years. Troops of reporters descended on his office and tried to get him on the phone—to no avail. The twenty-three-year-old director wisely went into hiding for several days.

Apparently the owners of radio station HCQRX in Quito, Ecuador, hadn't heard about the damage Welles caused with his reworking of *The War of the Worlds*—or perhaps they thought Ecuadorians weren't as gullible. In February

1949 the station put on its own version, using bulletins and spot coverage just as Welles had, and making it seem as if the Martians had landed in Quito.

Like their neighbors to the north, the Quiteños took the show at face value and panicked. But by the morning after, when they realized it had all been a joke, they took more direct action. An angry mob stormed the 3-story El Commercio building, where the station was housed, and set it afire. The structure burned to the ground; fifteen workers trapped inside died in the blaze.

In 1993, KZSC, a student-operated station at the University of California at Santa Cruz, aired a Wellesian drama about a massive earthquake striking the Los Angeles area. Fires, floods, and mud slides were out of control, the broadcast reported. Thousands were dead, and buildings were collapsing everywhere.

But in California, earthquakes are hardly the stuff of science fiction, and listeners panicked. "The phones began ringing nonstop," said Roger Takacs, the student who wrote the script. "A lot of people were calling me an idiot, saying it was inappropriate to create so much panic." Evidently his station manager agreed. The show was pulled off the air twenty minutes after it began; the remaining ten minutes were filled with apologies.

Stop the projector—I want to get out. Unfortunate ideas for movies:

1. *Incubus.* This dreary 1965 tale of a good man possessed by demons is the only full-length motion picture ever made in Esperanto. It left critics, audiences, and the actors themselves scratching their heads in bewilderment.

2. *Viva Knievel.* Three movies have been made about stuntman Evel Knievel; blessedly, this is the only one that's ever starred him. He portrays himself as a crash-helmeted Mother Teresa who battles drug dealers, cures alcoholics, and hands out gifts to children in a Mexican orphanage.

3. *The Terror of Tiny Town.* Hollywood's only all-midget Western. Released in 1938, it featured gunslingers riding Shetland ponies and walking *under* the swinging doors of the local saloon.

4. *Carmen.* There have been many movies based on Bizet's opera. The most bizarre was made in 1915 and starred movie vamp Theda Bara. It was silent.

5. *Sleep.* Andy Warhol's first film showed close-ups of a naked man getting his eight hours. It was, logically, eight hours long.

Vomiting as art.

Would you pay good money to watch someone throw up?

Thousands once did, gladly, on both sides of the Atlantic. Born in Egypt in 1892, Hadji Ali came to the United States in the early 1930s, appearing in fairs, carnivals, and vaudeville. Billed variously as "the Amazing Regurgitator" and "the Egyptian Enigma," Ali would swallow a variety of household objects—coins, buttons, stones, watermelon seeds, hickory nuts, costume jewelry, even live goldfish—and wash them down with copious amounts of water. Then as audience members called out specific items, he would spit them up, one at a time. Ali acquired a small but enthusiastic following; his grand finale brought down the house every night.

His assistant would set up a toy castle in a corner of the stage while Ali gulped down a gallon of water chased with a pint of kerosene. To the accompaniment of a dramatic drum roll, he would spit out the kerosene in a 6-foot arc across the stage, setting the castle on fire. Then, with the flames shooting high into the air, Ali would upchuck the water and extinguish all traces of the fire.

"Novelty is always welcome, but talking pictures are just a fad."

—Irving Thalberg, head of production at MGM

Ali remained more a sideshow curiosity than a true vaudeville headliner; according to Joe Laurie Jr. in his book, *Vaudeville: From the Honky Tonks to the Palace,* Ali "lasted four weeks" in one theater "before they got wise that he was killing their supper shows."

Even so, Ali's remarkable talent was recorded in at least two films: *Strange as It Seems,* a 1930 short subject and *Politiquerias,* a Spanish language comedy made in 1931. He was also featured at Grauman's Chinese Theater in Holly-wood from 1930–1931. He died during a theatrical tour of Great Britain in 1937.

To be sure, Ali's genius for selective regurgitation was not unique or unprecedented. A performer named McNaughton, headlined as "The Human Tank," made a living ingesting and disgorging live frogs on stage until his act was shut down by the ASPCA in the 1920s; around the same time, German-born Hans Rohrl gained fame as "the living hydrant." He wowed audiences by propelling a mouthful of water 15 feet across a stage in a spray nearly 7 feet wide.

In fact, voluntary upchucking, through controlled expansion and contraction of the throat and stomach muscles, has been a popular form of entertainment since the 1600s. A French medical text published in 1812 noted that a highly distinguished member of the Faculty of Paris was capable of vomiting the contents of his stomach at will, without nausea or excessive effort. Unlike Hadji Ali, however, there is no indication that anyone paid to see him perform.

Museums you may have missed:

1. **Buford Pusser Museum. Adamsville, Tennessee.** Buford Pusser was the small-town sheriff popularized in the *Walking Tall* movies. You can see his size 13D shoes, a map showing where he was born, lived, and died in a car crash, and other Pusserana. Buy a souvenir ax handle in the gift shop and whack a few bad guys, Pusser style.

2. **Philips Mushroom Museum. Kennett Square, Pennsylvania.** Watch an eighteen-minute video on mushroom farming, or see a diorama about shiitakes.

3. **American Mechanical Fan Museum. Dallas, Texas.** Most popular exhibit: the illuminated Funeral Fan, used to shoo flies—and the odor of putrefaction—from the deceased.

4. **Thermometer Museum. Sacramento, California.** Two hundred years of temperature-taking devices. Not so hot.

5. **American Angora Goat Breeders Association Museum. Rocksprings, Texas.** "Not a whole lot here," said museum spokesperson Patty Shanklin. "We have some papers, photos, and one old stuffed goat."

6. **Syphilis Museum. Liverpool, England.** The Syphilis Museum has long since been razed. But when it was in business, fathers took their sons there to gaze in horror at an endless display of the withered organs and shriveled remains of men and women who had flirted with Sin and met the grisliest of ends. Douglas Day describes the museum in his 1973 biography of novelist Malcolm Lowry, who was taken on several traumatic visits there during his boyhood.

7. **The Museum of Questionable Medical Devices. Minneapolis, Minnesota.** Located in a shopping mall. Prize exhibit: the amazing Prostate Warmer.

8. **Museum of Menstruation. New Carrollton, Maryland.** Alas, Harry Finley has closed his original bricks-and-mortar museum, which he established in the basement of his suburban Washington, D.C., home in 1995. In it you could view a genuine U.S. Army tampon launcher, a dress made entirely of "Instead" menstrual cups, and several vintage rest-room tampon dispensers. The collection is now viewable on the World Wide Web at www.mum.org.

Concerts for the nose.

Proclaiming himself a Japanese-German inventor, Sadakichi Hartmann was, briefly, a fixture in the New York theater in the early 1900s. His claim to fame: perfume concerts.

Using a battery of noisy electric fans, Hartmann blew great scented clouds of smoke out at his audience, explaining in Katzenjammer Kids English that each smell represented a different nation. Hartmann, who often had trouble with hecklers, rarely made it beyond England (roses) and Germany (violets) before being hooted from the stage.

Out, damned Portia!

Portia, the quick-thinking heroine of *The Merchant of Venice*, is among Shakespeare's most memorable characters. But that didn't stop director Orson Welles from filming the play with Portia's part completely eliminated.

Production on Welles' *Merchant* was set to begin on location in 1969, with his longtime companion, Yugoslavian sculptor Oja Kodar, cast as Portia. But Kodar's English was shaky, and she wisely declined the role. Rather than find a replacement, Welles simply edited Portia out, filling in the gaps with some creative rewriting. Welles himself played Shylock.

The good news is that Welles' adulterated *Merchant* has never been commercially released and never will be. Prior to final editing, both prints of the film were stolen from the production office in Rome. Somewhere Shakespeare must be smiling.

I'm going for more Jujubes, so don't bother saving my seat. More movies worth missing:

1. *Eegah* (1962). When a misunderstood prehistoric giant with bad skin tries to establish roots in a southern California town, he is hounded by panicky locals who eventually kill him. Along the way he falls in love with a local teenager, who screams as the giant is about to be gunned down, "Don't shoot—he doesn't understand." Arch Hall Sr. made the movie for $15,000; he later grossed over a million. Arch Jr. plays the sixteen-year-old hero.

2. *They Saved Hitler's Brain* (1964). Expatriate Nazis take over the island nation of Mandoras, where Hitler's disembodied head rules with an iron hand. They scheme to conquer the world by blanketing it with nerve gas. The premise is bad enough; what makes *Hitler's Brain* a standard at "Worst Films" festivals is its use of scenes scavenged from an old spy movie, spliced together with newer footage.

3. *Incredibly Strange Creatures Who Stopped Living and Became Mixed-Up Zombies* (1965). A crazed beatnik (played by director Cash Flagg) and a gypsy hypnotist terrorize a small-town carnival, primarily by putting them under and then rearranging their faces with acid. Filmed in "Bloody Vision."

> **"It is probable that television drama of high caliber and produced by first-rate artists will materially raise the level of dramatic taste of the nation."**
>
> *—David Sarnoff, founder and head of RCA (1939)*

4. *Plan 9 from Outer Space* (1959). This was Bela Lugosi's last movie: He died two days into the shooting. Rather than waste the footage, director Ed Wood kept it in the film and hired a taller, younger actor who looked nothing like Lugosi to do his remaining scenes. (Some said he was Wood's wife's dentist.) Plot: Aliens enlist corpses from a California cemetery in a war to conquer Earth. Special effects include the destruction of their flying saucers,

which, depending on which account you believe, were actually hubcaps, Mrs. Wood's good china, or paper plates soaked in gasoline and set on fire.

5. **The Cure for Insomnia (1987).** Few films more fully live up to their title than this eighty-five-hour monstrosity directed by John Henry Timmis IV. The title is taken from L. D. Groban's 4,080-page poem of the same name, which is read on screen by the poet; there is also some rock music and soft-core sex.

6. **The Longest, Most Meaningless Movie in the World (1970).** Sometimes described as the longest commercially released film ever, *Longest* was produced in Great Britain and premiered in Paris. It ran forty-eight hours.

The legacy of Hank McCune.

Probably not one person in a million remembers *The Hank McCune Show*, a primitive TV sitcom that ran for seven weeks in 1950, and then was never seen again. Hank played an amiable bungler who was forever exasperating his superiors at the candy company where he was employed. Even at the time, one critic called the series "eminently forgettable," but it does have one claim to posterity, however dubious. It was the first show ever to use canned laughter.

"Video won't be able to hold onto any market it captures after the first six months. People will soon get tired of staring at a plywood box every night."

—Daryl F. Zanuck (1946)

"Although the show is lensed on film without a studio audience, there are chuckles and yocks dubbed in," reported *Variety*. "Whether this induces a jovial mood in home viewers is still to be determined, but the practice may have unlimited possibilities if it's spread to include canned peals of hilarity, thunderous ovations, and gasps of sympathy."

We'd gladly invite you to tune in again next week, only there won't be a next week.

The annals of commercial TV abound with programming ideas no self-respecting broadcast executive would ever admit to. Consider:

1. *You're in the Picture,* possibly the most wretched idea for a TV series ever hatched; *TV Guide* called it "the biggest disaster since the Johnstown Flood." In this 1961 game show, celebrity guests poked their arms and heads through cutouts in painted backdrops and tried to guess what the scenes looked like. The show was panned so mercilessly after it premiered that a second episode never materialized. Instead, host Jackie Gleason spent the entire allotted half hour the following week apologizing for the fiasco.

2. *Turn-on,* another one-shot TV fiasco. Patterned loosely after Rowan and Martin's *Laugh-in,* and premiering in 1969, *Turn-on* ran heavily to animation, short videotaped blackouts, computer graphics, and synthesizer music. Its heavy reliance on sexual innuendo frightened off many ABC affiliates after the first week, forcing Bristol-Myers to drop its sponsorship.

3. *100 Grand,* touted upon its 1963 premiere as the first big-money giveaway show since the 1958 quiz show scandals. But no one was interested, and the show was dropped after three weeks.

4. *Land of the Giants,* a late-1960's sci-fi series about seven men and women marooned on a distant planet where they are kept in thrall by a race of humanoid giants. The earthlings spend every waking moment trying to repair their crippled spaceship and return home; meanwhile, they are tormented by gargantuan toddlers, pets, insects, and demented scientists. Wrote one critic of the series, "It looks like it was written in thirty minutes over a pastrami sandwich."

5. *The Survivors,* a cheesy adaptation of the Harold Robbins novel of the same name, starring Lana Turner and Kevin McCarthy. *Los Angeles Times*

critic Cecil Smith wrote, "There is not a character, a situation, a line of dialogue that is remotely associated with human beings." Evidently ABC
agreed: The series was yanked after three-and-a-half months.

6. *The Baileys of Balboa,* a sitcom whose lame plots turned on the inevitable
conflict between an unassuming fishing-boat owner, played by Paul Ford,
and the swells who moored their yachts nearby. "This had to be seen not
to be believed," wrote critic John Horn in the *New York Herald Tribune.* The
Baileys managed to stay afloat for six months in the 1964–1965 season
before CBS pulled the plug.

Grave oversight.

As a publicity stunt, promoters of Ernst Lubitsch's 1932 film *Broken
Lullaby* arranged for a stuntman to be buried alive for twenty-four hours.
But a storm blew away the grave marker, and when it came time to dig
the man out, it was impossible to find him. It took a team of thirty rescue
workers half a day to locate their man and disinter him.

"Freeway" to oblivion.

At first glance nothing about the 1981 comedy *Honky Tonk Freeway* particularly
seemed to doom it to failure. It featured a top-line director (John Schlesinger)
and a strong cast (Jessica Tandy, Hume Cronyn, Geraldine Page, Beau Bridges).

But the quirky plot, set in the dreary town of Ticlaw, Florida, turned off critics and kept audiences away in droves. Costing $24 million to produce, *Freeway* netted only $500,000 in North American rentals. On a percentage basis, that makes it the worst box-office flop in Hollywood history.

Other movies that should never have gone beyond the concept stage include *Contaminacion*, an aptly named Colombian opus filmed in 1982. By 1992 it had earned just under $1,500—the lowest box-office gross of any movie ever. *Heaven's Gate* (1980), the three-and-a-half-hour epic Western that destroyed United Artists, barely earned back $1.5 million of the $44 million it cost to make. No movie has ever lost more money.

The hills are alive with the sound of splicing.

A movie-theater manager in Seoul, South Korea, decided that the running time of *The Sound of Music* was too long. He shortened it by cutting out all the songs.

Officer, arrest that projectionist! More frightful ideas for movies:

1. ***Myra Breckinridge.*** "As funny as a child molester," is how *TV Guide* described this 1970 cinematization of the Gore Vidal novel. "It is an insult to intelligence, an affront to sensibility, an abomination to the eye." Film reviewer Rex Reed plays an actor who undergoes sex-change surgery and emerges as Raquel Welch. Critic Leonard Maltin called it "as bad as any movie ever made."

2. ***The Big Noise.*** The bubbles had pretty much fizzed out of Laurel and Hardy by the mid-1940s, and the legendary screen comics should have known better than to try to squeeze out one more film. This 1944 dud finds Stan and Ollie working as detectives, hired to guard a bomb. (The French title, self-referentially, was *Quel Petard*, or *What a Bomb*.) Bosley

Crowther wrote in the *New York Times* that the movie had "about as much humor in it as a six-foot hole in the ground."

3. *Robot Monster.* Extraterrestrials dressed in gorilla suits and diving helmets overrun planet Earth, bent on destroying mankind. Where did they come from? Hard to say, since the film was released under two other titles— *Monsters from the Moon* and *Monster from Mars.* Filmed in 1953 for less than $16,000, *Robot Monster* was possibly the most frugally budgeted movie in Hollywood history, though it grossed more than $1 million at the box office. Depressed over the scathing reviews and cheated by his partners, producer-director Phil Tucker attempted suicide.

4. *Santa Claus Conquers the Martians.* This 1964 low-budget bomb, shot entirely in an airplane hangar, is "without exaggeration one of the single worst films ever made," according to movie historians Jay Robert Nash and Stanley Ralph Ross. Pia Zadora made her film debut, accordionist Milton DeLugg wrote the score, and ex–Howdy Doody unit manager Paul Jacobs was the producer.

5. *The Thing with Two Heads.* A black-baiting scientist played by Ray Milland awakens from a coma to find that his head has been grafted onto the body of Los Angeles Rams tackle Rosie Grier. The two spend most of the 1972 film battling for control of their body, screaming threats and insults and punching each other in the head. (Not to be confused with the 1971 film *The Incredible Two-Headed Transplant,* in which the heads of a mentally retarded man and a sociopathic killer are attached to a single body.)

Pancho Villa, the film.

A Hollywood movie mogul hired Pancho Villa to overthrow the Mexican government on camera.

On January 3, 1914, Harry Aitken, head of the Mutual Film Corporation, met with Villa and offered him $25,000 to allow his next revolution to be filmed. It was to be a real revolution, Aitken stressed, with real bullets and real blood. At the same time Villa would be expected to reshoot scenes—and enemy troops—at the director's discretion, and otherwise aid in the making of a marketable film property.

As it turned out, Villa, together with Emiliano Zapata and Venestusiano Carranzo, was already leading an insurrection against the Mexican military dictator Victoriano Huerta. He took the deal, and Aitken hired D. W. Griffith to direct. When Griffith quit the project to direct *Birth of a Nation*, Aitken hired Christy Cabanne and Raoul Walsh in his place.

"Gone With the Wind is going to be the biggest flop in Hollywood history. I'm just glad it'll be Clark Gable who's falling flat on his face and not Gary Cooper."

—Gary Cooper (1938)

Villa was nothing if not cooperative. Without complaint he delayed an offensive at Ojinaga to allow Walsh's cameramen to set up, even though it gave Huerta's troops time to regroup. He agreed to limit most of his major fighting to the hours of 9:00 A.M. to 4:00 P.M., when the light was best, and even moved executions back to after sunrise.

"He used to have them at four or five in the morning, when there was no light," Walsh told a biographer. "I got him to put them off until seven or eight. I'd line the cameramen up, and they'd put these fellows against the wall and then they'd shoot them."

When Walsh and Cabanne had the scenes they needed, they thanked Zapata and his minions and returned to Hollywood. There they discovered that most of the footage was bland and unmemorable. So they reshot the battle scenes on a Hollywood back lot with a stand-in for Villa. Not a single print of *The Life of General Zapata* remains.

Nuking the Moon

Bad Ideas in Science and Medicine

A Nobel Prize for the father of lobotomy.

Brain surgery with an ice pick? That's exactly what a prefrontal lobotomy is—the surgical excision of a generous slice of healthy brain tissue, typically with an ice pick rammed through the eye socket into the cranium.

If it sounds unpleasant, it is. Aside from their evident barbarousness, lobotomies ruined the lives of thousands of mental patients and are no longer performed. But in its day the procedure was hailed as a miracle cure for severe anxiety and depression.

More incredibly, the man who developed it received the Nobel Prize.

He was Antonio Egas Moniz, a Portuguese neurosurgeon and statesman. By the early 1930s, the versatile Moniz had served his country as ambassador, cabinet minister, and member of Parliament, written more than 200 books (including a history of playing cards), and invented cerebral angiography, an X-ray technique still used to provide telling maps of the brain. But his greatest triumph was yet to come.

In 1935 Moniz poked a syringe through a hole drilled in the cranium of a sixty-three-year-old mental patient and obliterated her front lobes, which he deemed to be the seat of her unhealthy impulses. Afterwards the woman appeared calmer and less susceptible to hallucinations and delusions. Moniz pronounced her cured and went on to perform the same operation on hundreds more—initially with a syringe, later with a sharp surgical probe. When his hands became deformed by gout and exposure to radioactive dyes, a colleague did the cutting, with Moniz coaching from the side.

After World War II, Moniz's American disciples showed you could get at the lobes a lot faster by hammering a pointed instrument—an ordinary ice pick would do nicely—up through the thin bones of the eye socket and into the brain. Voilá: the instant lobotomy. The whole thing was over in eight or nine minutes, and, on a good morning, a nimble lobotomist could process a dozen or more patients by lunchtime.

"Jupiter's moons are invisible to the naked eye and therefore can have no influence on the earth, and therefore would be useless, and therefore do not exist."

—Francisco Sizzi, astronomer, rebutting Galileo's claim to have viewed the moons of Jupiter through a telescope (1610)

In the late 1940s and 1950s, more than 5,000 men and women had their lobes plucked in the United States and Europe, although the operation was banned in Moniz's native Portugal. But the good doctor's work sufficiently impressed the Nobel Prize Committee to win him a 1949 Nobel in Medicine—and $30,000 cash—"for his discovery of the therapeutic value of leucotomy [as the procedure was then called] in certain psychoses."

The Nobel committee had never been more wrong. Although the operation quieted some patients, it turned many more into zombies, and maimed and killed others. By 1960 lobotomies were largely a thing of the past, and "incurable" patients were treated far more effectively and humanely with drugs.

Sigmund Freud, coke pusher.

Sigmund Freud, father of psychoanalysis, was also the father of cocaine abuse.

Cocaine has been snorted as far back as 3000 B.C. But it remained little-used until 1884, when a German army doctor named Theodor Aschenbrandt gave it to exhausted soldiers, who perked up and grabbed their rifles, ready to party. Reading of Aschenbrandt's success in a medical journal, Freud decided to conduct his own field tests.

On a day when he was especially tired from overwork and in a generally sour mood, Freud took 200 milligrams of cocaine. Within minutes, he reported, he felt "light and exhilarated." He was able to work more productively, too.

He began using cocaine regularly, sharing his supply with colleagues and patients. He may well have been high when he wrote to his prim-and-proper fiancee, Martha Bernays, "I will kiss you quite red . . . and you shall see who is the stronger—a gentle little girl who doesn't eat enough or a big wild man who has cocaine in his body."

But cocaine was more than a recreational drug, Freud found. Its numbing effect made it an ideal pain suppressant. It could be used to treat anemia, asthma, nausea, indigestion, headaches, depression, fatigue, and impotence as well.

Following Freud's lead, thousands of people across Europe and the United States tried coke for themselves. Doctors and dentists prescribed it to patients; hawkers sold it door-to-door. Bartenders spiked drinks with the stuff, and it became the key ingredient of Coca-Cola and more than sixty knockoffs. Thanks to Freud, cocaine became a growth industry.

Inevitably, of course, people became addicted. Lives were ruined by the narcotic, and it was a contributing factor in the gruesome death of Ernst von Fleischl-Markow, a friend of Freud's who grew dependent on cocaine in the process of weaning himself off morphine. Freud himself continued doing coke for years with no ill effect. But a noted physician, Albrecht Erlenmayer, condemned the drug as "the third scourge of humanity" (after alcohol and morphine). And by the 1920s, its use was outlawed in the United States and most of Europe.

You are what you laugh.

The Italian astronomer Domascere published the results of a far-reaching study in 1692 linking the phonology of laughter with the humors of the human body. A laugh with a pronounced "I" vowel sound (as in "tee-hee") denotes a morose, melancholic disposition, he claimed. The "E" sound (as in "heh-heh") is symptomatic of a bilious character and chronic indigestion. The "A" sound ("ha-ha") suggests a cool, phlegmatic temperament. Most desirable is the deep, throaty "O" laugh ("ho-ho") emitted by cheerful, confident, sanguine individuals.

"Leave the boy alone, Martha. Who cares if he goes blind, as long as he wins a Nobel in physics?"

Ever wonder why more men than women pursue careers as plumbers and automobile mechanics? Bertrand Cramer, in a 1971 monograph, "Sex Differences in Early Childhood" (published in the *Journal of Child Psychiatry and Human Development*), explains it all for you:

"The capacity of the penis and testicles to move and retract presents the boy with a particular challenge in the development of the body image; this may contribute to his interest in machinery, physics and the like . . . The ability the boy has to perceive his sexual organ may also contribute to a better representation of space and to his better skill and greater interest in experimental sciences and mathematics." Notes New Zealand science writer Vicki Hyde, "One can only conclude from this that women should be overrepresented as mining engineers, tunnellers, and speleologists."

DDT for breakfast.

In an experiment designed to show that "DDT is harmless," pest-control executive Robert Loible and his wife Louise gulped down a ten-milligram capsule of dichloro-diphenyltrichlorthane with their morning coffee every day for six months.

The dosage of DDT consumed by the North Hollywood, California, couple was 300 times greater than the average daily intake by an American consumer during the days when the toxin was still legal. All told, they ingested as much DDT as individuals eating dusted produce for eighty-three years.

"X-rays are a hoax."

—*William Thomson, Lord Kelvin, president of the Royal Society (1900)*

Strangely, blood tests and urinalysis conducted by U.S. government physicians showed "nothing out of the ordinary." And Loible insisted, "We feel better than we used to. In fact, I think my appetite has increased since I began taking DDT."

The seat of intelligence.

A physician had his buttocks injected with gargantuan doses of Novocaine as part of an experiment to determine the truth of the old saw, "A pilot flies by the seat of his pants."

The subject, Hubertus Strughold, had formerly been director of Space Medicine for the National Aeronautics and Space Administration. With his derriere deadened, he boarded a jet plane. The pilot put the plane through a punishing set of maneuvers—rolls, loops, figure eights, and dives. Passenger Strughold became thoroughly ill, somehow proving, he claimed, that "the pants are one of the pilot's most valuable flight instruments."

Golly, Mr. Wizard!

1. Why bother reading when you can eat whatever you need to know? James McConnell, head of the University of Michigan's Planaria Research Group, trained several flatworms, ran them through a blender, and fed the pieces to untrained worms. Since the cannibal worms appeared to acquire some of the skills of their frappéd cousins, McConnell concluded that knowledge is edible.

2. Do desserts think? To find out, Canadian neurologist Adrian R. M. Upton performed an electroencephalogram test on a serving of lime Jell-O in 1976. Upton attached electrodes to the Jell-O in the intensive care unit of McMaster University Hospital, in Hamilton, Ontario. Faint brain waves were recorded.

3. Researchers at Ohio State University designed a three-week experiment to determine if rats are more sexually attracted to other rats than to tennis balls. Their findings: Yes, but only marginally.

4. At an international conference of organ transplant specialists in Fiuggi, Italy, Dr. Robert J. White of Cleveland proclaimed, "We must, we want to think of transplanting the head." White subsequently grafted new heads on several monkeys, claiming that some subjects survived the surgery for as long as thirty-six hours.

5. R. S. Ryback conducted an exhaustive study of the effects of heavy drinking on goldfish in 1969. After being taught to negotiate a simple maze, half the fish were transferred to a tank filled with a mixture of water and grain alcohol, where several eventually passed out, dead drunk. Sobered up and returned to tank number one a few days later, the hung over fish didn't remember a thing they'd been taught. The abstinent fish passed with flying colors.

6. Science achieved a historic breakthrough in 1972 with the discovery that male cats feel pain when their testicles are squeezed. In their seminal paper, "Afferent Neural Responses to Mechanical Distortion of the

Testis of the Cat," D. F. Petersen and O. Carrier Jr., observed the following: "Compression in lightly anaesthetized cats indicated a pseudo-affective pain-like response to distortion of the testis." They also noted that "a glancing blow to the testicle produced a burst of activity."

Physician, heal thyself.

As a rule, most physicians will not diagnose or treat their own infirmities. One who broke this rule was a Pennsylvania surgeon named Evan Kane. In 1921, at the age of sixty, he removed his own appendix.

Kane first had himself injected with a local anesthetic. Then, sitting upright, he sliced into his abdomen with a scalpel, pulled out his inflamed appendix, and snipped it. He let nurses suture the incision.

Kane had an uneventful recuperation and suffered no ill effects from the operation, which took place at Kane Summit Hospital, in Kane, Pennsylvania. Why did he do it? To prove that even major surgery could be performed as painlessly with local anesthesia as it could with ether—and a lot more safely.

"Everything that can be invented has been invented."

—Charles H. Duell, commissioner, U.S. Office of Patents (1899)

The appendectomy wasn't Kane's only do-it-yourself operation. In 1923 he amputated his own finger. And nine years later, at the age of seventy, he repaired his own inguinal hernia—a particularly dicey undertaking, since it involved cutting the femoral blood vessels. But the procedure went perfectly, and Kane was operating on another patient thirty-six hours later.

Self-surgery was only one of Kane's remarkable shticks. The other was designer surgery. Following an operation he would tattoo the Morse code symbol for the letter "K" near the wound, using india ink and a needle. He claimed no patient ever complained about the monogram and that many failed to notice it.

The taxing ordeal of Mr. Coffee and Mr. Tea.

Coffee was a popular drink throughout Europe by the eighteenth century, but King Gustavus III (1746–1792) of Sweden was convinced it was liquid death. To prove it he concocted a strange experiment, using two condemned prisoners as guinea pigs.

"MARTIANS BUILD TWO IMMENSE CANALS IN TWO YEARS. Vast Engineering Works Accomplished in an Incredibly Short Time by Our Planetary Neighbors."

—Headline in the New York Times *(1911)*

One was given only coffee to drink, the other tea. Two physicians were assigned to monitor the men and record their observations. The king had no doubt that it was only a matter of time before the coffee drinker died of acute poisoning.

But the experiment went on for months, with neither subject showing any ill effects. The first participant to die was one of the doctors; his colleague expired soon thereafter. Then the king was assassinated by a coterie of spoiled young nobles at the Stockholm Opera while he was attending a masquerade.

As for the two prisoners, they lived several years longer. The tea drinker died first.

Santa moves to Trenton.

During the Spanish-American War, a magazine editor hatched a plan for zapping Spain back to the Stone Age in seconds—and installing the United States as "dictator of the world."

Writing in an 1898 issue of *Electrical Age,* editor Newton Harrieson proposed wrapping a 25,000-mile-long cable around the earth. Then, by pumping a powerful electric current through it, it would be possible to reposition the earth's magnetic fields at will. Press a button and, poof, the North Pole is in New Jersey. Press it again and, presto, they're making snow angels in the Sahara. Hit it a third time and—hey, this is *fun*—Spain is an arctic wasteland, and the United States wins the war.

This is no gross oversimplification of Harrieson's scheme. As he saw it, once the Americans got the hang of electro-magnetically tilting the earth's axis back and forth, they could cool the tropics, turn the ice caps to toast, cure mosquito-born diseases, and grow wheat where glaciers used to be.

Never mind that some nations along the path of the proposed belt might not willingly grant access rights—or that the cost of constructing, maintaining, and patrolling it would be, in a word, astronomical. "Expense?" wrote Harrieson. "Nonsense! . . . There would be no trouble in laying this girdle over land and sea."

Harrieson seemed most excited about the cable's military uses. Whoever controlled it "could annihilate an enemy at will," he claimed. "In a single night a nation could be wiped off the earth—frozen to death. If the U.S. controlled the cable, it would be dictator of the world . . . The U.S. at a single touch of the button would transform [opposing nations] in turn to frozen wastes or torrid deserts . . . Ours would be the victory without the loss of a single life . . . And everybody would be happy."

"God save our gracious Queen and grant us Iceland's steam. . ."

In 1894 inventor R. W. Hill produced a fail-safe plan for meeting Great Britain's electricity requirements for all eternity.

But first Britain would have to conquer Iceland.

While burning coal was the preferred means of generating electricity in those days, Hill considered it a crude technology. A far richer power source, he felt, was steam. And it was available in limitless abundance within a network of geothermal springs beneath the surface of Iceland.

Hill urged Her Majesty's government to construct an 800-mile undersea pipeline to Iceland through which steam could be conveyed. Of course the cheeky Icelanders were not apt to hand their natural resources to a foreign power on a silver platter. So Britain's armed forces would first have to pound the rotters into submission and bring them under Crown rule. It would be worth it—and not just to solve Britain's looming energy crunch, but to show the Yanks a thing or two.

"Just think how envious would be our American cousins if an enterprising John Bull puts his steam batteries in all the geysers of Iceland," Hill said, aiming a few barbs in particular at "the so-called 'wizard,' T. A. Edison." In fact, he prophesied, "in ten or fifteen years hence, the present dynamo [will] be regarded as a great nuisance, nonsense and curiosity."

Captain Video meets Evelyn Waugh.

In 1964, the year it declared independence, the African nation of Zambia revealed its space program to the world.

"I'll have my first Zambian astronaut on the moon by 1965," promised Edward Mukula Nkoloso, Director General of the National Academy of Science, Space Research and Philosophy. Lest skeptics question his seriousness, Nkoloso, a grade-school science teacher, absented himself from independence day festivities in Lusaka. He was too busy getting ready to beat the United States and the Soviet Union in the race for space, he said.

Nkoloso trained his team of twelve apprentice astronauts using a simulated space capsule and firing system. Trainees curled up inside a forty-pound oil drum, which was rolled down a steep hill "to give them the feeling of rushing through space." In another exercise the capsule was swung around a tree on a long rope. "When they reach the highest point, I cut the rope," said the director. "This produces the feeling of free fall." Zambian astronauts also received intensive training in walking on their hands, "the only way humans can walk on the moon."

To date Zambia has yet to launch its first space mission, manned or otherwise. In a 1984 interview Nkoloso put the blame squarely on the nation's "space-men and spacewomen." As he explained, "They won't concentrate on space flight. There's too much love-making when they should be studying the moon."

The celestial power line.

In the late nineteenth century, many physicists imagined the universe to be filled with a vaguely defined substance called "ether." Unlike oxygen and other gases, ether was *everywhere*, occupying the voids between planets and every other available space in the cosmos. Some believed you could do nifty things with it.

In 1903 Albert Gallatin Whitney of Chicago devised a "method of collection putting to practical use the electricity from the interplanetary ether." His plan: build a 150-mile-long power line, anchor one end to planet Earth and launch the other into space via rocket or airship. Getting the line spaceborne would be as easy as flying a kite, Whitney explained: As soon as it attained an altitude of 17 miles, the ether itself "will raise the further end of the cable through the miles remaining without the necessity of employing any extra force."

Once the line was spaceborne, it could suck electricity from the ether and carry it down to earth to supply humanity's power needs for all eternity at pennies a kilowatt. Although Whitney was granted patents in the United States and Great Britain, the cable remained a pipe dream.

Edison's talk-to-the-dead machine.

Thomas Edison, inventor of incandescent light and the phonograph, also spent time working on a telephone for communicating with the dead.

As Edison figured it, human consciousness was simply an aggregation of electrons that survived intact after death. Cut loose from the brain, they floated around forlornly in space, looking for a receptive host. Some people were naturally attuned to such otherworldly emanations; Edison felt that with some fancy electrical wiring, anyone could tune in the dead.

"I have been thinking for some time of a machine or apparatus which could be operated by personalities which have passed on to another existence or sphere," he said in an interview with *Scientific American* in 1920. While he was vague about the form the device would take, he did offer that it would be "in the nature of a valve," and that it would amplify messages from the after-world "so as to give us whatever form of record we desire for the purpose of investigation."

"Every man who has sexual relations with two women at the same time risks syphilis, even if the two women are faithful to him, for all libertine behavior spontaneously incites this disease."

—Alexandre Weill (1891)

At one point Edison's friend Henry Ford arranged a meeting with Bert Reese, a self-professed psychic. Convinced that he could replicate Reese's tele-pathic feats scientifically, the inventor set up an experiment in which he and three associates wound electric coils around their heads and tried to commu-nicate telepathically from different rooms in the same house.

"We achieved no result in mind reading," Edison reported. Shortly there-after, Reese was publicly exposed as a fraud.

How much does your soul weigh?

The average human soul weighs one ounce. We know this thanks to the work of Dr. Duncan MacDougall.

At a Haverhill, Massachusetts, hospital in 1907, MacDougall moved the bed of a dying tuberculosis patient onto a large, highly sensitive balance scale. At the precise moment of death, the beam fell and the scale showed a weight loss of an ounce. MacDougall weighed five more terminal patients over the next two and a half years; at least two, and as many as four, also lost weight at the moment of death—between three-eighths and twelve ounces. There seemed to be no explanation other than the soul's flight from the body. Just to be sure, MacDougall ran the same experiment on fifteen moribund—and presumably soulless—dogs. Not one showed a weight loss.

Although he professed to be a man of science and not a spiritualist, MacDougall insisted that his experiments proved the existence of the human soul beyond question. Several newspapers urged that a convicted criminal be weighed as he was being electrocuted to corroborate MacDougall's findings. The grisly follow-up never took place, nor did anyone bother to weigh MacDougall's own departing soul when he died in 1920.

Faulty logic.

Portuguese children still have nightmares about the great earthquake of 1755, an eight-point-sixer that took 60,000 lives, caused fires that burned for days, and leveled the city of Lisbon. But that didn't stop a team of scientists from planning to stage a mini-quake in the waters off Oporto for the purpose of learning something new about the earth's inner structure. "Operation Combo" leaders offered assurances that the quake, triggered by twenty-two tons of TNT, would cause nary a ripple on the surface of the sea.

"There is absolutely no danger," said seismologist Luis Mendes Victor, who headed the venture. "If during the explosion you are in a very tall building and it's quiet and there are no vibrations from trucks passing, you might feel it." But the Portuguese weren't buying it, and the media carried credible reports that the tremors could cause coastal damage. "We're crazy if we allow this," said João Montenegro, director of the Institute of Geophysics of the University of Oporto. "Portugal needs schools, not dubious mega-projects." In the end the quake was canceled—largely in deference to national outrage. But it didn't help that the Portuguese company hired to detonate the TNT withdrew from the project on the grounds that it hadn't been paid for the work it had already completed.

"Yoo-hoo, Mr. Space Creature— over here!"

One of the most brilliant mathematical minds of the nineteenth century, Carl Friedrich Gauss spent his entire adult life mapping the heavens as director of the Göttingen Observatory and devising complex formulas to explain the movement of the planets. So it is understandable that his inability to reach out and touch the denizens of those planets caused him unceasing frustration. Finally Gauss came up with a way to get through: find a spot where undeveloped real estate was plentiful and cheap, and draw a mathematical diagram large enough to be visible from outer space. Who but the most jaded Martian could fail to take notice?

Gauss found his site in the steppes of Siberia. His idea was to plant a vast wheat field, at least 10 miles across and shaped like a right triangle. A block of trees would be set along each side, correctly sized to represent the Pythagorean formula—in a right triangle, the square of the hypotenuse can be found by adding the squares of the remaining two sides. Alien observers would be moved by the friendly, if immodest, expression of earthling intelligence, Gauss predicted, and might even beam back a reply. Unfortunately he failed to interest patrons in underwriting the project, and it never left the drawing board.

Neither did that of the Austrian astronomer Joseph von Littrow, who also sat up nights dreaming about networking with aliens. He hit upon the idea of digging immense circular, rhomboid, and trapezoidal trenches in the Sahara, which would be filled with kerosene and set ablaze for the delight and edification of anyone watching from outer space. Even more daring was the 1869 plan of French physicist Charles Cros to build a system of mirrors extending across Europe that would be used to reflect light spaceward. Arranged in the shape of well-known constellations, the mirrors couldn't help but attract interest from friendly spacelings, Cros said. That's assuming they weren't blinded first.

Nuking the moon.

To Alexander Abian the moon is little more than an unsightly mass of space crud that serves no other purpose than to foul up the earth's weather. He wants to blow it up.

Specifically it's the moon's gravitational pull, he argues, that causes the earth's twenty-three-degree tilt, the main factor in the planet's seasonal changes and climatic extremes. Relieved of this celestial gallstone, the earth would straighten up, the seasons would even out, and we would all enjoy "eternal spring."

These are not the ravings of a madman. Until his retirement, Abian was a respected Iowa State University mathematics professor with three theorems named after him and more than 200 scholarly papers to his credit. He believes it would be entirely feasible to fire enough nuclear-powered rockets at the moon to splinter it into small pieces or obliterate it altogether. We'd all be better off, and "it would make a great show for a few minutes."

Critics say such an act of destruction would melt the polar ice caps and cause global flooding. And the risk of Earth being showered with radioactive fallout or beaned with a chunk of shrapnel the size of India is not pleasant to contemplate. Worse, without the stabilizing influence of the moon's gravity, the earth could spin out of control and hurtle into the sun. "How does he propose to change the earth's angle of rotation without creating massive earthquakes?" asked Northwestern University physicist David Taylor. "He would destroy civilization, but we would have great weather."

Abian said such anxieties are unfounded. Yes, the ice caps would melt, but too slowly to be a problem. Given the moon's distance from the earth—240,000 miles—blowing it up would not endanger us in any way.

But what about the void that would be left in the hearts of poets and lovers?

Not to worry, he said. The moon's romantic qualities are vastly overrated.

"In some cultures, the moon is associated with ugliness and plainness," Abian told the *Wall Street Journal*. "In Russian, there is even an expression: 'To be as dull as the moon.'" But in any case, the operation is not irreversible: The same technology used to blow the moon to kingdom come could be used to replace it with moons appropriated from other planets. "To those romantics, I say, 'OK, you love the moon?' I will give you two."

Forty dollars for changing the world.

Sci-fi writer Arthur C. Clarke published the world's first detailed description of satellite communications in 1945. But he chose not to patent his invention, thereby forfeiting untold millions of dollars in royalties.

In a 1945 issue of *Wireless World*, Clarke suggested that radio waves—and, eventually, TV and phone signals, too—could be transmitted faster and more reliably by bouncing them off an orbiting space station. For the system to work, he said, the station would have to be placed exactly 22,248 miles up. At that altitude, it would rotate in tandem with the Earth, thus appearing to hover in the same position at all times. Since it would always remain in daylight, it could easily be powered by solar energy.

At the time scientists were toying with the idea of satellite-aided communications, using the moon as a relay point; no one paid much attention to Clarke's Tom Swiftian fantasies of rocket flights and cosmic hardware, which showed up again in his 1950 novel *Prelude to Space.*

In 1962 Clarke's fantasies became reality with the launching of Telstar, the world's first commercial communications satellite. But Early Bird, launched in 1965, bore almost uncanny similarities to Clarke's 1945 proposal, such as its 22,248-mile-high geosynchronous orbit—known today as the Clarke Belt—and its reliance on solar energy.

"It's a scientific fact that if you shave your moustache, you weaken your eyes."

—William "Alfa Bill" Murray, governor of Oklahoma (1932)

Since then satellite communications have revolutionized telephone, TV, and data communications and proven to be one of the twentieth century's most lucrative commercial successes. Clarke could have shared in the wealth. Instead his total earnings came to $40—his fee from *Wireless World* in 1945.

Hi. My name's Donic, and I'll be your wait-robot this evening.

The owners of the Kavio Restaurant in Leith, Scotland, added a robot named Donic to their staff in 1980. Dressed in tails and bow tie, the waist-high automaton was programmed to pour wine at the tables. But on the night of its debut, a glitch in the wiring caused the robot to spin out of control, darting chaotically around the restaurant, smashing furniture and crockery, spilling wine, and terrorizing the diners. Donic finally came to a halt after its head fell into a diner's lap.

The atomic mushroom farm.

A Texas businessman offered the U.S. government big bucks in 1994 for the 5-mile warren of tunnels built to house the superconducting supercollider.

He wanted to turn it into a mushroom farm.

Lined with concrete and buried 200 feet below the ground, the tunnels were to be the home of the world's most expensive atom smasher. Then in 1993 Congress cut off funding for the supercollider. Only 20 percent completed, the project had already soaked up more than $2 billion. Naresh Vashisht, president of Ominex, a Texas energy company, thought the subterranean passageways would make a neat place to grow mushrooms.

"We would save a lot of energy costs," he explained. Dark, damp, and continuously cool, the tunnels would never require air-conditioning, unlike the aboveground concrete-block mushroom farm his company owned in Colorado. "The 5 miles is exactly what we are looking for."

To the dismay of Vashisht and herbivores everywhere, the U.S. Department of Energy rejected his offer, preferring to abandon the tunnels.

Bonehead Plays in the Field of Sports

Game called on account of Heidi.

On the evening of November 17, 1968, millions of football fans were watching the New York Jets battle the Oakland Raiders in a game aired over NBC. At 7:00 P.M., with a minute left to go in the fourth quarter, and the Jets protecting a 32-29 lead, NBC programmers made the worst gridiron blunder since Roy Riegels carried the ball 98 yards in the wrong direction in the 1929 Rose Bowl: They aborted the telecast to begin a regularly scheduled showing of the movie *Heidi*.

Viewers must have thought they were hallucinating when their TV screens suddenly showed postcard scenes of Alpine meadows where a moment before there were grunting neanderthals tearing each other's lungs out. Thousands telephoned NBC headquarters to blister, rant, and bellow. When it became known that the Raiders had scored two last-minute touchdowns to pull out a 43-32 victory, the tide of calls swamped the NBC switchboard and the circuits went dead. Those who couldn't get through to NBC called the New York City Police Department, tying up the city's police emergency line for hours.

NBC executives later claimed that as Oakland started its remarkable comeback, they considered cutting back to the game, but before they could make up their minds, the clock ran out. *Sports Illustrated* called the programming gaffe "a memorial to the ability of network television to foul up."

At the 1975 Blue-Gray all-star college football game, it was the TV producers and not the quarterbacks who were calling the signals. Unbeknownst to the coaches or players, executives of Mizlou, the independent network covering the contest, had arranged to shorten the first quarter from fifteen to twelve minutes so it would fit neatly into its scheduled time slot. Later, as the tempo of the play picked up, Mizlou was afraid the game would actually end too early, and word went out to the timekeeper to slow things down if he could. In the fourth quarter the North mounted a dramatic last-minute drive and the last minute seemed to go on forever. As the clock stood still, the Blue scored on a 51-yard pass. With three seconds remaining, they kicked the extra point to win 14-13—long after regulation time should have expired.

They shoot pigeons, don't they?

Pigeon shooting was introduced at the Paris Olympics in 1900. Marksman Leon de Lunden of Belgium was the Gold Medalist, picking off twenty-one birds; Maurice Fauré of France won the Silver Medal with twenty. This was the only event involving the deliberate killing of live animals in the history of the games.

The Race to Death.

On an overcast morning in May 1903, thousands of Parisians turned out for the start of the great 870-mile Paris to Madrid automobile race. More than 200 of Europe's fastest drivers were at the starting line, and the mood of the crowd was festive. No one could know that the widely heralded event would quickly turn into the bloodiest spectacle in the annals of car racing.

All along the course spectators thronged the road shoulders and many spilled out onto the road. Roaring past at 90 and 100 miles per hour, the drivers tried futilely to steer around them—and plunged into ditches, crashed into trees and embankments, and drove head-on into the crowds. By the time the French government halted the race at Bordeaux, after 343 miles, there were 550 deaths and thousands of wounded.

The Race to Death, as it came to be known, was the last of the great "city-to-city" races. From that point on, automobile races were limited to enclosed courses, with the spectators safely confined to grandstands.

Nazi baseball.

American baseball was introduced to Europeans at the now-infamous 1936 Berlin Olympics. The crowd of more than 100,000 spectators didn't care much for it

> **"If Jesus were on the field, he'd be pitching inside and breaking up double plays. He'd be high-fiving the other guys."**
>
> —*Montreal Expos pitcher Tim Burke*

Despite pre-game lectures on the sport in three languages, most spectators watched the seven-inning night game in hopeless confusion, applauding with equal enthusiasm whether the ball was hit for extra bases or an easy out. The biggest cheer of the evening came *before* the game, when the players lined up on the field to give the Nazi salute.

Many spectators complained that there were too many players standing still at any given moment. Better lighting might have helped: In the overpowering glare of the lights, the crowd often had trouble following the ball. So did the players.

Chess grandmaster class: Lesson 1.

During a 1938 tournament in Plymouth, England, R. M. Bruce did what no man, woman, child, or computer has ever attempted before or since:

He challenged two world champion chess masters in a single day.

In the morning Bruce took on Vera Menchik-Stevenson, and, in the afternoon, the legendary Alexander Alekhine. Menchik-Stevenson, perhaps the greatest female chess player of all time, was women's world chess champion from 1927 until her death in 1944. Alekhine held the world chess championship from 1937 to 1946.

Bruce lost to both.

They throw grenades, don't they?

The noble sport of grenade throwing hasn't been featured in *Sports Illustrated* yet. But give it time.

Originating in the mid-1970s in the former Soviet Union, grenade throwing attracted some thirty-six million participants at its peak, according to Tass. The sport was part of a Kremlin-inspired fitness campaign called "Ready for Work and the Defense of the USSR."

More than 400 entrants, ages ten to forty-nine, showed up for the national grenade-throwing finals at Tashkent, capital of Uzbekistan, in 1976. Medal winners included Valentina Bykova, a thirty-nine-year-old housewife with the range (if not the accuracy) of an Estonian Carl Furillo. She hurled her grenade 132.8 feet.

Those magnificent men in their fartmobiles.

You wouldn't *believe* the assortment of vehicles that turned up at the starting line of the nation's first Los Angeles–to–New York "Future Fuels Challenge Rally" in 1977. There were vans, roadsters, trucks, and two seaters powered by firewood, methyl alcohol, and—gag me with a dipstick—soybeans and vegetable oil. (The emissions grossed out everyone for yards.)

Rally sponsor Bob Shepard, an upstate New York electronics magnate, wanted to inspire Americans to devise better, cleaner automotive fuels and put up $31,000 in prize money. It seemed like a good idea at the time. But in the end, only OPEC was smiling. Everything went wrong.

As early as the night before, Shepard might have known the rally was in the fast lane to Edselville: A monster publicity bash, held in a large convention hall that was rented for $5,000, drew eighteen people.

Then minutes before starting time, someone swiped the vials that were to have been filled with fuel samples to make sure none of the entrants was running on gasoline. Worse, the planners neglected to figure in the time-zone change from Pacific to Mountain and the drivers broke their necks—almost literally—trying to hit Albuquerque by 6:00 P.M. on the second day to avoid disqualification.

On the third day the rally coordinator was run over at a Phoenix intersection.

The drivers started dropping out long before the halfway mark, and Shepard seriously considered cutting the race short and catching the next flight back to Rochester. But somehow twenty of the thirty-eight starters made it to the finish in New York.

"None of them," reported the *Los Angeles Times*, "seemed in particularly good moods."

> **"Ruth made a great mistake when he gave up pitching. Working once a week, he might have lasted a long time and become a great star."**
>
> *—Cleveland Indians manager-outfielder Tris Speaker (1921)*

"Hey—you're both right. It's an airport *and* a golf course *and* a breath mint!"

Newcomers to Iowa's Laurens Country and Golf Club are advised to keep one eye on the ball and the other on the skies. The course also serves as the local airport.

It was built in the 1950s on what turned out to be a landing strip used by local crop-duster pilots, according to Bruce Nash and Allan Zullo in their book, *The Golf Hall of Shame*. Somehow golfers and aviators have managed to coexist over the years without a serious accident, even though the 1,200-foot runway cuts through the fairways of seven of the course's nine holes.

There have been some close calls, however. A pilot landing one moonless night looked in vain for his wife, who was supposed to have parked her car on the runway and kept the lights on. But she never showed up, and the pilot had to land in the dark. He missed the runway and wound up on the green.

"Mantle's a switch hitter because he's amphibious."

—Yogi Berra

Pilots usually circle the runway a few times before landing, to give anyone on the course a chance to clear the runway. But out-of-towners don't always get the hint. "They just gawk and wave as a plane gets closer and closer to them," said Ronald Harms, a longtime habitue of the course. "Sooner or later they run out of the way. After landing, the pilot usually gets out of his plane screaming and mad as the dickens." Local golfers who should know better sometimes play a perverse form of chicken, refusing to step aside to allow planes to land. When that happens, said pilot Glen Siddall, "then the planes just buzz them and scare them. They've all got electric carts and it's really something to fly down low and see them scatter."

Sometimes, though, it's the golfers who wreak the most mayhem. In

Livermore, California, for example, a golfer drove his ball through the cockpit window of an approaching plane and beaned the pilot. Miraculously, the aircraft landed without mishap.

Sonja + Omaha 4ever.

When Olympic figure skater Sonja Henie brought her ice show to Omaha, Nebraska, on the eve of Valentine's Day, 1941, a local booster commissioned an eighty-pound ice sculpture of her heart. He vowed that the city would keep it always—or at least until Sonja returned.

Sonja reacted lukewarmly to the frigid valentine, although she agreed to try carving her name into it with a heated nail. By the time of her death in 1969, she had never made it back to Omaha. But the city was true to its word and stowed the icy replica of her most vital internal organ in the Omaha Cold Storage Terminal. By the late 1990s the heart had melted to a fraction of its original size, and a futile effort was made to transfer it to a local museum. Before a new home could be found, the heart evaporated completely.

At the next games, let's make fiscal mismanagement an Olympic event.

The city of Montreal had never hosted an Olympics before 1976, so it is understandable that their cost estimates were somewhat rough. As it turned out, by the time the closing ceremony was over, the city was $1 billion in debt. That's 700 percent more than they'd planned.

What went wrong? For one thing the Montrealers had counted on continuing to reap a steady income from the stadium and the two first-class hotels built for the games. But bad weather, strikes, and cost overruns dogged construction, and the stadium and hotels were still uncompleted by the time the games were over. Designed by the French architect Roger Taillibert, the Olympic Stadium cost $1.2 billion to erect—more than any other building in the history of the world. It cost almost as much as all the other roofed stadiums in North America combined—and that was before its own fabric roof was installed. (When it was, it ripped almost immediately.) Montrealers call the stadium "The Big O" (rhymes with "Owe").

Also left over from the games was a $50 million velodrome that proved to be a total bust as a drawing card. Three hundred spectators showed up for the first national cycling championships held there; the stands could hold 10,000. Other mindless extravagances included $1.5 million spent on walkie-talkies for the security guards, and an even million to rent thirty-three cranes. (Purchasing them would have been cheaper.)

But the city fathers had a plan to recoup their losses. They held a giant tag sale, selling off 3,700 tons of used Olympic supplies, including TV broadcast equipment and shoelaces, and they levied a twenty-year Special Olympic Tax on property owners. But the money pit only got deeper: According to Quebec sports minister Claude Charron, it would cost $5.5 million a year to run the Olympic complex, with projected earnings of only $2 million. "It is a monstrous heritage," he said, "born of outrageous expense, socially unjustified and economically unrealistic."

Personal fowl.

Craig Rodenfels, of the Los Angeles Kings, hurled a live chicken in a Kings uniform onto the ice during a 1988 regular season game.

Rodenfels was tossed from the game and also arrested on a charge of malicious mischief and cruelty to animals. (Arena officials who saw him holding the chicken in a sack before the game took no action because carrying a chicken without obvious intent to hurl it is not illegal.)

The annals of academe.

At its 1989 commencement ceremonies, Ohio's Central State University awarded Mike Tyson an honorary doctorate in humane letters.

"I don't know what kind of doctor I am," Tyson said in his acceptance remarks. "But watching all these beautiful sisters here, I'm debating whether I should be a gynecologist."

Selling the Babe.

Baseball team owners, rarely known for their munificence, have struck some improbably generous deals in their day. The St. Louis Cardinals traded the great Steve Carlton to the Philadelphia Phillies for Rick Wise in 1972, and the New York Mets handed Nolan Ryan to the California Angels on a silver platter the same year. But by far the most incredible giveaway since the Dutch sold Manhattan was the one that sent Babe Ruth from the Red Sox to the Yankees in 1919.

Ruth had not only batted .322 and belted a record twenty-nine home runs for Boston that year, he'd also posted an impressive 9-5 record as a pitcher. But the Sox's wealthy owner, Harry Frazee, needed cash fast to prop up some failing investments and gave the Babe to the Yankees for $100,000—a pittance by today's standards but twice as much as had ever been paid for a player at the time. The deal nearly set off street riots in Boston; had Frazee dared show his face in public, he would surely have been lynched, despite his insistence that he was doing the Red Sox and their fans a favor.

"Ruth has become simply impossible," he told reporters, "and the Boston Club could no longer put up with his eccentricities. I think the Yankees are taking a gamble."

Some gamble: In his first season in Yankee pinstripes, the Babe batted .376 and hit an astonishing fifty-four home runs—more than any other *team*. The rest of his epic career—the 714 home runs, the "called shot" in the 1932 series—is familiar even to people who don't know a slide from a slider.

Frazee meanwhile continued to sell off Boston's best to the hated New

Yorkers, helping to build the great Yankee dynasty of the 1920s and 1930s, and crippling his own team in the process. By 1921 the Ruthless Sox had settled comfortably in the bottom half of the league, often finishing dead last and never making it higher than fifth place until 1934. They haven't won a World Series since Ruth pitched them to victory in 1918.

Frazee himself did better. He sold the club in 1925 and invested the proceeds in a smash Broadway production of *No, No, Nanette*. He made millions.

The electronic football helmet.

In 1956 several pro football quarterbacks wore radio-equipped helmets to receive instructions from the bench.

They could have done better with smoke signals.

The Cleveland Browns introduced the idea during an early-season game against the Detroit Lions. From the sidelines, coach Paul Brown called the plays into a microphone; on the field, quarterback George Ratterman tuned in through a tiny wireless receiver tucked in his helmet. Though the system did what it was supposed to, the Browns did not. They lost 31-14.

Undaunted, they took to the airwaves again a week later against the Chicago Bears. This time the radio went dead in midgame. When the Bears went electronic against the San Francisco 49ers a few weeks later, they won 31-7, despite the fact that their assistant coach spent much of the game transmitting defense signals while his team was on offense. In New York that same day, the Browns' radio signals were

> **"Last night I neglected to mention something that bears repeating."**
>
> —*Ron Fairly, San Francisco Giants announcer, during a play-by-play account of a game*

intercepted by a Giants reserve end with a receiver of his own. Final score: Giants 21, Browns 9.

A few weeks later Chicago Cardinals quarterback Lamar McHan's receiver was knocked loose during a tackle, so he tossed it aside. Unaware of the move, coaching assistant Charlie Trippi continued broadcasting anyway. The Cardinals won 35-27.

For the most part, neither fans nor players were enthusiastic about electronic helmets and NFL president Bert Bell received a fair amount of static over them. On October 19, he banned their use for the rest of the season. It wasn't until 1994 that the ban was lifted. Today radio helmets are as common a fixture of NFL game gear as mouth guards and shoulder pads.

Game called on account of flying LPs.

White Sox owner Bill Veeck lured more than 30,000 fans out to Chicago's Comiskey Park for a 1979 doubleheader against the Detroit Tigers with a unique promotion: Bring a disco LP to the ballpark and get in for 98 cents. Veeck's plan was to burn the records in a spectacular outfield bonfire between games—his way of joyously proclaiming the death of disco music.

But things didn't work out as planned. Before the first game was over, 7,000 crazed fans started scaling the LPs like frisbees at the field and at each other. By the time the second game was about to begin, there were still hordes of fans on the playing field, frolicking among jagged shards of vinyl and basking in the glow of a huge toxic bonfire. On order of the umpires, the flames were doused, and the White Sox forfeited the second game. Thirty-seven fans were arrested.

Playing hardball with the Goodyear Blimp.

It happened on July 3, 1939, at the Golden Gate Exposition in San Francisco. The San Francisco Seals, of the Pacific Coast League, were on hand, and manager Lefty O'Doul thought the crowd might get a kick out of seeing one of his stars try to catch a ball dropped from the Goodyear Blimp, circling above the fairgrounds at 1,500 feet.

He had only one taker—catcher Joe "Mule" Sprinz, who stood below, while O'Doul released a baseball from the airship. "I saw it all the way," Sprinz later said from his hospital bed. "But it looked about the size of an aspirin tablet."

Gaining speed at 32 feet per second^2, the ball slammed into Sprinz's upraised catcher's mitt with the force of a howitzer shell, driving his gloved hand into his face. He suffered severe lacerations of the mouth and nose, fractured his jaw, and lost five teeth. But he remained conscious and fielded the ball cleanly.

Why did he do it?

"All the other players refused and walked off the field," Sprinz said. "But I said to myself, 'God hates a coward.'"

Chess grandmaster class: Lesson 2.

Seventeen-year-old Joe Hayden announced he would play 180 simultaneous chess matches at a Cardiff, New Jersey, shopping mall in 1977. But there were only twenty takers and Hayden was trounced by all but two of them. Among the eighteen victors was Stowell Fulton, age seven, who polished the teenager off in a half-dozen moves.

One of the two Hayden beat was his own mother.

Couldn't he have just said thank you?

Virtually no one picked Soviet oarsman Vyachesla Ivanov to win the single sculls at the 1956 Olympics in Melbourne. At eighteen he was too inexperienced, and the competition was formidable. But in the closing minutes of the race, Ivanov came from behind to beat the favorite, Australian Stuart Mackenzie (a professional chicken sexer in the off-season). So thrilled was the winner that he heaved his Gold Medal high in the air after the official presentation ceremony.

Unfortunately Ivanov had miscalculated the trajectory, and the medal fell into Lake Wendouree. He jumped in after it, and later a corps of trained divers scoured the lake bottom, but it was never found.

In a related story, after sinking an especially difficult putt at the 1957 Bing Crosby National Pro-Am golf tournament, Tony Lema leaped for joy and toppled off an 18-foot cliff. He escaped with bruises on his elbows and shins.

What if they gave a heavyweight title fight and no one came?

Jack Dempsey hadn't fought in more than two years when he agreed to defend his world heavyweight title against Tommy Gibbons in Shelby, Montana, a torpid little cow town in the middle of nowhere. The bout, which took place on July 4, 1923, turned into the biggest fiasco in boxing history.

Shelby boosters concocted the idea as a way of putting their town on the map. To lure Dempsey they promised him $250,000 plus half the gate receipts. It was a rather bold gesture, considering the town didn't even have a boxing arena.

To raise the funds to build one, the promoters borrowed heavily, sold stock in a very iffy oil exploration scheme, and cadged donations from local merchants, many of whom thought the fight was a stupid idea. They scraped up enough cash to construct a 45,000-seat stadium.

> **"Women play about 25 percent as good as men."**
>
> —*Former tennis star Bobby Riggs, prior to being defeated by Billie Jean King at the Houston Astrodome (1973)*

But by fight day, nowhere close to 45,000 tickets had been sold.

Desperate to fill seats, the organizers delayed the start of the fight more than an hour, slashing admission prices and practically dragging people in off the street. Finally cowboys pulled down the fences with lassos and let spectators in for free. But by the time the boxers threw their first punches, the arena was three-quarters empty.

Dempsey was the favorite, and an early-round knockout would have surprised no one. But Gibbons went the distance and lost on a decision. In a postfight ceremony, a delegation of Blackfeet Indians crowned him with a war bonnet made of eagle feathers.

It was all that the challenger got for his trouble; he wasn't paid a cent. Dempsey was also shortchanged by $50,000, but he cut his losses and got out of town in a hurry, afraid the promoters would want their money back. He never returned. Meanwhile four banks and several local businesses in Shelby went bankrupt.

Vidiot.

Major-league wanna-be Ron Kravitz sued Mickey Mantle Sports Productions, Inc. for injuries he claimed were caused by their instructional video on base-stealing techniques. According to Kravitz, while watching the tape, he tore several ligaments and a tendon when he slid headfirst into a heavy table in his basement. He said he was trying to beat Tom Seaver's pick-off throw to first.

Pantyhose Night at the ballpark.

It started with Ladies' Day. Then came Ball Day, Cap Day, Bat Day, and Ten-Cent Beer Night. Finally, in a desperate effort to draw fans to the ballpark, the hapless Washington Senators offered Pantyhose Night, distributing a free pair to every woman who bought a ticket.

It was degrading to women, to baseball, and to the memory of Walter Johnson. Even Bill Veeck, the flamboyant baseball magnate who once sent a midget to pinch hit, was disgusted. "I wouldn't have something like that because that's like having Deodorant Night," he said. "You embarrass people who need large ones. It's also, I think, in bad taste. And, anyway, you can't have all sizes."

"Iron man" Smoltz.

Atlanta Braves pitcher John Smoltz suffered second-degree burns on his chest in 1990 when he tried to iron a shirt while he was wearing it.

Smoltz was in his hotel room during spring training when the mishap occurred. "I've ironed my shirt while wearing it five or six times before and never was burned," he said later. "I couldn't believe it."

Smoltz's off-the-field miscue is matched by that of teammate Tom Glavine, who suffered a cracked rib in 1992 when he vomited too strenuously. . . Mark Smith, of the Baltimore Orioles, received nasty cuts on his hand when he inserted it in a hotel room air conditioner to see why it wasn't working properly. . . Terry Harper, also of the Braves, dislocated his shoulder waving home a base runner. . . José Valentin of the Milwaukee Brewers wound up on the disabled list after cutting his hand on a pineapple. . . Brewers pitcher Steve Sparks dislocated his shoulder attempting to rip a phone book in half. . . And Florida Marlins infielder Bret Barberie was sidelined after accidentally rubbing chili juice in his eye.

The farting golfer.

Golfer Tommy Bolt reached the peak of his career in 1958 when he won the U.S. Open. He hit something of a low the following year when he was disciplined for farting during a tournament in Tennessee.

A respectful hush had fallen over the spectators at the 1959 Memphis Invitational Open as one of Bolt's opponents prepared to tee off. Suddenly Bolt—nicknamed "Thunder"—let loose with a rock-shivering blast that crashed through the silence and sent the crowd into hysterics.

"That's disgusting," one of the other golfers protested, and the officials agreed. Although the PGA rules did not explicitly prohibit premeditated farting during tournament play, Bolt was slapped with a $250 fine for "conduct unbecoming a professional golfer." For his part Bolt felt he had nothing to apologize for. "Damn it," he railed at the judges. "You guys are trying to take all the color out of the game!"

Later, when asked by reporters about the episode, he said with a straight face, "It was blown out of proportion."

The witch of Cleveland.

The Cleveland Indians, perennial cellar dwellers of the American League, hired a witch in 1984 to get them out of last place.

Before a night home game on Friday, July 13, the witch, known to her followers as Elizabeth, built a fire behind second base, where she burned charcoal, herbs, and incense and prayed for the removal of a twenty-six-year hex on the Indians. According to local lore, after being fired as manager in 1958, Bobby Bragan had pronounced a curse on the Indians, condemning them to never again winning an American League pennant. Elizabeth asked the "supreme goddess" to grant the Indians "intelligence, strength, and virtue to win their games." She then announced that the curse was gone.

> **"Heavyweight prizefights have gone the way of the tournament and the duel. We have outgrown prizefights; that's all there is to it."**
>
> —Life *magazine (1910)*

The Indians ended the season in seventh place, twenty-nine games behind the league-leading Detroit Tigers.

Someone's idea of fun: Ten very strange sports.

1. **Bullfighting on wheels.** In 1901, promoter Henri Deutsch staged the world's first vehicular bullfight in Bayonne, France. The *coche del torero* was a twelve-horsepower Peugeot, driven by Deutsch's chauffeur; the bullfighter, a man named Ledesma, sat next to him. The Peugeot was reinforced with steel plates—a needless precaution, it turned out. The bull panicked when he saw the car and the bullfight turned into a protracted chase, with the bull zigzagging across the arena, and the Peugeot futilely trying to keep up with him. As the stink of exhaust fumes filled the air, the crowd quickly grew bored and began to leave.

2. **Roller basketball.** Basketball originated in 1891; a decade later roller skating enjoyed a surge in popularity. That's when someone got the idea to combine the two. Roller basketball attracted a small but loyal following. There was even talk of a roller basketball league, with fifty clubs applying for franchises, and some went so far as to predict that it would replace pedestrian basketball. It didn't.

3. **Equestrian basketball.** Basketball on horseback had a small following in the 1920s. The rules were much the same as horseless b-ball, except that dribbling was eliminated and the foul line was pushed out to 30 feet. Not surprisingly, not many points were scored. In one 1929 contest, Battery D, of the 104th Field Artillery in New York City, trounced Battery F 9-4. Game highlight: a nasty third period collision between Horton (Battery F) and Van Iseghan (Battery D), with the former breaking his leg, and the latter suffering spinal damage.

4. **Equestrian boxing.** Joe Edwards, an American expatriate living in Berlin, invented boxing on horseback in 1912, and the German army staged several matches, mostly for training purposes. "The new sport will be valuable for the soldier in time of war, as when he loses his

weapons he will have to fall back on his natural means of defense," the German War Ministry explained.

5. **Aerial golf.** A creation of the 1920s, aerial golf required four players—two in the air and two on the ground. The airborne duffers took off in separate craft, each with a generous supply of balls, and at an altitude of 50 feet or so, dropped the ball as close to the cup as possible. Then each golfer's earthbound partner played the ball from where it landed.

6. **Robot sumo wrestling.** The All-Japan Robot Sumo Tournament has been sponsored annually by Fuji Software since 1989. Entrants compete in one of two classes—radio-controlled and stand alone. Either way, robots that are more than 20 centimeters wide or hurl objects at their opponents are ineligible. First prize: one million yen.

7. **The Eskimo ear-pull.** A fixture of the annual Eskimo-Indian Olympics. Two opponents face each other, connected by a length of sealgut fishing line tied to each person's ear. Each pulls back on the line, trying to force the other to give up. Other events include the four-man carry, wherein each entrant must lift and carry four men; and ear–weight lifting, the object of which is to carry a sixteen-pound weight suspended on a string from one's ear.

8. **Purring.** In this ancient Welsh contact sport, two opponents stand face-to-face, grasping each other firmly by the shoulders. At the starting signal, they begin kicking each other smartly in the shins with shoes reinforced with metal toeplates. First one to release his opponent's shoulders loses.

9. **Face slapping.** Nothing complex about this sport, which was in vogue in Russia in the early 1930s—just two guys slapping each other silly until one or the other cried uncle. The most celebrated match took place in Kiev between Wasyl Bezbordny and Michalko Goniusz in 1931. They went at it for thirty hours until spectators intervened and separated the bloody-faced competitors.

10. The fifty-six-pound rock throw. Introduced at the 1904 Olympic games and won by Canadian policeman Etienne Desmarteau with a manly heave of 34 feet, 4 inches. Why fifty-six pounds? Good question.

We're number two! We're number two!

The Cleveland Browns kicked off against the Detroit Lions on New Year's Day, 1961, in a postseason contest expressly designed to determine the *second-best* team in professional football. The game was called "the Bert Bell Benefit Bowl," after the late lamented NFL commissioner, who had suffered a fatal coronary while watching a Steelers-Eagles game on TV the year before. Though a poignant tribute, it remains nonetheless the most spirited celebration of mediocrity in modern sports.

A month earlier the regular season had ended with the Baltimore Colts edging out the New York Giants 31-17 in overtime to win the NFL championship. Desperate to prolong the playing season and wring out a few extra dollars of profit, league executives decided to pit the Eastern and National Conference runner-up finishers against each other. The winner, presumably, would be hailed as the second-best team in football—or, strictly speaking, *third* best, behind the Colts and Giants.

"A gun is a recreational tool—like a golf club or tennis racket. You can kill someone with a golf club, you know."

—NRA official Martel Lovelace

As it turned out the first Bell Bowl was the most closely fought, with Detroit nipping Cleveland 17-16. Thereafter the games were as exciting as lint, with the also-rans using the games to try out new plays but otherwise just going through the motions. After Baltimore's 35-3 drubbing of Dallas in 1965, the NFL shut down the Bell Bowl for good.

Good judgment strikes out.

Fewer than 300 major-league pitchers have struck out more than 1,000 batters. The Atlanta Braves' Charlie Liebrandt reached that milestone during a 1992 contest with the Philadelphia Phillies. After receiving the ball from the catcher, Liebrandt tossed it into the dugout for safekeeping, realizing too late that he'd neglected to ask for time out. As Liebrandt futilely chased the ball, the runner on first scampered to second. Liebrandt was charged with an error.

Greed hits a home run.

Major-league baseball came up with a winning idea in 1933—a midseason contest between teams made up of the best players from the American and National Leagues. It was called the All-Star Game, and it was an instant hit.

More than 49,000 fans were at Chicago's Comiskey Park on July 6 to see the American League All-Stars, including Babe Ruth, Lou Gehrig, and Al Simmons, beat the Nationals (Carl Hubbell, Lefty Grove, and Pepper Martin) 4-2. While fat-cat team owners hardly lost money on the deal, most of the profits went toward the players' pension fund.

Except for a wartime break in 1944, the All-Star Game was played annually until 1959, when the players had an algebraic revelation: If we can make X dollars from *one* All-Star Game, we can make 2X dollars from twice as many All-Star Games. And so, from 1959 through 1962, there were two All-Star contests each season.

Despite the game's obvious appeal, there was no masking that (1) it had no impact on the standings, nor any real significance at all, and (2) its only purpose was to fatten the players' nest eggs. Tacking on a sequel struck most fans as a wretched excess.

Some of the players, editorialized *Sports Illustrated,* "would be willing to play a third, or even a fourth All-Star Game, but the fans . . . evidently feel that two games are one too many. So do we." After the 1962 season the players went back to a one-game-a-year schedule. It's been that way ever since.

A Miscellany of Moronic Stunts, Pointless Heroics, and Unsafe Practices

The pushpin crucifixion.

A California minister had himself nailed to a cross as a protest against crime in the streets.

In 1978, the Reverend Willie Dicks, of St. John's Missionary Baptist Church in San Jose, set up a 9-foot by 12-foot wooden cross in Oakland's Arroyo Viejo Park. Removing his white cotton gown, he leaned against the cross and extended his arms. Using carpenter's nails sprayed with Bactine, an assistant affixed the pastor to the cross, hammering the nails through the skin between the third and fourth fingers of each hand, and between his first and second toes.

While a small crowd formed, Reverend Dicks remained on the cross for ten minutes, lecturing about crime and morality. "I would like to say from this cross that I'm disgusted that our senior citizens cannot walk through the streets of the cities they helped to build without being robbed and raped," he said. "I'm asking you here today to refrain from all crime."

In a related story, following his fiancée's miraculous recovery from a paralyzing illness, Paulo Cesar Bonfion expressed thanks by hiking the width of Brazil bearing a heavy wooden cross on his back. During his absence his fiancée married another man.

"Oh, Victor, you shouldn't have!"

As the first king to rule over a united Italy, Victor Emmanuel II (1820–1878) might well have achieved historical prominence even if he hadn't distinguished himself as the bestower of one of the most vulgar gifts imaginable.

For some unfathomable reason, the monarch allowed the nail of his big toe to go untrimmed for a year at a time. Each New Year's Day was the occasion for the grand Paring Ceremony, by which time the nail had grown a good half an inch beyond the end of the toe, or even farther in good years.

The royal clipping was then passed on to the king's jeweler, who took the "gem," polished it, shaped it, edged it with gold, and encrusted it with precious stones. In the hands of the skilled craftsman, the nail was transformed into a valuable if unsavory bauble. Victor Emmanuel made it a custom to turn over this little piece of himself to his favorite mistress of the moment. The most stunning collection of *ongles de roi* was accumulated by the Countess Mirafiori, whom the king ultimately married.

Stupid primate tricks:

1. A despondent man set himself afire in a park in Biella, Italy. Then, evidently experiencing second thoughts, he threw himself to the ground and rolled around on the grass in an effort to extinguish the flames. Onlookers gasped in horror as he rolled off a cliff and fell to his death.
2. Rip Howell, a.k.a. "The Human French Fry," sat naked in a bathtub filled with ketchup for thirty-four hours in 1980 to establish a new world record. (No one remembers what the old one was, who set it, or why.) "I'm totally insane," the University of Southwest Louisiana undergraduate told reporters.
3. A man in Hamilton, Scotland, was hospitalized with frozen tonsils after devouring fifty scoops of ice cream in sixteen minutes in an ice cream–eating contest.

4. A farmer in northern Kenya was forced to cancel his wedding when he discovered that the money he'd saved for the dowry—$150 in paper currency—had been eaten by ants. Rather than put the money in a bank, he had buried it for safekeeping.

Hazelwood rides again.

Three years after the Exxon *Valdez* spilled eleven million gallons of oil into Alaska's Prince William Sound, Capt. Joseph Hazelwood was hired to teach cadets how to stand watch on a ship.

Hazelwood was commander of the *Valdez* when it tripped over Bligh Reef in March 1989, causing one of the worst environmental disasters in history. Hazelwood admitted to having a drink shortly before the incident and assigning a third mate to stand watch in his place. Although his license was suspended by the U.S. Coast Guard, he was found not guilty of navigating while intoxicated.

Not surprisingly, Skipper Joe wound up on the hit lists of environmentalists, politicians, and stand-up comics everywhere. But that didn't stop State University of New York's Maritime College from hiring him as an instructor in 1992. The job, which paid $5,000, involved supervising cadets on the bridge of the 17,000-ton *Empire State* during a training cruise from New York to Gibraltar.

"This is truly amazing," said a spokesman for the Sierra Club. "I hired him, I guess I'm the one who should take the flak," said the head of the school, Admiral Floyd Miller.

The man who would be bat food.

The English naturalist Charles Waterton was without question one of the nineteenth century's most bizarre personalities. He erected a 9-foot wall around his estate and turned the grounds into a wildlife sanctuary. On jungle treks he would bare-handedly wrestle alligators and pythons into submission, disemboweling them on the spot to the horror and edification of his companions. Back home he slept on the bare floor, using a wooden block for a pillow. For fun he liked nothing better than to hide behind the foyer draperies, leaping out with a snarl at visitors and biting them on the shins.

"Three-quarters of [the oil] was contained within the ship. There's been very little reporting on that."

—*John Sununu, White House Chief of Staff, to reporters after the Exxon* **Valdez** *spilled 250,000 barrels of oil into Alaska's Prince William Sound*

During his explorations of the South American rain forest, Waterton was intrigued by stories of the blood-sucking proclivities of vampire bats. He wanted to see for himself. So he pitched camp near a bat cave, daubed his big toe with blood, and slept night after night in a hammock with the digit exposed, desperate to be bitten.

But not a single bat showed the least interest in Waterton's toe. His Indian manservant, however, was bitten with gusto nightly. "His toe held all the attractions," Waterton lamented.

On another occasion, while visiting upstate New York, Waterton bruised his foot hiking, but luckily, he knew exactly what to do: A doctor had advised him once to treat injuries with cold water. If a water pump was effective, Waterton reasoned, a water*fall* would work twice as well. So he cooled his sore foot under Niagara Falls.

There's nothing like home-baked bread.

In 1988 the *San Francisco Chronicle* reported the sad tale of a chef who inadvertently cooked his salary.

Employed in the kitchen of the New House Hotel, in Haverdfordwest,

Wales, the chef parked his earnings in an oven before closing up one night. He had been too exhausted to climb upstairs to the hotel safe. Arriving at work the following morning, he turned on the oven, forgetting that it wasn't empty. The resulting fire incinerated the money and filled the hotel with smoke.

Stupid primate tricks II:

1. In its issue of November 17, 1850, the *Times* of London reported the gruesome death of young Richard Bolton of Yorkshire. The boy had been playing with a friend "who was pretending to place a pea in his ear and make it come out of his mouth," the *Times* noted. Attempting to copy the trick, Richard pushed the pea in too far. A doctor was summoned, who accidentally pushed it in farther. The boy died four days later.

2. During a parade in Ventura, California, a drum major threw his baton as high as he could. It struck an overhead power line, causing a 10-block blackout, putting a radio station temporarily off the air and starting a grass fire.

3. Thomas Waddell of Baltimore was arrested with twenty-one live homing pigeons stuffed in his pants; police found five more—all dead—when they frisked him. "He looked like the guy in the Michelin tire ad," said arresting officer Ronald Pettie. Waddell, who had stolen the birds from two neighbors, was charged with grand theft and cruelty to animals.

4. When his wife left him, a Thai construction worker stationed in Bahrain cut off his penis. Friends found the man bleeding profusely, packed the severed organ in a bottle of water, and drove him—and it—to the hospital, Reuters reported. Man and member were surgically reunited in a three-hour operation.

5. With a large crowd cheering him on, twenty-four-year-old Floyd Malacek attempted to jump Minnesota's 40-foot-wide Lacque Park River on a power lawn mower. He missed by 35 feet.

Just when you thought it was safe to take up smoking again.

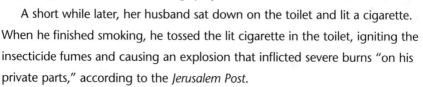

In Tel Aviv, Israel, a woman squashed a cockroach in her home, tossed it in the toilet, and finished the job by emptying an entire canister of bug spray into the bowl.

A short while later, her husband sat down on the toilet and lit a cigarette. When he finished smoking, he tossed the lit cigarette in the toilet, igniting the insecticide fumes and causing an explosion that inflicted severe burns "on his private parts," according to the *Jerusalem Post*.

It gets worse. Ambulance workers placed the man on a stretcher and proceeded to carry him out of the house. When they asked him how the burns had occurred, he told them. Convulsed with laughter, they dropped the stretcher, breaking two of the man's ribs and cracking his pelvis.

The water test.

In Haruku, Indonesia, two neighbors, named Djambi and Hasnuddin, argued over who was the rightful owner of a sago tree. They agreed to resolve their dispute in the traditional manner: Each man would load up his pockets with heavy stones and jump into the river. The one who remained submerged longest would be the winner.

It was a tie. Both drowned.

"Honey, I drained the canal."

A work crew dredging the Chesterfield Canal in Nottinghamshire, England, in 1978 was not having an easy time of it, struggling to fish out rusted car doors, household appliances, and bicycle frames stuck in the mud. When the dredge hooked onto a heavy chain, the laborers knew they had their work cut out for them. Finally they hauled it out, along with a heavy wooden block attached to the end. Then they broke for tea.

In their absence a passerby noticed that the water in the canal was swirling violently and the level was dropping fast. The workers had removed the plug, set in place when the canal was built 200 years earlier.

Before anyone could think what to do, all the water drained from a mile-and-a-half stretch of the canal into the River Idle. Several pleasure boats, along with the dredge, remained behind, stuck in the mud.

"Hazards are one of the main causes of accidents."

—U.S. Occupational Safety and Health Administration booklet

When in doubt, hide.

In 1947 Vladimir Zenchenkov, a government accounting clerk in Kishinev, U.S.S.R., returned home from a night of drinking to discover that he had misplaced 400 ration cards owned by his boss.

This was not a good thing. Ration cards were a prized commodity in postwar Russia. With Siberia beckoning, Mrs. Zenchenkov advised her husband to make himself scarce. The next day she told his coworkers that he had run off with another woman. For the next twenty-two years, according to the newspaper *Sovetskaya Moldavia,* the terrified Zenchenkov never once left his house.

In 1969 Mrs. Zenchenkov died, and her husband went to the local police station to turn himself in.

He was told that the ration cards had turned up in his desk drawer the day after they disappeared in 1947.

Stupid primate tricks III:

1. In Sacramento, California, a man tried to conceal a lit firecracker from county police by placing it between his legs. The device exploded, and the man wound up in University Medical Center with serious burns.

2. A man left a loaded pistol on the seat of his car in San Angelo, Texas. When he got back in the car, he accidentally fired the gun when he sat on it. The bullet missed him, but he was so startled that he jumped up and cut his head on the ceiling.

3. The directions on the box note that Alka Seltzer must first be dissolved in water. But that didn't stop a Boston man from popping two in his mouth like a couple of Tylenol and washing them down with a glass of cold club soda. The resulting chemical interaction tore two holes in his esophagus, according to the *New England Journal of Medicine*.

4. Two men were getting quietly drunk in a Jackson, Mississippi, garage, when the buzzing of flies threatened to spoil their fun. So they loaded their pistols and tried to blow the insects away. The spray of bullets sent neighbors ducking for cover, and when the police arrived to arrest the marksmen, they found more than seventy bullet holes in the walls. Not a single fly was killed, but one of the bullets struck a passing Pepsi truck.

5. A Tasmanian man jumped into the gorilla cage of the Royal Melbourne Zoological Gardens, shouting, "I've come to kill a gorilla!" He then pummeled and kicked a 220-pound ape before security guards restrained him.

A shattering experience.

The world's first roller skates were perfected more than two centuries ago by Joseph Merlin—who, regrettably, neglected to perfect the art of skating as well. His first public demonstration of the invention ended in disaster.

A renowned maker of violins and harpsichords, the Belgian-born Merlin moved to London in 1760, where he dreamed up the idea of replacing the blades on ice skates with metal wheels. Dressed as a minstrel, he made his entrance at an elegant Soho masquerade ball on skates and dazzled the guests as he wheeled gracefully about the ballroom floor playing a violin. Then as his admirers watched in horror, Merlin lost control of himself and sailed headlong into a costly crystal mirror, demolishing it and his handcrafted violin. Merlin himself was badly cut up.

Any chances of creating a market for the new invention were quickly shattered by the mishap. Europeans took little notice of roller skating, and it wasn't until the late 1860s, when a skating craze swept the United States and the Continent, that the sport enjoyed real popularity.

Over the Falls in a barrel.

If such things must be proven, schoolteacher Anna Edson Taylor established once and for all, in front of a thousand witnesses, that a woman can be as reckless as a man.

On October 24, 1901—her forty-third birthday—the ex-schoolteacher squeezed into a 42-foot by 3-foot wooden barrel, which was well-cushioned within and fitted with a rubber hose that allowed her to breathe. A boat towed her out into the turbulent Niagara River. At exactly 4:05 P.M. the line was cut and the barrel shot downstream, bobbing crazily. At 4:23 P.M. it reached the brink of Horseshoe Falls on the Canadian side, seemed to pause for a moment, and then plummeted 176 feet into the swirling eddies below.

When the barrel was recovered, it had to be sawed apart to extricate the dizzy daredevil. She had been knocked unconscious and blood was pouring from a gash on her forehead. Later she warned others "not to attempt the foolish thing I have done."

Ms. Taylor, who hoped her feat would bring her fame and fortune, died penniless in the Niagara County Infirmary in 1929. She was buried between two other Falls jumpers in a Niagara Falls, New York, cemetery.

In 1980 Michigan's Bay City Chamber of Commerce sued to have Ms. Taylor's remains exhumed and reinterred in Bay City, where she had taught grade school, and where her barrel was built. An ugly legal battle ensued, but the move was successfully blocked in court by a group called "The Remaining Friends of Annie Taylor."

The man who thought he could outrace a horse.

On July 4, 1880, having toasted the nation's birthday many times over at a saloon owned by George Atkins of Charleston, Arizona, a prospector named George Warren challenged his host to a 200-yard race. To make it interesting Warren would run on foot and Atkins would ride on horseback.

Should he win, Warren would take Atkins' horse. Should Atkins win, his prize would be Warren's one-ninth share in the Copper Queen mine in Bisbee, Arizona.

Warren knew he couldn't outrun a horse on a straightaway. But the course they laid out ran to a stake and back, and he assumed his ability to negotiate the turnaround more tightly would give him the edge. He assumed wrong. He lost the race, his claim in the mine, and what would eventually come to $20 million in profits.

It wasn't all he lost. The following year the courts judged Warren insane and allowed creditors to strip him of three other mining claims. He lived out his life in penniless vagrancy, ultimately winding up in—and dying in—Bisbee, a stone's throw from the mine that would have made him a millionaire.

Texaco goes drilling for salt.

Having located substantial reserves of oil beneath Lake Peigneur, in Iberia Parish, Louisiana, in 1980, Texaco erected two drilling platforms and began boring into the lake bed.

After several hours the pumps were still dry. At that point the company should have packed its rig back in the box and gone home. Better yet, they should never have set foot within a hundred miles of the place. Instead they kept drilling.

Suddenly the lake's waters started whirlpooling violently, like some giant toilet. Workmen and others watched in horror as the entire 1,300-acre lake was sucked into a sinkhole, along with five lakeside homes, eight tugboats, nine barges, both drilling rigs, a mobile home, a tourist garden, and a large chunk of a nearby island.

Texaco's geologists had overlooked the presence of an abandoned salt mine beneath the lake, owned by the Diamond Crystal Salt Company. The day after the disaster, the crater that had formed in Lake Peigneur's place refilled with sea water, and the nine missing barges popped back up to the surface like bath toys. Meanwhile Texaco and Diamond slapped each other with multibillion dollar lawsuits, each charging the other with responsibility for the mishap.

> **"If I could drop dead now, I'd be the happiest man alive."**
>
> *—Samuel Goldwyn (1882–1974)*

Stupid primate tricks returns.

1. A Hindu yogi named Rao announced his intention to walk on water in Bombay in 1966. Some 600 prominent members of Bombay society were invited to witness the spectacle. Garbed in flowing robes, the bearded mystic stood majestically at the edge of a 5-foot-deep pond, prayed silently, and stepped boldly forward. He sank immediately to the bottom.

2. Herostratus burned down the temple of the goddess Diana at Ephesus in 356 B.C.—one of the seven wonders of the ancient world—for the sole purpose of ensuring that his name would live forever in history books.

3. Janusz Chomatek of Warsaw, Poland, bounced a tennis ball on his head for forty-five minutes in 1990, setting a new world's record. Total bounces: 15,225, according to the newspaper *Dziennik Ludowy*.

4. On August 21, 1977, Dan Cameron Rodhill alerted the news media that he was about to jump off the Brooklyn Bridge, and then did exactly that. His objective: to attract attention to his unproduced drama, *The Dry Season*. Police fished him out of the harbor with thirteen broken ribs and lung damage. To the best of our knowledge, *The Dry Season* has still not been staged.

5. In Kenmore, New York, a thirty-year-old man tried to kill himself by jumping from a fourth-story window but survived when he landed on the roof of a parked car. He tried again and landed on the same car, fracturing his ankle and wrist.

6. To win a $500 bet in 1929, Bill Williams of Hondo, Texas, spent thirty days pushing a peanut 22 miles along the ground and up to the summit of Pikes Peak with his nose.

Swimming to oblivion.

With no publicity, organized backing, or apparent rationale, twenty-seven-year-old sign painter Fred P. Newton from Clinton, Oklahoma, waded into the Mississippi River north of Minneapolis on July 6 and began swimming south.

For reasons that remain a mystery, he wanted to become the first person to swim the Mississippi lengthwise.

Newton had hoped to complete his watery marathon before the first frost. But bad weather and stomach cramps forced him to make more stops than he'd anticipated, and it was December 29 when he finally climbed out of the water in New Orleans. He was shivering with cold, despite the protective layer of petroleum jelly coating his entire body. He had spent more than 740 hours in the water.

Newton insisted to reporters that he had no point to prove, nor any interest in fame when he decided to swim the Mississippi. He quickly vanished from public view and earned no money for his effort. His official welcoming party at New Orleans consisted of three motorcycle policemen.

The short rain of Elegabalus the awful.

Fabled for his eccentric tastes, the Roman emperor Elegabalus (A.D. 218–222) often served fake food made of glass, ivory, and marble at state dinners; other delicacies included tarantulas in aspic, pickled camels' feet, ostrich brains, and pastries filled with lion's dung. Lest they enrage their maniacal host and risk death, guests ate up and licked their lips.

But the worst party idea Elegabalus ever hatched started out as a seemingly innocent jape: He decided that a light sprinkle of rose petals would add a nice touch to a palace feast. The sprinkle swelled out of control and turned into a torrent, flooding the hall. Many guests were buried alive.

Later, when Elegabalus' excesses got too much for his own grandmother to bear, she had him murdered in his bathroom by the Praetorian Guards and thrown into the Tiber. He was eighteen.

The horror, the horror.

"EXEC IN TOPLESS CLUB DIES IN FREAK MISHAP WITH PIANO, WOMAN," read a headline in *Variety* in 1986. Jim Ferrozzo, assistant manager of San Francisco's famed Condor nightclub, had decided to make love with his girlfriend atop the piano. The club was closed, the patrons had left, and the hour was late: With no one around, the amorous couple coupled amorously in total privacy.

Unfortunately the piano was mounted on a hydraulic lift, which was somehow set in motion. But with other things on their minds, the two never noticed that they'd become airborne. When they were discovered the next morning, Ferrozzo lay dead, pinned under his lover, who was lodged tightly between him and the ceiling. Coroners said Ferrozzo had died of asphyxiation; his girlfriend suffered only minor bruises, although it took a fire department rescue team nearly three hours to pry them loose.

Even more stupid primate tricks:

1. After downing a bowl of chili, two martinis, and a glass of wine in 1979, a Washington, D.C., man drank a glass of baking soda to ease his indigestion—and his stomach exploded. The victim later sued the manufacturers of Arm & Hammer baking soda.

2. In Jackson, Mississippi, in 1972, police who flagged down a car zigzagging randomly through traffic discovered that the driver was blind. He was being directed by a friend in the passenger seat who said he was too drunk to drive himself.

3. Convicted murderer Michael Anderson Godwin was serving a life sentence in a Texas prison, having narrowly escaped death in the electric chair. Attempting to repair a pair of headphones while sitting on a steel toilet seat, he was electrocuted.

4. Wayne Reynolds, a police officer in Brooklyn, New York, accidentally shot himself in the leg while dropping his gunbelt in the station house men's room.

5. While dreaming of chasing fly balls, turn-of-the-century Philadelphia Phillies outfielder Sherry Magee bolted from his hotel bed and jumped through an open window. Luckily he landed on a setback 12 feet below and was not seriously injured. "It was one of the most exciting games I ever played, even though I was asleep," he told reporters.

Annals—that's *two* n's—of Medicine.

A forty-nine-year-old man appeared at the Letterman Army Medical Center in California in October 1973 with a baseball lodged in his rectum. An acquaintance had planted it there, he explained, to celebrate the Oakland A's World Series triumph over the New York Mets that day. Ingeniously, emergency room doctors removed the ball with a long-handled corkscrew, pulling off what is surely one of the most unusual come-from-behind victories in major league history.

Jerk-in-the-box.

Heartbreak is one of Robert Mannah's middle names. The other is *meshuganah*. Gunning for a berth in *The Guinness Book of World Records*, Mannah had himself buried alive in Dover, Delaware, on April 1, 1977, intending to stay buried for at least the 102 days he would need to break the world's record.

But Mannah had barely made himself comfortable when he learned he had inadvertently played a cruel April Fool's prank on himself: The record wasn't 101 days but 217. Still reeling from that blow, he was then informed that the editors of *Guinness* had decided to exclude live burials from all forthcoming editions because they are too dangerous.

"After that, I didn't see any sense staying down," Mannah said, cutting short his effort after twelve days.

Plennie Wingo's get-rich-quick scheme.

In 1931 a 35-year-old Texan named Plennie L. Wingo wrote to several shoe manufacturers requesting backing for a first-of-its-kind expedition. Although he got no takers, he remained determined. On April 15, 1931, Wingo set out from Fort Worth headed east but looking west. His plan was to walk around the world backwards.

For hindsight, Wingo wore a pair of specially designed reflective glasses. Arriving in New York City, he caught a freighter bound for Germany, resuming his walk upon disembarking in Hamburg. But Turkish immigration officials refused him entry to Istanbul, unimpressed by a letter of introduction he carried from the Fort Worth Chamber of Commerce.

His hopes of orbiting the planet quashed, Wingo sailed back to New York, hitched a ride to Santa Monica, and then proceeded to walk home to Fort

WHAT WERE THEY THINKING?

Worth. He arrived there on October 24, 1932, having worn out thirteen pairs of shoes and having traversed more than 8,000 miles. He learned on returning that his wife had left him while he was away.

The twenty-seven-pound pocketknife.

A 10-foot-long jackknife weighing twenty-seven pounds was built by Bill Farley of Phoenix, Arizona. The knife took him fifteen years to build, has four blades, and is totally useless.

Cherchez le pomme: four rash, witless, and misguided acts involving potatoes:

1. In an ambitious but ultimately futile re-education initiative funded by U.S. taxpayers, the United States Department of Agriculture tried to convince opium growers in Thailand to grow potatoes instead.

   The USDA and the State Department had already failed in efforts to turn Thai poppy growers onto the profit potential of strawberries and castor beans. But they felt hopeful about their 1987 campaign to sell them on Russet Burbank potatoes. The reason: U.S.–based fast-food chains were becoming increasingly popular throughout the Pacific Rim nations, creating a booming market for french fries.

2. During a KP stint at Fort Meyer, Virginia, in 1959, Pfc. Andrew God was caught lopping the eyes off potatoes with too free a hand. According to U.S. Army regulations, he should have excised them surgically with the point of his knife. For such wanton profligacy, God's commanding officers ordered him arrested on charges of having "willfully suffered potatoes of some value, the military property of the United States, to be destroyed by improper peeling." He was court-martialed, though ultimately acquitted.

3. Minor league catcher Dave Bresnahan tried to throw out a base runner with a potato.

Bresnahan's Williamsport Bills were playing the Reading Phillies in a 1987 Eastern League game. In a phony pickoff attempt, the catcher fired what appeared to be a legitimate baseball over the outstretched glove of the third baseman. It was actually a potato Bresnahan had sculpted to look like a baseball. When the base runner scampered home, Bresnahan was holding the real ball and tagged him with it.

The runner was called safe and Bresnahan was tossed from the game. The next day he was fined $50 by his team, and the day after that he was fired by the Bills' parent club, the Cleveland Indians, on grounds of "unprofessional" conduct.

"There's nothing in the rule book that says you can't throw a potato," Bresnahan protested.

> **"I must have put it there when I was a child."**
>
> —*Somerset, England, factory worker, complaining of lifelong deafness, upon having a cork extracted from his ear by a physician*

4. According to author Jay Kaye, one way to cut your monthly electric bills is to run your appliances off the power generated by potatoes. Though a battery connected to a single spud could barely get a flashlight to flicker, a properly wired array of 1,500 potatoes could probably fire up a sixty-watt light bulb. "Larger potato agglomerations could power the rest of the house or, for that matter, the whole neighborhood," he adds. He does concede, however, that "this method of power production . . . is both messy and grossly inefficient."

Trashing the Queen's parade.

A British sanitation worker impulsively crashed a 1950 parade for Princess Elizabeth in Bebington, England. Driving behind Her Majesty's limousine in a bright orange garbage truck, the interloper waved and bowed to the crowd in mockery of the young monarch, later boasting to friends that he had gotten more cheers than Elizabeth herself.

He was fired.

Just sitting on top of the world.

Frank Perkins of San Jose, California, believed he could win fame and fortune by spending a year perched atop a 60-foot-high flagpole. He actually stayed up for more than 400 days, during which time the company that hired him for the stunt went bankrupt and Perkins' phone and electricity were turned off for nonpayment. Also, his girlfriend left him for another man.

The tunnel to nowhere.

William Henry Schmidt—"Burro" to his friends—spent more than three decades hand-digging a tunnel through half a mile of solid granite in California's El Paso Mountains.

The tunnel turned out to be totally unnecessary.

Born in Rhode Island in 1871, Schmidt grew up frail and sickly, barely surviving an outbreak of tuberculosis that killed six siblings. In his twenties he went west to improve his health and prospect for gold. He made a lucky strike in Copper Mountain, near Randsburg, California, but decided it would be pointless to work his claim until he had first tunneled through to the mountain's far side, where he could pick up a road to the smelter.

He began digging in 1906, his sole companions a pair of pack burros. Working with only a pick, a four-pound hammer, a hand drill, and dynamite when he could afford it, Schmidt labored day and night in total isolation year after year. Often he worked in darkness, the damp air so thin that candles wouldn't burn. Along the way he struck several veins of gold, silver, iron, and copper but refused to be distracted by them. Meanwhile, with the tunnel half-finished, overland road and rail links between the mountain's north and south sides were built, rendering the tunnel unnecessary. But Schmidt continued to dig.

In 1938 after thirty-two years, 1,872 feet, and 2,600 cubic yards of rock, Schmidt broke through into daylight on the south side of Copper Mountain. He was sixty-six years old. Reporters, geologists, and curiosity seekers descended on the site en masse, and Robert "Believe-It-or-Not!" Ripley dubbed him "The Human Mole." Later Schmidt turned the tunnel into a tourist attraction, which he ran until his death in 1954.

Burn cattle, win valuable prizes.

Suppose a neighborhood kid told you to torch all your old Grateful Dead records, or else you'd turn into a fruit fly—would you listen? In nineteenth-century Africa, hundreds of thousands of presumably rational adults went along with a no-less-bizarre ultimatum posed by a hallucinating fourteen-year-old and her uncle. The results were catastrophic.

She was a Xhosa girl named Nongquase, and in April 1856 she was bathing in South Africa's Gxara River when she saw several gauzy apparitions who tried to engage her in conversation. The girl fled in horror to her uncle, a local prophet and witch doctor, who returned with her to the river the next day. There he recognized the wraiths as those of his dead friends and relatives, who offered him and the Xhosas the deal of the century: The spirits would rise from the afterworld to create heaven on earth for the Xhosas. The fertility of their fields would be restored, grain pits would overflow, no one would ever again get sick, and happiness would last in perpetuity. Best of all, the British colonialists who had put the Xhosas in thrall would be swept out to sea by a tidal wave.

But for all this to happen, the Xhosas would have to burn their grain, cattle, and belongings and cease working the fields. If they did the sun would reverse direction across the sky on a date to be announced, signaling the resurrection of the dead and the beginning of the promised paradise. If they nixed the deal, they'd be turned into bugs and squashed.

Some Xhosas harrumphed at the prophecy and went about their business. But many more bought it outright, and obediently began murdering their livestock and trashing the grain stores. On the morning of February 16, 1857, hundreds of thousands of Xhosas awoke early to watch the sun begin its passage across the heavens. By then, some 300,000 cattle lay dead and hunger and disease were rampant; presumably, at least some of the Xhosas were beginning to have second thoughts about taking Nongquase's rantings so seriously. When the sun covered its normal east-west course without a detour, there was widespread dismay; the Xhosas, hoping they'd gotten the date wrong, tried again the following morning. Still, nothing happened.

The nonevent later became enshrined in African history as "The Great Disappointment." No spirits appeared, no paradise arose, and the Xhosas came increasingly under the thumb of European colonialists. Meanwhile their suicidal gullibility had caused a famine that took as many as 40,000 lives. Nongquase, the girl whose hysterical fantasies had started it all, was banished for life to the Eastern Province. Her uncle went into hiding and died of starvation.

Stupid footwear tricks.

During a scheduled shutdown in 1977, a worker tossed a rubber rain boot into an atomic reactor at the Browns Ferry Nuclear Power Plant in Alabama.

Concerned that the plant's cooling system could become clogged, the Tennessee Valley Authority closed down the facility for seventeen days so that the errant galosh could be removed. Total cost: $2.8 million.

And Other Marketplace Excesses

Keeping Lady Liberty regular.

The nation's leading manufacturer of laxatives once tried to buy advertising space on the Statue of Liberty.

A centennial gift from France to the United States, the statue was completed and ready for shipping by the summer of 1884. All that remained was the construction of a pedestal, which the Americans were working on. But money ran out with the work only one-sixth done, and production halted. Another $100,000 was needed to finish the job.

Then the Centaur Company, makers of Castoria, offered $25,000 in exchange for the right to place the name "Castoria" in large letters across the top of the pedestal. "Thus, art and science, the symbol of liberty to man, and of health to his children, would be more closely enshrined in the hearts of our people," the company's executives said.

But the statue committee turned the offer down, evidently feeling that the concept of "liberty" had loftier associations than bowel regularity. By the summer of 1885, the fund-raisers had their $100,000 thanks to the contributions of more than 121,000 Americans. The pedestal was completed, and the statue was dedicated on October 28, 1886.

Board games from hell:

1. *Titanic.* Introduced by the Ideal Toy Corporation, it was based on the 1912 sea disaster of the same name and billed as "the game you play as the ship goes down."

2. *Mafia.* Made and marketed in Italy, where it was a major *scandale.* Each player represents a crime "family" vying for control of Sicilian businesses, airports, construction sites, and heroin profits while trying to bump off rivals and stay ahead of the police.

3. *Is the Pope Catholic?* Players move around the board "Chutes & Ladders" style, en route to becoming Pope. Getting drunk on sacramental wine or blowing the church's money on Hershey bars will cost you a turn; minor miracles advance you extra spaces.

4. *Twinkies and Trolls.* "T&T" was described by its creators—owners of a popular gay bar in Boston—as "a lighthearted reflection of the gay lifestyle." Players come out of the closet, haunt bars and bathhouses, and summer in Provincetown and San Francisco. The player who picks up the most "Twinkies" (handsome young men) and the fewest "Trolls" (ugly old men) wins.

5. *Group Therapy.* Game equipment includes a stack of cards that contains such instructions as "Tell the person on your right a secret you've never told anyone before," and "Hold each player in a way that shows how you feel about him." Only for the *very* secure.

6. *Civil War.* Re-create war-torn Beirut in your own living room. Players win extra points for smuggling arms, taking hostages, and reselling goods sent as foreign aid. "Civil War," in both French and English versions, was the 1989 brainchild of Naji Tueini, a Lebanese businessman.

7. *Death Race.* This 1976 video game put players behind the wheel with the object of running over pedestrians. Every hit was accompanied by a shriek; scores were displayed on a gravestone. When the National Safety Council

called the game "morbid" and "sick," programmer Phil Brooks protested. "We could have had screeching tires, moans and screams for eight bucks extra," he said. "But we wouldn't build a game like that. We're human beings too."

8. ***Chess for microbes.*** Nikolai Syadristy, a craftsman from Uzhgorod, in the former Soviet Union, spent several years hand-carving a set of chess figures so small they could be distinguished only when magnified 2,000 times with an electron microscope. Syadristy also specialized in forging horseshoes for fleas.

Jailhouse abs.

Charles Bronson, a convicted killer who has spent twenty-four of the last twenty-eight years in solitary confinement, has written a fitness guide for people working or living in cramped spaces. The book, *Solitary Fitness,* offers exercise tips geared toward agoraphobic readers as well as those with minimal room to exercise— such as oil-rig workers and office cubicle dwellers.

Considered one of Britain's most dangerous prison inmates, Bronson does 3,000 sit-ups a day in his cell in Great Britain's Wakefield Prison. "It sounds inhuman and amazing," he conceded. "But remember that it's killing time for me." His book emphasizes the importance of a balanced diet with lots of fruits and vegetables and takes a dim view of steroids and expensive weight-training equipment. Bronson, whose own diet consists largely of porridge and stew, was jailed for robbery in 1975 but was placed in solitary after violent attacks on staff and inmates.

Soft drink. Softer heads.

The Coca-Cola Company figured they were only giving consumers what they wanted when they "updated" the flavor of the ninety-nine-year-old soft drink in 1985. Marketing research had proven that people wanted more sugar and less fizz, so Coke changed the formula accordingly and waited for sales to jump.

Sales did jump, more than 14 percent—but they were sales of Pepsi, Coke's archenemy in the cola wars. All Coke got for its efforts was an F-minus in marketing. Everyone, it seemed, hated the new taste.

"This is the man who was not only the president of the National Council of Shopping Centers, but the International Council of Shopping Centers . . ."

—*U.S. senator Rudy Boschwitz (Minnesota), urging the appointment of Melvin F. Sembler as ambassador to Australia*

Worse, people took it personally. Some 40,000 protesters sputtered at the company via a toll-free phone line set up by the company; one angry loyalist said tampering with the formula was "like spitting on the flag"; others likened the new taste to that of sewer water, furniture polish, even flat Pepsi.

At the Houston Astrodome, crowds lustily booed a Coke commercial projected on the giant TV screen; massive protest rallies were organized by a group calling itself the Old Cola Drinkers of America. Meanwhile, cokeheads scavenged for the last remaining supplies of the old Coke, willingly paying exorbitant markups. A California man bought one hundred cases, then rented a $1,200 wine cooler to keep them in.

Where the company had erred was in believing that popular soft-drink preferences can be quantified as precisely as the mean annual rainfall in

Sandusky, Ohio. Give consumers a choice between sweet and not-so-sweet in blind taste tests and they will almost always go for the former; but that preference won't necessarily play out in the marketplace, or erase the kind of powerful emotional allegiances that Coke has enjoyed among consumers. Smart marketers would have known this, but Coca-Cola, as *Newsweek* said, had succumbed to "a bad attack of the MBAs."

In the end the company made things right by bringing back old Coke—repackaged as "Coke Classic"—while continuing to push the newer version. Said one marketing savant, the introduction of New Coke was "the marketing fiasco of the decade."

Maybe so. But using it as a birth control device is an even worse idea. Because of its high pH count and easy availability, Coca-Cola is widely used as a spermicidal douche in Third-World countries. But in their *Textbook of Contraceptive Practice*, authors Peel and Potts note that Coke Classic is a significantly more potent contraceptive than New Coke. In their experiment the authors added live sperm samples to test tubes filled with four different formulations of the soft drink—Classic, New, Caffeine-free, and Diet. After one minute, only 41.6 percent of the New Coke sperm were still moving, but the Coke Classic sample had immobilized all but 8.5 percent.

Still, if you're really serious about birth control, Diet Coke is the soft drink of choice: *None* of the sperm dunked in the Diet solution were moving sixty seconds after splashdown.

In all fairness, it should be pointed out that the Coke people aren't the only soft-drink marketers with bubbles in their brain. In the 1980s, Pepsi Cola introduced Pepsi A.M., a high-caffeine beverage targeted at the breakfast soft-drink market. According to Pepsi's marketing rationale, there are millions of Americans who dislike the taste of coffee and tea but still need a hit of caffeine each morning to jump-start their neural synapses; research showed that early-morning soft-drink consumption is especially common in the South. Not surprisingly, though, the idea of Colas and croissants never caught on.

Scratch, sniff, 'n' run for cover.

A 1989 issue of *The Armed Forces Journal* included a scratch-'n'-sniff advertisement for BEI Defense Systems' Hydra 70 weapons system. The ad depicted two fighter choppers in armed combat; the scent strip, when scratched, released the pungent odor of cordite, an explosive used in bombs.

How to market a sea monster.

The town of Seljord, Norway, sent a twenty-person task force to Loch Ness, Scotland, in 1992 to study how to turn a sea monster into a growth industry.

Ever since its first modern sighting in 1930, the Loch Ness Monster has proven a priceless boon to the town of Inverness, bringing in millions of dollars in tourism and outside trade. For centuries a Nessie-like monster has similarly prowled the depths of Lake Seljord, but no one ever made a single krone off of it. The purpose of the Seljord delegation to Loch Ness was to learn how "to develop our monster tradition into a tourist activity and build up the identity of the town," according to Seljord Trade Association spokesman Rune Handlykken.

The fact finders met with Inverness city officials and business leaders. In addition, a 90-foot Norwegian research boat was dispatched to Loch Ness to determine if a monster indeed lurked beneath the surface. The vessel was equipped with a battery of high-tech equipment, including sonar and underwater cameras; the project was estimated to cost more than $5 million.

A third-class idea.

In 1994, Nynex—formerly New York Telephone—concocted a marketing campaign that had scam artists thinking they had died and gone to heaven.

Most third-class mail is tossed out with the trash, and that includes the letters Nynex sent to three million customers throughout New York State in 1994. In each was a paper replica of the recipient's telephone "calling card," complete with his or her secret "personal identification number" (PIN).

"Honest businessmen should be protected from the unscrupulous consumer."

—Lester Maddox, former governor of Georgia

By punching in their phone number-plus-PIN, users could charge long-distance calls to their calling card. Which is why Nynex warns customers to assiduously guard the secrecy of their PINs and phone numbers, especially from "shoulder surfers," who stalk public phones, spying on callers and noting the credit card digits as they're punched in. The shoulder surfer then sells the numbers to people who like to phone faraway places, and the illicit calls wind up on the customer's bill.

Nynex's promotion made the job easier by printing out PINS in black and white. All a scam artist had to do was pluck a discarded envelope from a trash can and look up the cus-

"Bargain basement upstairs."

—Advertisement for London department store

tomer's phone number. With Nynex's generous, if unwitting, assistance, he now had a highly marketable commodity to sell.

Predictably many customers were aghast and complained loudly to Nynex. "The minute I saw it, I thought 'blunder,'" said one. The company immediately suspended the promotion and agreed to change the PIN of any customer who so requested, and to bear the cost of any illegal calls. "In hindsight," said a Nynex spokesman, "maybe we should have done it differently."

Lost in translation.

Smart advertising people know it's almost *always* a bad idea to translate English-language ad copy for use in non-English-speaking countries. But that doesn't stop some ad agencies from trying anyway—with often disastrous results:

1. When Pepsi Cola introduced a new ad campaign in Germany, the line "Come Alive with Pepsi" was translated as "Come out of the grave with Pepsi." In China the same words came out as "Pepsi brings your ancestors back from the dead."

2. The makers of Mercury cars scored such great results with the phrase "the Big M" that they exported it to Latin America as "el Grande M." But south of the border, "el Grande M" is short for "el grande mierda"—a common slang term meaning "the big shit."

3. Buyers steered clear of the Chevy Nova when it was introduced in South America. Small wonder: In Spanish, "No va" means "It doesn't go."

4. In Brazil the Ford Pinto broke down on the highway to success. There, "pinto" is a slang term for "small male appendage." The car was quickly redubbed the Corcell—Portuguese for "horse." Ford also had a hard time selling its Fiera and Caliente models in South America. In Spanish street slang, Fiera means "ugly old hag," and "caliente" is a streetwalker.

5. A popular brand of German chocolate failed to win much popularity among Americans. Its name: Zit. A similar fate befell a French soft drink briefly marketed in Great Britain called "Pschitt."

6. In the 1950s, a commercial for Arid underarm deodorant showed a cartoon octopus freshening up with eight dabs

of Arid—one for each armpit. But in many parts of the Far East where the ad subsequently ran, it was discovered too late that people commonly think of those octo-appendages not as *arms*, but as *legs.*

7. Sumitomo, a Japanese steel manufacturer, introduced its new line of high-grade industrial pipe—Sumitomo High Toughness—to the U.S. market with a series of full-page newspaper ads that generated more smirks than sales. Headlining the ads and taking up much of the page were the letters SHT. The copy noted that the product "was made to match its name."

8. A U.S. soap maker packaged its laundry detergent in a box that showed a pile of soiled clothes on the left, followed by a box of detergent, and a pile of clean clothes on the right. But in the Middle East, where people read from right to left, shoppers assumed the product would make clean clothes dirty.

9. Cans of Pet milk did not exactly leap off the shelves when it first appeared in French stores several years ago. "Pet" is French for "fart."

> **"Hark, the herald angels sing, Beecham's Pills are just the thing. Peace on earth and mercy mild, two for man and one for child."**
>
> —*Ad for Beecham's Pills, early-twentieth-century English laxative*

Good food, bad food.

It seemed like a good idea at the time: To encourage Americans to eat healthier, the American Heart Association bestowed a seal of approval—a nifty little heart-shaped logo—on name-brand foods with acceptably low levels of sodium, cholesterol, and fat.

But the 1990 program, called HeartGuide, was doomed from the start.

Many advertisers and nutritionists carped about the arbitrariness of its standards, and the U.S. Food and Drug Administration claimed it "could mislead consumers." At one point the FDA threatened to confiscate foods bearing the HeartGuide label if it felt the labels were deceptive.

Worse yet, qualifying for the seal wasn't simply a matter of meeting nutritional guidelines. Food manufacturers had to fork over between $15,000 and $640,000 for it.

Dogged by FDA warnings, harsh criticisms, and manufacturer defections from the half-baked program, HeartGuide died an early death less than two months after it was introduced. To show there were no hard feelings, the Heart Association refunded all the enrollment fees it had collected.

I'll take two pints, please, and a package of breath mints for the cat.

If your baby's innate fragrance needs a boost, try Ptisenbon, marketed by Parfums Givenchy of Paris.

Advertised as the first French perfume for infants and toddlers, it has what a Givenchy spokesman describes as a "citrus scent that simply enhances the natural smell of a baby."

Kids with more discriminating tastes might prefer Gregory, a designer fragrance for three- to ten-year-olds marketed in 1986 by Randy Pernini of Miami. Sold for $15.50 an ounce, Gregory is redolent of citrus, lavender, and vetiver, and it's packaged in a scaled-down bottle so kids can handle it easily. The product was named after Pernini's nephew.

Bass ackwards.

Memo to advertisers: Before hyping your product's role in a historic event, it helps to make sure the event *actually took place.*

A 1993 radio ad for Bass Ale recalled that Bass was the beverage of choice on Sir Ernest Shackleton's expedition to the Antarctic in 1921. It was a grueling voyage lasting "several months," the ad noted, and when the explorers finally reached the South Pole, "they toasted their achievements with pints of Bass."

A lovely image—but it never happened. Chances are Shackleton and his crew had heard of Bass Ale. They may even have packed a few cases along with their frozen penguin patties and blubber knives. But on that 1921 voyage—Shackleton's fourth try at reaching the South Pole—they got no closer to their destination than the Falkland Islands. Shackleton suffered a fatal heart attack there on January 5, 1922.

> **"Warning: Never use while sleeping."**
>
> —*Warning in hair dryer manual, as noted in* **U.S. News & World Report**

But historical truth did not chill the enthusiasm of Weiss, Whitten, Stagliano, the ad agency that created the bogus campaign. Said its president, "Bass's unprecedented past allows the brand to use reality as a resource."

Hiroshima, the toy.

In 1968 a Japanese manufacturer introduced a toy atomic bomb that flashed, banged, and emitted a minimushroom cloud of real smoke.

Eau de Sammy's armpits.

A New York company called Starclone introduced a private label perfume in 1995 whose main ingredient was country singer Sammy Kershaw's armpit sweat.

During concerts the singer wore absorbent pads sewn into the armpits of his shirt; the pads were then raced off to a University of Colorado laboratory, where his bodily secretions were separated out, distilled, and sent to Starclone for further processing. The cologne (priced at $19.50 for a two-ounce bottle) was marketed as "an expression of the sharing nature of country music."

My parents went to Laguna Beach on their vacation, and all they brought me was this lousy Charles Manson T-shirt.

Inc. editors take note: With mass murder no longer a viable means of earning a living, Charles Manson has gone into men's beachwear.

In the early 1990s, Zooport Riot Gear, of Newport Beach, California, introduced a line of souvenir T-shirts showing the convicted cult killer's face on the front and the words "Charlie don't surf"—a line from the movie *Apocalypse Now*—on the back. The shirts, priced at $17 each, were an instant hit among surfers up and down the California coast. Manson, serving a life sentence for his role in the 1969 murder of actress Sharon Tate and six others, licensed his name and picture to the Zooport company and signed a royalty agreement that paid him 10 cents a shirt. But those old enough to remember his crimes weren't buying.

"It defies belief," said Stephen Kay, the district attorney who sent Manson and his accomplices to jail in 1971. "The kids today weren't alive at the time, and they don't know how bad

> **"Replacing battery:**
>
> **Replace the old battery**
>
> **with a new one."**
>
> —*Instructions on battery replacement in an insect-repeller-device manual*

Charles Manson was . . . Anybody who really knows about his beliefs will burn the T-shirts as fast as they can." Zooport co-owner Richard Lemmons, however, didn't see a problem.

"We did it as a joke," he told the Associated Press. "You can't see it without laughing. I mean, 'Charlie don't surf'—he's in prison."

Hanging up on Bell.

Western Union once had a chance to purchase Alexander Graham Bell's telephone patents at bargain-basement rates—and they blew it.

Though the telephone was the headline story of 1876, Bell wasn't having much commercial success with it. Short on cash and heavily in debt, he called on William Orton, chairman of Western Union, then the nation's communications behemoth, to offer his company full rights to the telephone for a paltry $100,000.

It was a no-lose proposition for Western Union, but Bell evidently had the wrong number. Some believe that Orton was put off by Bell's low-tech background—that he was only a teacher of the deaf and not a world-class inventor. Others point to Bell's

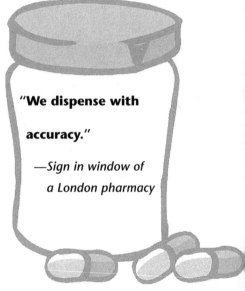

"**We dispense with accuracy.**"

—*Sign in window of a London pharmacy*

alliance with Orton's longtime foe, Gardiner G. Hubbard. Whatever the reason, Orton turned him down. "What use could this company make of an electrical toy?" he said.

The following year Orton had a second chance to do a deal with Bell and again walked away. Instead he hired inventors Thomas Edison and Elisha Grey to devise an alternative phone system, setting up a new business—the American Speaking Telephone Company—to go up against Bell. Orton was backed by vast financial resources and marketing clout, but Bell ultimately beat him on technology. A few years later, according to Bell biographer Catherine Mackenzie, Western Union "would have been glad to pay $25 million for the patents which Bell and his friends were then so eager to sell for one-hundred thousand dollars."

A paragon of integrity, decency, and clearheadedness, Bell nonetheless had a couple of strange ideas of his own. Perhaps the strangest was his insistence that people answer the phone by saying "Ahoy, Ahoy!" rather than "Hello."

Jesus Christ, action figure.

The Ideal Toy Corporation introduced a "Christ Child Doll" in 1958, just in time for Christmas. The 9-inch plastic newborn was garbed in white swaddling clothes and came with a cardboard manger, Mary and Joseph figurines, and a bevy of barnyard animals. Not surprisingly, playing with a creche was no kid's idea of a good time, and the dolls remained quietly on the shelves throughout the shopping season, while G.I. Joes and repeat-action burp guns flew from the stores. A few days before Christmas, Ideal gave a Christ Child Doll to each of its employees; the rest of its unsold inventory was buried in a landfill.

O Pioneers!

In 1919 advertising copywriters for Odo-Ro-No, an underarm deodorant, created the first ad to discuss body odor.

A Smorgasbord of Unappetizing Ideas

Diet of Worms.

Many of the world's gravest ills—warfare, famine, boredom, and flatulence—could be cured overnight, argued Vincent Holt, if only Europeans would work up an appetite for insects.

In his 1885 book, *Why Not Eat Insects?*, Holt noted that insects were a dietary fixture throughout the so-called "primitive" world. Among the Hottentots, for example, grasshopper egg soup and white ants were a prized delicacy; in Zanzibar, gourmets favored a pastry made from sugar, banana flour, and termites. Mexican Indians snacked on giant waterbugs, North American Indians on boiled locusts.

Lest his European readers be repulsed, Holt quoted Leviticus 11:22: "Of these you may eat the following: locusts of every variety . . . crickets of every variety; and all varieties of grasshopper. . . ." But bugs were more than good Christian fare, he wrote; they were *delicious:* "What a pleasant change from the laborer's unvarying meal of bread, lard, and bacon . . . would be a good dish of fried cockchafers or grasshoppers." Moreover, insects could provide a nutritious staple for the poor. And eating insects would eliminate them as pests.

In 1992 a banquet marking the one hundredth anniversary of the New

York Entomological Society was prepared entirely from recipes found in *Entertaining with Insects: The Original Guide to Insect Cookery,* by Ronald L. Taylor and Barbara J. Carter. On the menu were mealworm California rolls with tamari dipping sauce, wax worm fritters with plum sauce, and cricket tempura. Nothing with cockroaches, though. "Nobody eats cockroaches," said University of Wisconsin entomologist Gene Defoliart. "They're unsanitary. Kind of disgusting, when you think about it."

Oddly, the Bible says nothing about barbecued pork rinds and General Tan's Shrimp.

Crickets and grasshoppers may pass the kosher test, but these fifteen animals are explicitly banned from the dinner table in Leviticus II:

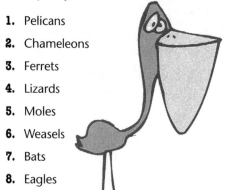

1. Pelicans
2. Chameleons
3. Ferrets
4. Lizards
5. Moles
6. Weasels
7. Bats
8. Eagles
9. Owls
10. Four-legged poultry
11. Cuckoo birds
12. Storks
13. Camels
14. Ospreys
15. Ossifrages

Is this vegetable necessary?

In 1924 a Soviet geneticist named Karpechenko successfully crossed a cabbage and a radish to produce an entirely new vegetable. He called it the *Rephanobrassica,* or rabage. (Admittedly an unfortunate name, but clearly rabage is preferable to cadish.)

Given the questionable appeal of both vegetables, a child of their union, no matter how lovingly nurtured, would seem doomed from the start. To be sure, the rabages turned out in Karpechenko's experiment could in turn generate little rabages, and the scientists held out great hope for a plant with a plum, edible root, and a succulent, leafy head.

But much to the world's misfortune, and despite Karpechenko's tireless efforts at selective breeding, the rabage yielded only the straggly greens of a radish and small useless roots of a cabbage.

The sad tale of the rabage suggests another about selective breeding. Seated next to George Bernard Shaw at a London dinner party, Isadora Duncan suggested that theirs would be the eugenically perfect marriage. Just imagine, she said, the offspring produced by her beauty and his brains.

"Yes, Miss Duncan," Shaw replied politely. "But what if the child should have my body and your brains?"

> **"Foods will, by 1976, be sterilized by split-second exposures [to atomic radiation], thus extending the shelf life of fresh foods practically indefinitely. Fission rays will immunize seeds, oats and other grains against disease."**
>
> —*Morris L. Ernst, attorney and author (1955)*

Why not just take along a gross of Mars bars?

If America ever revives its manned space exploration efforts, keeping astronauts well-fed on intergalactic journeys could be a difficult problem. According to the British weekly *New Scientist,* the Japan Livestock Institute, working with the National Aeronautics and Space Administration, has come up with one possible solution: a new breed of very small pigs to take along on the trip.

An equally novel plan—which would not pose a problem for astronauts observing any dietary laws—was advanced by Theodore Dufur in 1955. He suggested that spaceships be constructed of edible substances, such as cheese or frozen margarine. When the interplanetary explorers land on Mars, Dufur explained, they could simply nibble away at the craft until the next expedition arrives.

Guns don't kill people. And they make tasteful table adornments.

The National Rifle Association announced plans in 2000 to open NRASportsBlast, a gun-based theme restaurant, in New York City. "Imagine a new, exciting, total shooting sports and sporting goods experience," said NRA executive vice president Wayne LaPierre. The idea was ultimately shot down by New York's City Council, which passed a resolution officially declaring the store unwelcome.

Thanks, but I had a big lunch:

1. In the 1950s, when Roman Catholics still observed meatless Fridays, McDonald's created the "Hula Burger"—toasted bun, melted cheese, pickles, relish, and a slice of pineapple instead of a hamburger. The idea turned out to be a major McFlop.

2. Hires introduced milk with just a hint of root beer in the 1960s. Around the same time, Robert Cade, originator of Gatorade, gave the world "Hop 'n' Gator," a blend of Gatorade and beer. And a few years later, the Lone Star Brewing Company came out with a line of flavored beers, including lemon-lime and grapefruit. They must have been drinking the stuff on the job.

3. Coq au cola is Weight Watchers' low-calorie answer to coq au vin. It's skin-less chicken breasts marinated in diet cola.

4. Cholent is a traditional Jewish sabbath meal consisting of potatoes, beans, vegetables, and beef cooked at low heat for twenty-four hours. In Israel you can buy new Instant Cholent—just add hot water, bless, and serve. The *New York Times* called it "a dehy-drated product much like dried pet food."

5. Armour Food Service Systems intro-duced "Sir Broil" to cost-conscious restaurant owners in the 1970s, billing it as "the low-cost answer to the high cost of steak." Sir Broil was actually steak-size patties of beef leavings, held together with adhe-sives, texturizers, and preservatives and stamped with authentic-looking grill marks. An advertisement proclaimed that Sir Broil "is hard to tell from a strip steak, and you can serve it at a menu price that will build traffic while it builds profits."

> **"All free men, wherever they may live, are citizens of Berlin. And therefore, as a free man, I take pride in the words, 'Ich bin ein Berliner.' "**
>
> *—President John F. Kennedy in a 1963 speech in Berlin, unaware that, in German parlance, a "berliner" is a jelly doughnut*

The great chewing mania.

While they had little else in common, John D. Rockefeller, Upton Sinclair, and Prime Minister William Gladstone of Britain all shared one distinctive habit: At breakfast, lunch, and dinner, they obsessively chewed every morsel of food a minimum of thirty-two times—once for each tooth.

The man who instructed them in this laborious and questionable prac-tice was Horace Fletcher (1849–1919), whose philosophy of life is epitomized in the slogan he composed: "Nature will castigate those who don't masticate." Fletcher believed that unless food is chewed into a liquid state, one cannot possibly derive from it its full nutritional value. Even soup and milk should be sloshed around the mouth a full fifteen or twenty seconds to give the saliva ample time to do its work, he said. Although it made for tedious meals and tired jaws, thousands of people in the United States and Europe engaged enthusiastically in the practice in the 1890s, and mothers dutifully exhorted their children to "fletcherize" every bite on their plates.

> **"Copulation is . . . danger-**
>
> **ous immediately after a**
>
> **meal and during the two**
>
> **and three hours which the**
>
> **first digestion needs . . ."**
>
> *—Bernard S. Talmey, M.D.*
> *(1919)*

"Horace Fletcher saved my life," crowed novelist Henry James. "And, what is more, he improved my disposition." Fletcherism also worked wonders for Fletcher, it seems. In 1903, testing his legs on the Yale University ergometer, he raised 350 pounds, double the record of the school's most powerful athlete; and to celebrate his fiftieth birthday, Fletcher bicycled 200 miles in one day. His meals, consisting principally of milk, prepared cereals, and maple sugar, cost an average of 11 cents a day, and once, as an experiment, he subsisted on potatoes alone for two months.

Every aspect of digestion engaged Fletcher's interest. At one point in his life, he arranged to send periodic samples of his feces to the United States Department of Agriculture for testing and analysis.

Breakfast of champions.

Prime Minister Morarji Desai of India started each day by drinking his own urine. Addressing a 1977 meeting of India's Tuberculosis Association, Desai claimed to have cured his brother's TB with regular doses of liquid wastes, and admitted imbibing freely himself. "For the past five or six years," he told a reporter, "I have drunk a glass of my own urine—about six to eight ounces—every morning. It is very good for you, and it is free."

It turns out the prime minister was not alone. In past years urine was the soft drink of choice among participants in the "Urine Dance" of the New Mexico Zunis, and was similarly favored by medieval pagan revelers in a ritual known as the "Feast of the Fools." Even in the Bible, Desai pointed out, "it says to drink from your own cistern. What is your own cistern? It is your own urine. Urine is the water of life."

Drink up, drink up!

1. The Uape Indians of the upper Amazon cremate their dead. Then, to absorb the admirable qualities of the deceased, the ashes are mixed with casiri, the local alcoholic beverage, and drunk by members of the funeral party with great reverence.

2. Paiwari, another mildly intoxicating brew from the Amazon, is made by scorching meal from the cassava plant. The Indian women chew this preparation, then expectorate it into a vat to ferment. Paiwari chewing is a highly esteemed profession, whose practitioners have their lips specially tattooed to keep evil spirits from entering their saliva.

3. Masai tribespeople in East Africa mix blood drawn from their cattle with sweet milk. (Blood is actually an indispensable part of their diet because it provides salt, which is scarce in the Masai territories.)

And an honorable mention to Brussels sprouts.

A recent Gallup Poll reveals that the most widely detested food in the United States is beef brains.

Runner-up: Snails.

I'm stuffed—really. Couldn't eat another thing:

1. Tundra Chocolates, in Eagle River, Alaska, sells bonbons designed to look exactly like moose droppings. Sales are brisk—especially to tourists. "We have some people with a strange sense of humor out here," said company head Karen Underwood.

2. Wang Guang, a restaurant in Sichuan Province, China, was reported to have served its patrons sandwiches made from human buttock meat.

3. "Possibly the worst food creation of the century." That's how the *New York Times* described Tube-A-Goo, an aim-and-squeeze dessert topping introduced in the mid-1970s by Amurol Products Company, of Naperville, Illinois. Packed in see-through tubes, Tube-A-Goo came in several flavors, including cherry, grape, and raspberry, all of which looked and smelled "exactly like hair waving lotion," said the *Times*.

4. When Kellogg's Frosted Rice was first introduced in 1977, it contained so much iron that consumers found they could pick it up and eat it with a magnet. After the problem was fixed, a company spokesman assured the *Wall Street Journal* that the new, improved—and demagnetized—version of the cereal could not be lifted with magnets "unless they are very, very strong."

5. The advertisements exclaimed: "Oh, my gosh, it's Frothingslosh!" Old Frothingslosh beer, bottled only around the Christmas holidays by Iron City Brewing Co., was billed as "the pale, stale ale with the foam on the bottom." But it wasn't a brewing breakthrough that enabled Iron City Brewing to make that revolutionary claim; they simply pasted the label on upside down.

Eviscerating the Oreo.

Score another high-tech first for the Japanese: the creamless Oreo.

Introduced in 1991 by Yamazaki Nabisco, the noncookie was a big hit in Japan, where sugary confections are less of a national mania than they are in the West. It was called Petit Oreo Non-Cream, and a five-ounce package sold for $1.75.

Undoctored Oreos are the biggest-selling cookie in the world; Americans alone eat more than five billion a year. But Yamazaki Nabisco's market research indicated that Japanese Oreo-philes tend to eat "just the base"—in contrast to their American cousins, who often discard the base to get at the filling.

From where we sit, *both* practices are sacrilege. If God wanted Oreos to be broken open and eaten like coconuts, he'd have grown them that way.

Know a better way to quench a youngster's thirst for violence?

In the 1970s marketers introduced, and quickly withdrew, Chilly Bang! Bang! Juice, a sugary beverage bottled in a plastic water pistol. Kids drank it by sticking the barrel in their mouths and pulling the trigger.

Lemme have a large Emu McNuggets and a Diet Yak Sweat.

1. In the 1920s, health faddists with a sweet tooth snacked on "Vegetable Sandwich Bars," made from tomatoes, celery, bell peppers, and cabbage. Ad slogan: "Will not constipate."
2. Buffalo Burgers served at Al's Oasis, a restaurant in Oacama, South Dakota, are guaranteed "100 percent pure buffalo" from "the herd that appeared in *Dances with Wolves.*"

3. In a 1994 report, animal husbandry experts at Pennsylvania State University urged U.S. farms to raise emus. The meat of the hairy, flightless mega-birds, which resemble ostriches, "is low in fat, calories, and cholesterol," the report said.

4. A nonalcoholic tequila-flavored lollipop called "Hotlix" made its debut in 1992. In place of a worm, each one contained a quick-fried beetle larva.

5. True to its name, each Heublein's quick-serve "Wine & Dine" dinner included a small bottle of wine. Most buyers assumed the wine was intended to be sipped with the meal, and bought the product on that basis. It turned out to be *cooking* wine, salty and sharp to the taste, and unfit for imbibing.

The decontaminant that's less filling.

Following the Chernobyl nuclear disaster in 1986, scientists at the Bulgarian Defense Ministry introduced Lulin Special Light Lager—the beer that gives you more taste and less strontium. Unlike other brews, Lulin Light is made with the secret ingredient kantatonic, which helps purge radioactive strontium-90 from the bones and teeth.

George Pauli, a chemist with the U.S. Food and Drug Administration who studied the impact of the Chernobyl meltdown on local populations, wasn't sure he'd reach for a Lulin to quench his thirst, even after a week of yard work: "I expect that anything that removes strontium would probably remove calcium from bones and teeth as well," he said.

Rat food.

Barbecued rat meat is the latest fast-food fad in China. In a country where rats grow as big as Studebakers and devour some fifteen million tons of grain a year, their popularity as a snack food isn't hard to understand: Apart from their wholesome, mouthwatering tastiness, every rat that winds up on a sesame bun means one less rat in the grain bin. If only the best will do, Fujian Province is considered the rat-meat capital of China.

Rodents are also a prized delicacy in many areas of Africa. Inch-long voles and field mice are often trapped, skinned, and roasted in open pits and served as hors d'oeuvres. But the most popular varieties by far are the larger and meatier Gambian and canecutter rats.

The government of Zaire recently enlisted the aid of the University of Wisconsin in promoting rat ranching. According to Jane Homan, a university veterinarian and research associate, rats, or "micro-livestock," as she called them, offer all sorts of practical advantages over poultry, hogs, and beef cattle. Among them: They feed on natural plants and require no special feed. They also have no harmful effects on the environment.

"Fifty years hence . . . we shall escape the absurdity of growing a whole chicken in order to eat the breast or wing, by growing these parts separately under a suitable medium."

—*Sir Winston Churchill (1932)*

Nectar of the pharaohs.

When traveling in Egypt, ordering a bottle of domestic wine in a restaurant is not necessarily a bad idea. *Drinking* it most certainly is.

Some of the earliest wines were brewed in ancient Egypt, nearly 5,000 years ago. Evidently no one complained much about them at the time, at least not as far as hieroglyphic records indicate. In fact wine was considered safer than water back when the pharaohs reigned. But these days, according to the *New York Times*, the United States Embassy in Cairo issues directives to foreign tourists and expatriates to avoid homegrown wines at all costs. A glass or two is likely to bring on epic hangovers and nausea at the very least, and moderate-to-heavy imbibers risk blindness and death. "Things were especially bad after President Mubarak's pilot drank our wine and went blind," said winery manager Raouf Abu Kila.

> **"A nuclear power plant is infinitely safer than eating, because 300 people choke to death on food every year."**
>
> —*Dixy Lee Ray, former chairman of the Atomic Energy Commission*

Why is Egyptian wine so beastly? Virtually all of the nation's output—some 240,000 bottles a month—is produced by the Egyptian Vineyards Company, a government monopoly. Many believe the absence of competition has not helped the taste, bouquet, or color of the product. According to John Rees, a British subject living in Cairo, "I mix the rosé with Seven-Up to give it some taste, but even then I get terrible headaches and diarrhea. The wine tastes and smells like vinegar. It is often a musty, brown color and the corks are dirty." At the Gianaclis winery, home of such favorites as Cru des Ptolémées, Nefertiti, and Reine Cléopâtre, official Said Ibrahim admitted, "I don't let it in my house. I have to taste it here. That's enough."

Sweet hereafter.

In Qazvin, Iran, a bridegroom choked to death when he licked the honey from his bride's finger—a traditional wedding custom—and ingested one of her press-on nails.

Monsieur Sauvage's
Flying Egg

Transportation Ideas That Hopped the Track

The romance of flight I: More wings, less gravity.

Before the Wright Brothers, most inventors at work on a heavier-than-air flying machine knew that wings would probably have to be involved. But how many? Two? Six? Fifty-nine? One Britisher decided that the more wings, the better the chance of getting airborne. He went with one hundred.

Horatio Phillips flew his first "polyplane" near Harrow, England, in May 1893. The steam-powered contrivance, which carried no pilot, sported fifty pairs of wings, making it resemble a monster air conditioner. Phillips managed to get the thing moving arthritically along the ground and then airborne for a few seconds, but it hardly counted as a real flight.

Strangely, even after Orville and Wilbur's success at Kitty Hawk, North Carolina, in 1903, Phillips stuck with his more-wings-less-gravity approach. None of his planes flew, though, and most didn't even move along the ground very efficiently. But the design was only part of the problem; for some reason Phillips thought he had the best chance of taking off from an *oval* runway. Built of wood and looking like a giant toilet seat, the airstrip did not serve his purposes very efficiently, although he did manage to get one 200-wing colossus off the ground briefly in 1907.

An American named Roshan who also liked his airplanes with lots of wings tried to fly one with two sets of thirteen wings in 1908. As the contraption taxied, the wings flapped out of control and the entire thing collapsed in a pile of splinters. It was the last recorded attempt by anyone to fly a multiwinged aircraft.

Exceeding the speed limit on the road to obscurity: A list of abysmal ideas for automobiles that doesn't mention the Edsel even once:

1. **The BMW Isetta.** Despite its reputation for automotive elegance and craftsmanship, BMW laid a multimillion dollar egg in the 1950s with its Isetta minicar, sneeringly dubbed "das rollende Ei," or "the rolling egg." The Isetta's engine was in the rear; passengers exited and entered through the nose of the car, as if it were a D-Day troop carrier. In fact, when the front door swung open, the steering column and dashboard came with it. As for safety, the entire vehicle, front to back, was one big crumple zone.

    Steering the Isetta was difficult, largely because its body was tapered toward the rear, like a wedge of Emmenthaler cheese. Most models had only three wheels, which didn't make the car any easier to control. But the design enabled the manufacturers to have the Isetta officially classified a motorcycle and thus taxed at cheaper rates.

2. **The Trabant.** A nasty little runt of a car, the post–World War II East German Trabant was equipped with an engine that spewed nine times more hydrocarbons and five times more carbon monoxide than the average car. It also had a plastic body that tended to melt, rather than burn, in fires, further poisoning the atmosphere.

    Manufactured by government monopoly, the "Trabi" saw virtually no design changes in its thirty-two years of existence, though one wag suggested a practical improvement: add a second exhaust pipe, and the car could be used as a wheelbarrow.

3. **The Amphicar.** Half car, half boat, the Amphicar wasn't bad to look at and actually performed reasonably well on land and sea. It wasn't the first amphibious auto ever designed, but it was the only one to go into mass production. Created by the West Germany–based Quanat Group in the early 1960s and priced at $3,400, the Amphicar had two rear-mounted propellers, which could be folded out of sight when it was on land.

    Unfortunately it also had a tendency to rust quickly—an undesirable quality in any water-going conveyance.

4. **The AV.** There was no mistaking an AV when it passed you on the high-way: The single-passenger runabout was shaped like a darning needle, with a nose that tapered to a sharp point. In addition to lacking a reverse gear, the AV also wanted for effective brakes; automotive writer Timothy Jacobs suggested that the quickest way to stop an AV was to aim it at the nearest tree, "where the car would no doubt stick like an arrow . . . if it survived the impact." (Presumably, a pedestrian struck head-on by an AV would have to go to the hospital to have it removed.) Manufactured by British-based Ward & Avery from 1919–1921, the AV, said Jacobs, "would have given Ralph Nader convulsions."

5. **The Henry J.** The Henry J was a no-frills compact manufactured by the Kaiser-Frazer company in 1951. Named for, and by, company chief Henry J. Kaiser, the Henry J was overpriced and underequipped: In magazine ads the auto was angled to conceal the fact that it lacked either a glove com-partment or trunk lid.

    The Henry J sold no better than it deserved to and was discontinued in 1954. But it was reincarnated the following year as the "All-State." In this version the car was sold by retail giant Sears Roebuck in its automotive supply stores. Although the All-State added a trunk lid and other accou-trements, it was still the same old plain-Jane Henry J in party clothes. It didn't help that the American buying public wasn't comfortable shopping

for cars in department stores. Not surprisingly, the All-State vanished without a trace within two years.

6. **The Studebaker Dictator.** In 1934, the same year Hitler became German
    führer and Mussolini began planning an Italian assault on Ethiopia,
    Studebaker introduced a new model called "The Dictator." Despite hor-
    rendous sales and expressions of outrage from U.S. consumers, the
    automaker kept the name for three years.

Didn't something similar once happen to Ralph Kramden?

The Cunard Line planned to name its grand new ocean liner, scheduled to
be launched in 1934, the *Queen Victoria*. But first the company's board of
directors agreed to seek the approval of King George V.

Meeting privately with the monarch, Cunard director Sir Thomas
Royden asked if His Majesty had any objections to naming the ship "after
the greatest queen this country has ever known." Answered the king,
"That is the greatest compliment ever paid to my wife. I'll ask her."

The ship was named the *Queen Mary*.

The Ford soymobile.

Henry Ford dreamed of mass-producing automobiles made of soybeans and
spent hundreds of thousands of dollars attempting to make that dream a reality.

Soybeans were Ford's passion. He ate them at every meal, drank soymilk
by the gallon, and even appeared at a convention dressed in a suit made
entirely of soy-based synthetic fabrics, down to his necktie and handkerchief.
At the 1934 Century of Progress Fair in Chicago, his company served a
sixteen-course soybean dinner, featuring puree of soybean, soybean cro-
quettes, and soybean coffee.

But the industrialist regarded soybeans as more than mankind's last best hope for nutritional salvation. They were the building blocks of America, adaptable to an infinite range of products—furniture, farm implements, houses, and, especially, cars.

Ford had first experimented with soybeans and soybean oil in his Dearborn, Michigan, workshop in the late 1920s. A few years later he purchased thousands of acres of soybean fields from local farmers and built mammoth bean-processing plants in River Rouge, Saline, and Milan, Michigan. These factories extracted millions of gallons of soybean oil, which was used in the manufacture of horn buttons, control knobs, switch handles, distributor housings, and paint for Ford cars.

Ford hoped someday to manufacture an all-soy car—the world's first true soymobile. But his dream never came to pass, and by the end of World War II, the company had closed its soybean factories for good.

A warm welcome for aliens.

In observance of America's bicentennial in 1976, the town of Lake City, Pennsylvania, built a $6,000 landing strip for flying saucers.

"Everyone else is looking back 200 years and restoring buildings and writing books," said Jim Maeder, director of Project UFO Port. "We wanted to look in the other direction—the future."

The romance of flight II: Dr. Christmas' Magic Bullet.

William Christmas of North Carolina professed to have a medical degree and a track record as a builder of quality airplanes. He couldn't prove either claim, but that didn't stop the U.S. government from commissioning him to build a bizarre plane he swore would win the Great War. But it never flew a single raid against the Germans. And it may have been the worst aircraft ever built.

In 1918, Dr. Christmas, who boasted of having refused a $1 million offer from Germany to revamp its aviation industry, took his proposal to Alfred and Henry McCrory, prominent Wall Street brokers, who agreed to back him. He also got the army to part with a hard-to-find aircraft engine, but only on the condition that army test pilots be given first shot at trying out the aircraft.

> **"With the possible exception of having more pleasing lines to the eye while in flight, the monoplane possesses no material advantages over the biplane."**
>
> —*Aviation pioneer Glenn Curtiss*

Christmas' design eliminated struts and wing supports, allowing the wings to flap freely like a pterodactyl's. By the time a prototype of his plane—he called it "the Bullet"—was ready for testing, the war was over. Despite his promise to the army, Christmas hired his own test pilot, an unemployed army veteran named Cuthbert Mills, who got the Bullet airborne, at which point the wings fell off, sending the fuselage into a dive. Mills died in the crash.

With incredible chutzpah, Christmas now approached the army and, rather than apologize for violating his contract, asked for a replacement propeller and engine with which to build a second plane. They gave him what he wanted. At the New York Air Show in 1919, he hailed his new and improved Bullet as "the safest, easiest controlled plane in the world." On its first flight it crashed into a barn, killing the pilot. Shortly thereafter, Christmas billed the army $100,000 for "wing design."

They paid.

The "Monster Wreck."

In the early years of steam locomotion, Americans traveled miles to gape at train wrecks. In 1896 one railroad line decided to profit from this mania by staging a head-on collision as a publicity stunt.

The "Monster Head-end Collision," as it was billed, was the brainchild of William G. Crush, a passenger agent with the Missouri, Kansas & Texas Railroad. A savvy marketer, Crush arranged for an all-out media blitz to promote the event.

By the morning of September 15, 50,000 people had poured into Crush City, Texas, a tent village erected alongside an isolated stretch of track outside Waco. There was a restaurant, a telegraph office, and a railroad depot. "A wonderful wrecklessness marked the conduct of many," wrote one reporter.

Two seven-car trains, gaily painted and weighted down with railroad ties, faced each other on the track, cowcatchers kissing. Spectators jockeyed for a good view, crowding as close as they could get to the action.

> **"With over fifty foreign cars already on sale here, the Japanese auto industry isn't likely to carve out a big slice of the U.S. market for itself."**
>
> **—Business Week *(1968)***

As the sun began to set, the trains backed up until they were a mile apart. At Crush's signal, the engineers threw the throttles open and jumped clear.

The trains were doing 60 miles per hour when they collided. The two engines reared up against each other like fighting stallions, tore themselves apart, then toppled off the track. The impact was deafening. The crowd went wild.

But that was only the beginning. After a few seconds of silence, both engine boilers exploded, hurling shrapnel over the crowd and beyond. Two people died and many were injured; the rest fled for their lives. A smokestack landed on a grazing cow a quarter-mile away.

Afterwards many of the survivors returned to snatch up shards of debris as souvenirs of the most sensational—and reckless—public relations stunt of the millennium. The man who dreamed it up was fired the next day.

The romance of flight III: The Eagle has landed (with a resounding thud).

Good thing General Motors' World War II Eagle fighter plane never went into mass production. If it had it would undoubtedly have killed more American pilots than Germans.

But then, GM had no intention of ever putting the aircraft into combat. The company's sole purpose in making it, at huge expense to itself and taxpayers, was to get out of another aviation project.

In 1942, Gen. Oliver Echols, head of the USAAF Materiel Command, was enlisting industrial help in designing and building the B-29 Superfortress, the world's biggest bomber to date. Echols particularly wanted GM to be part of the action. GM, however, would just as soon have gotten poked in the eye with a stick.

"Next year's cars should be rolling out of Detroit with plastic bodies."

—L. M. Bloomingdale in Yale Scientific Magazine *(1941)*

Aware that Echols could draft their company against their will, GM's management concocted an excuse: They claimed they were working on an even hotter project and couldn't spare the personnel. The project, they said, was a twin-engine fighter plane dubbed the Fisher (as in Body by) P-75 Eagle. Echols bought the story and let them off; under contract to the government, GM began producing a prototype.

It was an odd motivation for building an aircraft; the way GM went about it was odder still. Basically, their engineers cobbled together a pastiche from parts cannibalized from other planes. Incompetence and indecision dogged the effort, but the Eagle was ready for testing in November 1943, five months late.

Predictably, the Eagle was more like a turkey—slow, lumbering, unstable, and hard to handle. The army demanded improvements, but GM's engineers still came up short. GM finally pulled the plug on the Eagle in October 1944. By then six had been produced at a cost of $9 million, of which Washington paid more than half. None of the planes ever saw action, but that hardly mattered to GM. They'd gotten out of the B-29 project.

The car that couldn't.

"Looks right! Built right! Priced right!" Such was the overheated prose with which Ford Motor Company advertised the all-new Edsel in 1957. But *Time* magazine saw it differently. They called it "a classic case of the wrong car for the wrong market at the wrong time."

History sides with *Time*. In the annals of marketing, few products have ever been so closely identified with failure and fiasco.

It all started in 1954 when Ford's management decided to create a new car to compete with General Motors and Chrysler in the mid-size market. They weighed and rejected 6,000 possible names, including several suggested by poet Marianne Moore. Ford had hired her to conjure up a name that evinced "some visceral feeling of elegance, fleetness, advanced features and design," and she offered Bullet Cloisonné, Utopian Turtletop, Pastelogram, Andante con Moto, and Mongoose Civique. In the end the company dubbed the car "Edsel" (rhymes with "pretzel"), after Henry Ford's only son.

A year before the Edsel was to be introduced, Ford launched a $10 million media campaign that revealed nothing about the car, except that it would be a breakthrough in automotive technology. Interest mounted; when the Edsel was unveiled in September 1957, curiosity seekers thronged the showrooms.

As it turned out, they came to look—but not to buy. For one thing, Ford's timing was rotten. Hoping to get a jump on the competition, the company brought out the 1958 Edsel a month early—and wound up competing with the 1957 models, which dealers were clearing out at bargain prices.

Quality control was also a problem from day one—horn buttons stuck, brakes jammed, pumps leaked, oil pans dropped out, paint peeled, hubcaps fell off, heaters continued to heat after they were turned off. A company spokesman admitted that no more than half the 1958 Edsels sold functioned properly. By year's end many Edsel dealers were already filing for bankruptcy.

Things didn't improve the following year. The company created dealer incentives, doubled their advertising budget, and even offered deep discounts to state highway officials to get more cars on the road. But it was a case of too little too late. By the time ads began to proclaim, "The Edsel is a success. It's a New Idea. It's a *You* idea," the car was already a laughingstock. In 1960 Ford mercifully halted production, having sold fewer than 110,000 Edsels in three years—mostly to dealers, Ford executives, and ad-agency employees—and having lost a quarter of a billion dollars.

The Edsel was a lousy idea from the outset. Though conceived during an economic boom, it was marketed during a recession, when "economy" cars were becoming popular and wide-bodied gas guzzlers were on the way out. Meanwhile its breathless ad hype had raised expectations no automobile could ever meet. The Edsel, the public quickly discovered, was no world-of-tomorrow marvel—just another horsey, overpriced "family car" with lots of cheap push-button gadgets and superficial styling refinements. Critics likened its signature oval-shaped grille to an egg, a horse collar, and a toilet seat. One famous simile described the Edsel as "an Oldsmobile sucking a lemon."

Three days after its premiere, police reported that an Edsel had been stolen in North Philadelphia. It was the first, last, and only Edsel ever to be stolen. Not even thieves took it seriously.

The romance of flight IV: Loveboat takes wing.

Gianni Caproni was a respected aircraft designer whose main claim to fame was a class of jumbo bombers flown with great success by Italian pilots during World War I. After the war, the bomber-king turned his talents to building big planes for peacetime uses.

Caproni's most ambitious project was the CA-60 *Transaereo,* a gargantuan amphibious craft designed to carry one hundred passengers across the Atlantic. Three times the size of Caproni's biggest military transports, the twenty-seven-ton seaplane looked like something out of a Fellini dream sequence—a Mediterranean cruise boat bearing three full sets of triwings, or eighteen wings in all.

On the morning of March 4, 1921, a large crowd of dignitaries, reporters, and aviation enthusiasts gathered on the shores of Lake Maggiore, in the Italian Alps, to witness the *Transaereo's* maiden flight. The pilot started the plane's eight 400-horsepower engines; the giant craft taxied along the lake and then, miraculously began to rise. But 60 feet above the water's surface, it rolled sideways and crashed. Though the *Transaereo* shattered on impact, all aboard survived.

Afterwards some speculated that the accident was anything but: The pilot, they said, had taken the *Transaereo* down deliberately to save lives when he realized it probably wouldn't make it across Lake Maggiore, much less the Atlantic Ocean.

Kids in the cockpit.

Note to commercial airline pilots: It is almost never a good idea to let your kids fly the plane.

After the 1991 disintegration of the U.S.S.R., Aeroflot, the Soviet airline giant, was split into more than 150 mini-lines. With no centralized system of servicing, inspections, or quality control, the baby Aeroflots have collectively posted the worst air safety record since Icarus. Once, to show off his skill, a pilot tried to land a jet with the cockpit windows shuttered. The resulting crash took sixty lives. Another flight, illegally carrying passengers transporting canisters of gasoline, crashed and burned in Armenia, killing thirty-four.

"Heavier-than-air flying machines are impossible."

—*William Thomson, Lord Kelvin, president of the Royal Society (1895)*

Then in 1994 an Aeroflot Airbus 310 en route from Moscow to Hong Kong inexplicably fell out of the sky over Siberia and slammed into the Atali Mountains, killing all seventy-five passengers and crew members. It took investigators two weeks to figure out what went wrong: The pilot, trying to teach his children how to fly a jet, had handed the controls to his fifteen-year-old son. Either the boy or his sister had accidentally switched off the automatic controls, stalling the aircraft in midair and sending it into a nosedive.

"Flying Aeroflot is about as safe as playing Russian roulette," *Pravda* editorialized.

The romance of flight V: The Spruce Goose.

Twice the length of a B-29 bomber, the HK-1 was the biggest warplane ever built, a 200-ton monstrosity costing taxpayers millions. Washington invested in the amphibious craft in the early days of World War II in the hope that it would beef up Allied fleet strength in the North Atlantic. But as it turned out, the plane wasn't ready until 1946 and flew only once before being hangared for good.

One more thing: It was made entirely of wood. Detractors called it "the Spruce Goose."

It was aviator-industrialist Howard Hughes who came up with the idea of a giant ship that could simply rev its engines and fly away when things got too hot on the water. In 1942 Hughes took his idea to car czar Henry Kaiser, who secured an $18 million contract from the federal government to build the plane, but only on the condition that it not be made with aluminum, which was in short supply.

Hughes sent teams of engineers traipsing through the forests of the Pacific Northwest collecting samples of tree woods and testing them for flexibility and tensile strength. Ultimately he went with resin-infused birch. The term "Spruce Goose" was a misnomer.

Production schlepped along slowly, and it wasn't until June 1946, almost a year past V-J Day, that the plane was completed. It was more than another year before it flew. On November 2, 1947, the Spruce Goose was towed from its hangar in Long Beach for taxi trials. Hughes took the controls, chauffeuring thirty reporters on a spin around the harbor; then he dropped them off on shore and, to the surprise of 50,000 spectators, accelerated the engines and took off.

The Spruce Goose reached a cruising altitude of 70 feet and remained airborne for about a minute. Then it was returned to its hangar, never to fly again. The all-but-flightless bird had cost more than $25 million to build.

Hughes, quite the playboy in his younger days, later became a reclusive madman with long hair, uncut nails, and an obsessive fear of germs. He spent his last years in isolation, watching endless reruns of the movie *Ice Station Zebra,* dying in 1976. As for the Spruce Goose, it remained in its hangar in Long Beach until 1993, when it was transported in pieces by ship, barge, and truck to a museum in Oregon. The 1,000-mile trip took 138 days.

Icarus in a lawn chair.

"It was something I had to do to find inner peace," Larry Walters explained to reporters. He was talking about achieving the first manned flight in an aluminum lawn chair in 1982.

Walters lifted off from the backyard of his girlfriend's home near Long Beach, California, on July 2. Borne aloft by forty helium-filled balloons, he leveled off at 16,000 feet. His flight plan routed him northeast to the Mojave Desert, where he planned to land. But countervailing winds were strong, and Walters began drifting to the southeast, veering dangerously close to Long Beach Airport.

With a BB gun he had packed for the purpose, Walters began popping balloons to hasten his descent. In the process he and his lounge chair became hopelessly tangled in a power line, which had prudently been turned off by the local utility. Upon landing, Walters was reprimanded by the Federal Aviation Administration and fined $1,500. He never attempted to leave the earth's surface in any form of outdoor furniture again.

> **"I'm an old Navy man;**
>
> **the bow is the rear end,**
>
> **isn't it?"**
>
> —*Richard Nixon in an interview with David Frost*

The exploding traffic signal.

The world's first traffic light was installed in London in 1868. It wound up causing more accidents than it prevented.

Invented by J. P. Knight, the device was placed atop a 22-foot-high pillar at the corner of Bridge Street and New Palace Yard near the Houses of Parliament. Its sole purpose was to protect British MPs as they crossed the street; everyone

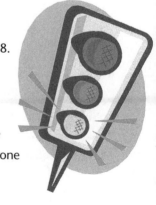

else hated the thing. One hansom cab driver called it "another of them fakements to wex poor cabbies."

The gaslit signal—red for "stop," green for "caution"—was manually operated by a full-time police officer who stood at the base. Less than a month after the thing was activated, it exploded, killing its attendant. The signal was removed shortly thereafter, and London didn't get its next traffic light until 1926.

The romance of flight VI: The flying tailor.

More than 300 people have jumped to their deaths from the Eiffel Tower since it was built in 1889. Most have been suicides, but the very first was an amateur inventor named Teichelt who had no intention of doing himself in. Equipped with an aerodynamic cape of his own design, he fully expected to fly.

A tailor by trade, Teichelt had built the contraption in his shop in Longjumeau, just outside Paris. The tower authorities initially rejected his request to use the structure as a launch pad. But they gave him the go-ahead after he agreed to indemnify them in the event of mishap and to obtain police authorization.

On a frigid morning in December 1911, the would-be aeronaut stood on the first platform of the tower, 600 feet above the Seine. With a crowd of journalists and sensation seekers urging him on, he strapped himself into his spring-loaded bat-wing cape, stepped onto the ledge, took a deep breath, and leaped.

Teichelt flapped his mechanical wings noisily, but the only direction he traveled was down. According to Joseph Harris, author of *The Tallest Tower: Eiffel and the Belle Epoque,* "the hole he dug in the frosty earth beneath the tower was nearly a foot deep."

Teichelt's leap isn't the only bizarre stunt performed on or about the Eiffel Tower. In 1981 Silvain Dornon climbed 363 steps up to the first platform on stilts, and in 1923 Pierre Labric bicycled down. In 1958 the famous stuntman Coin-Coin made the descent on a unicycle.

But to some critics the building of the tower in the first place was the most asinine stunt of all. It was designed by engineer Alexandre-Gustave Eiffel, who aimed to combine strength, lightness, and beauty in a single structure. But in a letter of protest, some of France's leading intellectuals, including Alexandre Dumas, Guy de Maupassant, and Charles Gounod, railed against the "useless and monstrous Eiffel Tower," and its "irreparable ugliness and disgrace." Asked why he ate so many meals in a restaurant in the tower, the English art critic William Morris said, "because it's the only place in Paris where I can avoid seeing the damn thing."

That burning sensation.

Beginning in 1986, Parisian taxicabs were equipped with a device designed to zap unruly passengers with a nasty shock.

Known as "le siege que brule," or "the seat that burns," the Israeli-made apparatus included an electrified pad under the rear seat that was wired to a powerful battery. At the first hint of conduct unbecoming a passenger, a catchall category covering everything from pointing a gun at the driver to skimping on the tip, the driver could deliver a 52,000-volt shock to the offender's spine by depressing a foot pedal.

"Man will not fly for fifty years."

—*Wilbur Wright (1901)*

Paris taxi drivers hailed the contraption as a potent and needed means of self-defense. "We are not like sheep waiting to be slaughtered," said hack spokesman Norbert Ben-Arous, noting that assaults on drivers were averaging forty a month. But police, Mayor Jacques Chirac of Paris, and consumer advocates were less enthusiastic.

"The danger of such a demented project is obvious to anyone who is sane," said a spokesman for the Federation of Transport Users. "Why not also install a cobra in a cage in the back seat?" Six months after its debut, "the seat that burns" was outlawed in Paris. Although no mishaps had been reported, the apparatus was a disaster waiting to happen, said Police Prefect Jean Paolini—especially for passengers with heart conditions or wet clothes.

Why couldn't they just shake hands?

A bill was introduced to the Philadelphia City Council in 1954 calling for construction of a "Kissing Room" at Philadelphia International Airport. The room would be available to couples "who need privacy for their good-byes."

The proposal was defeated.

The world's worst safety film.

British Aircraft Corporation produced a film in 1976 that emphasized the importance of wearing protective goggles and instructed factory workers in their proper use. According to Stephen Pile in *The Book of Heroic Failures,* the depictions of on-the-job eye injuries were so graphic that one worker fell off his chair and opened a gash in his head requiring stitches. Thirteen others fainted.

"Rail travel at high speed is not possible because passengers, unable to breathe, would die of asphyxia."

—Dr. Dionysus Lardner (1827)

The romance of flight VII: Monsieur Sauvage's flying egg.

In 1932 a French inventor named Sauvage concluded that air travel was so hazardous because planes were shaped like zucchinis, when they should be shaped like eggs. To prove his point he built a prototype aircraft with an ovoid fuselage. If a hen's egg were to be enclosed within an ostrich egg, he explained, the whole affair could be dropped from a great height without harming the chick. His crash-proof egg-o-plane was conceived along the same lines.

The French government was skeptical and went so far as to impound the wheels from Sauvage's aircraft to keep him from taking off. He got around that ploy by hauling the craft to a 90-foot cliff near Nice. As friends and supporters crowded around, he climbed into the cockpit and, when he was comfortably settled, signaled them to push him off.

Like the egg after which it was fashioned, Sauvage's crash-proof plane dropped like a stone, shattering on impact. Sauvage, too, was badly injured and had to be rescued with ropes.

Look Younger — and Have Fewer Hemorrhoids!

Bad Ideas for Better Living

Dressed to (be) kill(ed).

During the Reign of Terror, fashionable young women in England and France bobbed their hair and shaved the napes of their necks in imitation of the tonsures given to Marie Antoinette and other victims of French Revolutionary justice preparatory to being guillotined. They called the style *coiffure à la victime*. For an added touch of drama, some women wore blood-red ribbons around their necks.

Look younger— *and* have fewer hemorrhoids!

Whether or not Preparation H is effective at shrinking and soothing hemorrhoids is of little concern to some users. They put it on their face.

In the 1970s, word circulated among Hollywood glitterati that modest applications of Preparation H, the mother of all over-the-counter hemorrhoid salves, could smooth facial wrinkles and restore a youthful look to the complexion.

One Beverly Hills woman reported that she saved the ointment for chic gatherings, "when I want to look extra special." A Manhattan druggist told of selling out her entire stock in one day soon after the craze hit the East Coast: "Everybody left with one lipstick and one tube of Preparation H.

Nobody with hemorrhoids could buy it because everybody with wrinkles had grabbed it up."

Some cosmeticians note that Preparation H contains shark liver oil, a rich source of Vitamins A and D, which were thought to be beneficial to the skin. Nonetheless, the bottom line is that many physicians doubt the efficacy of Preparation H for its *advertised* purpose, and its use as a face cream is a decidedly bad idea. Said one New York dermatologist, "Women could become sensitized to it after not much use. The skin could redden, burn, scale, and blister after a week of use."

Full classrooms, empty coffers.

To boost sagging attendance in 1984, Indiana's Richmond High School made students an offer they couldn't refuse: show up every day for a year, and collect $100.

The bribe worked—far better than school officials could have hoped. Two hundred kids had perfect attendance, and the school had to pay out $20,000.

Patent nonsense.

From the files of the U.S. Patent and Trademark Office:

1. **Invention: Silent movie dialogue balloons. *Patent No. 1,240,774. Date: 1917. Inventor: Charles F. Pidgin.*** More than a decade before the first talking motion pictures, Pidgin devised a breakthrough way to simulate speech on screen. Before filming, balloons "made of rubber or any other suitable material" are concealed in each performer's mouth. The balloons are imprinted with dialogue; characters simply blow up their balloons on cue, allowing their lines to be read just as if they were comic-strip figures. Coiled party favors, the kind that unfurl when blown, would also work nicely, Pidgin said. Either way the technique will "add to the realism of the picture by the words appearing to come from the mouth of the players."

2. **Invention: Dimple maker.** *Patent No. 560,351. Date: 1896. Inventor: Martin Goetze.* Dimples were a precious social asset in the 1890s. For those unfortunate enough not to have been endowed with a proper set at birth, Goetze contrived a mechanical dimple maker. Patterned after a carpenter's brace, the device was fitted with a hard rubber knob, rather than a drill bit, to be held fast against the skin while the handle was cranked. For the price of a few moments' intense discomfort, the user would be endowed with a comely indentation guaranteed to last for several hours.

3. **Invention: Self back-patting machine.** *Patent No. 4,608,967. Date: 1986. Inventor: Ralph Pire.* There are frustrating times—we've all experienced them—when our most heroic efforts go unrecognized by others. It is for such emergencies that Pire invented his "mechanical pat-on-the-back apparatus." It incorporates a hinged arm that hangs over the shoulder and terminates in a simulated hand. With a bit of practice, the user can easily control the device to administer hearty, congratulatory pats on his or her back.

4. **Invention: Emergency toilet bowl breathing device.** *Patent No. 4,320,756. Date: 1982. Inventor: William O. Holmes.* In the event of a fire in a high-rise hotel, most people would instinctively rush for the doors. The more prudent course would be to walk calmly to the bathroom and insert Holmes' emergency breathing device, a long, flexible tube, into the toilet. The tube can then be snaked through the water trap until it reaches the vent pipe that connects to the sewer line. Remain crouched at the bowl and breathe normally until help arrives.

5. **Invention: Musical condom.** *Patent No. 5,163,447. Date: 1992. Inventor: Paul Lyons.* Lyons' condom contains a tiny sound transducer, similar to the microchips found in musical greeting cards. On contact, it plays *The 1812 Overture,* Handel's *Messiah,* or whatever other tune has been programmed.

6. **Invention: Preventive toilet seat.** *Patent No. 90,298. Date: 1869. Inventors: Francis Peters and George Clem.* Standing on a toilet seat was considered a heinous breach of social etiquette in the 1860s. Peters and

Clem's solution was a square toilet seat consisting of four wooden rollers, each mounted on its own axle. Should a user attempt the unthinkable, the rollers would spin under his feet and throw him to the floor. A couple of nasty encounters with the rollers, and even the most recalcitrant toilet stander would probably be cured for good.

7. **Invention: Device for shaping the upper lip.** *Patent No. 1,407,342. Date: 1924. Inventor: Hazel Mann Montealeagre.* "Betty Boop lips" were

considered the essence of female sensuality in the Jazz Age. Montealeagre's handheld device was engineered to make the look available—temporarily, at least—to even the most thin-lipped biddy. At the front end was a steel template that would be locked tightly against the upper lip by means of a spring clasp. The user would wear the mold there for a few minutes until the skin had "set."

8. **Invention: Method for minimizing facial aging.** *Patent No. 2,619,084. Date: 1952.* Wrinkles got you down? Forget greasy vanishing creams or costly cosmetic surgery. In this system a set of tiny anchors are imbedded in the scalp and connected by rubber bands. Worn this way for several hours, the rigging pulls the skin taut over the face and smoothes out wrinkles. For a while, anyway.

9. **Invention: Device for inducing sleep.** *Patent No. 313,516. Date: 1885. Inventor: F. W. Paul.* Can't seem to fall asleep at night? Why pollute your body with toxic drug-store potions when you can ease yourself into slumber the natural way—by cutting off the circulation of blood to your brain? Paul's brainchild is essentially a spring-wound collar that fits snugly around the neck; size adjustments are made by a thumbscrew. Within minutes of slipping it on, the flow of blood is "quieted," and sleep comes.

Otke Notive, Otke Notive, It's a Helluva Town. Kye Shonkil is up and Cheni Rotsha's down.

The way we christen towns and cities is all wrong, an English architect named Stedman Whitwell argued in the early 1800s. Derivative place names like "New Jersey" and "Indianapolis" may have a vague aesthetic appeal, he maintained, but they're no help to the perplexed traveler trying to locate them on a map.

"Radio has no future."

—William Thomson, Lord Kelvin, president of the Royal Society (1897)

As an alternative, Whitwell devised a complex labeling system, wherein each town was assigned a new name based on its precise latitude and longitude. Pittsburgh was thus redubbed Otfu Veitoup; Washington, D.C. became Feili Nyvul. And the Big Apple was Otke Notive.

The revolutionary spelling scheme would do more than take the mystery out of map reading, Whitwell claimed. It would also eliminate the mindless duplication of place names such as "Springfield" and "Madison" and give each and every town in the nation a unique moniker. However, there is no record of any town, anywhere, Whitwellizing its name.

The light that failed.

When the international energy shortage reached crisis proportions in the early 1970s, Congress came up with an easy way to save millions in fuel costs: year-round Daylight Savings.

It seemed so logical. After all, if it was possible to steal an extra hour's daylight by turning the clock ahead in the summer, think of all the money that could be saved on lighting by keeping the clock turned ahead *all* the time.

So, in September 1973, Congress decreed that the following January 6, the whole nation, with a few maverick states such as Indiana, Hawaii, and Arizona exempted, would go on Daylight Savings Time (DST).

The problem of course is that DST didn't create extra daylight—it simply shifted it from morning to evening, forcing people to commute to work in the dark. Not surprisingly the number of early-morning crimes and traffic accidents increased, and parents worried about the safety of children walking to school before dawn. In the first month alone, eight children died in early-morning traffic accidents in Florida—four times as many as normal. One TV commentator called Daylight Savings Time in the winter "Daylight Disaster Time."

Nor did the predicted benefits materialize. According to the Federal Transportation Department, power consumption dropped barely 1 percent for the first four months of the year; a decline of 5 percent or more had been forecast. Most of the savings was supposed to come from industry, but, according to the *New York Times*, "for the majority of companies, savings were either minimal or non-existent." Small wonder: The same lights that could be turned off in the evening now had to be turned on in the morning.

Acknowledging its folly, Congress put the country back on Standard Time that October, ordering a return to DST on the last Sunday of February 1975. The normal April starting date for DST was restored the following year.

Airmail's dismal start.

Airmail service was introduced by the U.S. Post Office in 1918. It could as easily have been introduced by Wrong-Way Corrigan with an assist from the Three Stooges. Everything went wrong.

On the morning of May 15, crowds gathered at a large polo field in Washington's Potomac Park to witness the departure of the world's first airmail flight. President Woodrow Wilson was on hand, along with many other notables. Pilot George Boyle settled into the cockpit of his single-engine Curtis Jenny, which carried a 140-pound sack of mail, and, at 11:00 A.M., he was ready to take off.

But the finely tuned Hispano-Suiza engine wouldn't start. Mechanics sweated over the stalled aircraft for nearly thirty minutes, while the president grew visibly irritated. Finally someone suggested checking the fuel tank. It was empty.

The tank was filled, the engine started, and Boyle took off. But instead of flying north to Philadelphia, his destination, he followed the wrong set of railroad tracks and flew southeast. Totally disoriented, he prepared to land in a Waldorf, Maryland, cornfield, 25 miles *south* of Washington, intending to ask directions. But he wrecked his propeller taxiing, turned the plane upside down, and couldn't get off the ground.

> **"If excessive smoking actually plays a role in the production of lung cancer, it seems to be a minor one."**
>
> —W. C. Heuper, M.D., of the National Cancer Institute (1954)

The mail was delivered to Philadelphia by truck.

PS: Twelve years after Boyle's remarkable nonflight, a candy bar called the Air Mail Bar was introduced. It lasted on the market about as long as Boyle stayed in the air.

Just the fax, ma'am.

When residents of Seoul, South Korea, complained that police emergency phone lines were often busy, the Metropolitan Police Administration added two emergency *fax* lines.

America goes underground.

When Eisenhower was in the White House and Uncle Miltie ruled Tuesday night, the specter of nuclear war frightened some 200,000 families throughout the United States into taking their government's advice and building concrete-reinforced bomb shelters beneath their homes.

Also known as fallout shelters, the subterranean bunkers were drab, windowless affairs, stocked with drinking water, medical supplies, food, clothing, blankets, board games, Perry Como records, and anything else needed to survive a week's confinement physically and psychologically intact. Many owners also kept a pistol or high-powered rifle handy against the possibility of an invasion by an unsheltered neighbor who demanded to be taken in and given refuge. Indeed, debating the merits of shooting your best friend between the eyes rather than letting him elbow his way into your shelter and suck off your family's oxygen supply was a favorite dinner-table diversion in the 1950s.

Shelters were expensive to build and maintain; in 1951 a shelter built for the Colhoun family of Los Angeles cost $1,995—a hefty sum in those days. But Mrs. Colhoun, mother of three, had no qualms about the outlay. "It will make a wonderful place for the children to play in," she said. "And it will be a good storehouse too. I do a lot of canning and bottling in the summer, you know."

Brace yourself.

Chemist Merlyn Starley of San Francisco patented the world's first condom suspenders in 1993. Designed to keep the condom securely in place, they include a pair of plastic clips and a special adhesive tape that attaches to the user's legs.

Brushing your teeth with a virus.

There's a better way to scour your choppers than brushing them with toothpaste, said Alan Morris.

Scrub them with viruses.

A chemical engineer in Rome, Georgia, Morris noted that tooth decay is caused primarily by bacteria, specifically the *sanguis,* *faecalis,* and *mutans* strains of streptococcus. It's common knowledge among microbiologists that certain strains of virus eat certain strains of bacteria. Ergo, to get rid of decay-causing germs, all you need to do is sic the right virus on them—which Morris is attempting to cultivate.

Once he succeeds he plans to package the little buggers in toothpaste form. All that's needed, he said, is to create the right virus for the job "to prevent 90 percent of dental cavities."

Thus far the American Dental Association has not issued a ringing endorsement of Morris' plan, nor has the Food and Drug Administration given its blessing. Anyway, Morris thinks he can move ahead without FDA clearance, since the agency's authority extends only to drugs and not to microorganisms. If he does manage ultimately to score some supermarket shelf space for his product, the real challenge will be to convince the toothbrushing public that viruses are good for them.

Cuisine by Rubbermaid.

Can't take the washed-out flavor of nuked food one day longer? Junk your microwave and cook your meals in the dishwasher instead.

According to Jim Kaye, author of *Light Your House with Potatoes,* an automatic dishwasher makes a nifty fish poacher. "Rather than exposing the delicate texture of fish to the open flame of a broiler or the direct heat of a pan," he wrote, "fish wrapped in foil and placed on the top rack of your dishwasher will come out moist and tasty." One complete wash-and-rinse cycle is enough to do most fish to a turn, he claimed, though cooking times will vary with the brand of machine. Hint: For best taste, omit detergent.

Another apostle of dishwasher cooking, *Fort Worth Star-Telegram* columnist Sheila Taylor, said vegetables also come out perfectly when they're steamed in dishwashers. Carrots, asparagus stalks, and zucchini strips will fit nicely in the silverware caddy; artichokes and potatoes can be impaled on the prongs where cups and glassware usually go.

But dishwashers aren't just for cooking, author Kaye pointed out. If you can find the water valve, shut it off, he suggested, and use the dishwasher to toss and dress the perfect salad. (The dressing goes in the detergent dispenser.) The greens may have to be picked off the walls of the machine, he conceded, "but messy salads are often the best-tasting ones."

Rats in space.

Most rattraps dispatch their prey by squashing, frying, or poisoning them. They're effective, sure, but they also inflict an unconscionable degree of pain and suffering on the critters. And they oblige the trapper to somehow dispose of the mangled remains.

Ann Koenig and Alan Gross of Oakland, California, have built what they consider a better rattrap. This one catches the rodent alive and rockets it 50 feet into the air, where it's trapped in a bin suspended from the ceiling (presumably a warehouse ceiling). They call it the "Ratapult."

Although the device may play havoc with a rat's equilibrium and overall sense of security, its effects would appear less jarring than those of conventional traps. So it is somewhat bewildering that Koenig and Gross have come in for harsh criticism from the San Francisco Society for the Prevention of Cruelty to Animals. More puzzling is why anyone would bother slam-dunking a rat into an overhead bin when it could be contained just as effectively at ground level.

Edison's concrete love seat.

The fertile mind of Thomas Edison produced hundreds of brilliant ideas during his lifetime—and a few duds.

Consider cement furniture.

In 1898 the inventor formed the Edison Portland Cement Company and built a huge cement works in Stewartsville, New Jersey. By 1905 the investors had sunk some $3 million in the venture and not seen a penny's profit. Auditors advised them to suspend operations at once and cut their losses. Edison wouldn't hear of it.

Instead, he simply altered his game plan. Rather than market his cement to builders, he now decided to become a builder himself. His idea was to mass-produce prefab concrete houses and sell them cheaply—$1,200 for a three-story, six-room home. Pouring wet cement into cast-iron molds, same as if they

"Nuclear powered vacuum cleaners will probably be a reality within ten years."

—*Alex Lewyt, vacuum cleaner manufacturer (1955)*

were making waffles, workmen could put up a house in six hours. Drying and hardening would take four days. Everything but the wiring, plumbing, and heating pipes would be made from a single piece of Portland cement—floors, doors, stairways, roof, window frames, and bathroom appliances.

But to keep prices down, the homes would have to be built in clusters of one hundred or more, as close as possible to where the raw materials were quarried. Not even the most house-hungry Americans were excited about the prospect of living cheek by jowl with one hundred other families on the edge of a gravel pit. Nor was Edison's idea of decorating each home with poured concrete furnishings much of a crowd pleaser, either. The inventor devised plans for refrigerators, divans, love seats, and pianos all made from concrete. To show it could be done, he even turned out a number of concrete phonograph cabinets. The public yawned.

He finally pulled the plug in 1907, never having built a single concrete home.

How do they stay up?

Chest wigs for men, starting at $200, were available from Roger's Hair-Styling Salon in New York City in the early 1970s.

No substitutions:

1. If the local Pick-N-Pay is out of Pampers, try diapering your infant with peat moss, according to the 1914 edition of *Infant Care*, published by the U.S. government.
2. Peanut butter is a serviceable substitute for shaving cream, according to U.S. Senator Barry Goldwater (1909–1998).

Great concept, weak execution.

Menelik II (1844–1913) was the George Washington of modern Ethiopia. Crowned in 1889, he expanded the country's boundaries, fought off the Italians at the Battle of Adowa in 1896, and established Ethiopia as a secure and independent state. Most important, he engineered a far-reaching program of modernization that took his empire from the middle ages to the twentieth century in less than a decade.

Penal reform was a big item on Menelik's agenda, and following the introduction of the electric chair at New York's Auburn State Prison in 1890, he eagerly ordered three of the devices for use in Ethiopia. But the move proved an embarrassment to the ruler: The electric chairs wouldn't electrocute because the country lacked electricity.

Unwilling to mothball his new purchase, Menelik had one of the chairs installed for use as his throne.

Just make sure you wash your hands before you reach out and touch someone.

There are more than one hundred million bathrooms in America's homes. AT&T would like to put a telephone in every one.

A marketing campaign launched in the early 1980s focused on making the phone a standard bathroom fixture. "The once inviolate taboos on bodily functions and intimate elements of personal hygiene are falling away," explained Judith Kuriansky, a psychologist retained by AT&T. "Therefore, the bathroom, where these needs are taken care of, is being opened up as well."

According to an AT&T spokesman, Americans are spending more time decorating and furnishing their bathrooms than ever before. They're also logging more time there—time that can be productively spent reaching out and touching someone. The fact that many people go to the bathroom to *escape* the phone does not figure into their market plan.

"I'm sure some people—pardon the expression—will take pot shots at us," said the company's media manager. "But we're very serious about it."

Bathroom talk.

Looking to liven things up in the smallest room in your house? You could do worse than installing a "Talking Tissue" on your toilet-paper dispenser. First marketed by a North Carolina company in 1989, it plays one of four messages every time the roll is turned: "Stinky-Stinky," "Yuk-yuk," "Nice one, nice one!" or a loud alarm.

Relieve cold symptoms—*and* have fewer babies.

Scientists at the Medical Research Institute in New Delhi, India, are developing what they claim to be the world's first decongestant-contraceptive nasal spray.

According to an institute spokesman, antihistamines in the spray reduce swelling in the nasal membranes, while contraceptive hormones travel directly to the ovulation centers of the brain. In experiments, five inhalations a month helped relieve the cold symptoms of sexually active rhesus monkeys while preventing them from getting pregnant.

Dress for success. Look like a schmuck.

The *Wall Street Journal* predicted in 1967 that one-piece jumpsuits would soon replace the suit and tie as standard business attire in the United States.

A picture of a jumpsuit-clad executive accompanied the front-page story, which quoted a motivational research expert as saying that tomorrow's innovative, hard-driving business leaders would want clothing they could put on in less than thirty seconds.

Now if they can only come up with a canine breath mint . . .

Laboratoire Alfamed of France introduced a bottled fragrance for dogs in 1981. Labeled "Monsieur Chien," the perfume was introduced with a $150,000 advertising campaign that ran in European magazines. Product spokespooch was Mycroft, an English bulldog.

Elvis has left the crisper.

Bell peppers that look like Elvis? It's possible with the Elvis Vegiform, a plastic mold that fits over garden produce, casting it in the king's shape as it grows. Vegetables shaped like Elvis "are more weighty," claimed inventor Richard Tweddell III, "and the flavor is enhanced."

Ever wonder why there are so many Indians?

The Indian Health Ministry conducted a countrywide campaign in the 1960s, replete with TV and print advertising, seminars, and home demonstrations, to promote birth control. After a year there was no measurable decline in the birth rate.

A survey showed that nearly 80 percent of the men had taken the birth control pill, and 98 percent were wearing the condoms on their finger, just as the government instructors had demonstrated.

Cooking the books.

It isn't enough for librarians to check the due dates of books as they're returned, argue two university researchers. They feel the books should also be cooked.

Books are public feeding troughs for silverfish, termites, roaches, lice, and other pests, who come for the paper and glue and stay for the crumbs and scraps that fall between the pages. According to entomologist Jerome Brezner and Philip Luner, professor of paper engineering at the State University of New York (Syracuse), one way to evict the buggers is to install microwave ovens at library return desks and nuke every book for sixty seconds as it is brought back.

Not everyone in the library business thinks microwaving books is such a hot idea. Gerald Garvey of the Library of Congress noted that some books have metal inserts, which could catch fire when zapped. Sheila Jackson of the Carnegie Library in Pittsburgh fears that "to open and shut the oven door every time is going to be a pain." Also, nuking would invariably melt the glue in some books and damage the leather bindings of rare volumes. If a library is determined to debug its holdings, Garvey said, it should use "the preferred method of freezing."

However, he does not recommend installing an Amana freezer at every return desk.

The mommy track.

Until the early years of the twentieth century, Muslim peasant women in Upper Egypt still believed it was possible to terminate an unwanted pregnancy by lying face down on the railroad tracks and allowing the next scheduled train to pass over them. Conversely, a woman who had difficulty conceiving would lie on her back on the tracks and allow the next scheduled train to pass over her and impregnate her.

The smokeless cigarette.

In 1989 in an effort to appeal to health-conscious smokers, R. J. Reynolds introduced the world's first smokeless cigarette, which it called "Premier." What RJR's marketing savants failed to grasp was that the very term "health-conscious smoker" was pure oxymoron. Smokers expected flavor from a cigarette—not the key to eternal life.

To smoke a Premier, which looked like a regular cigarette but had a plastic casing, you lit the carbon tip and then inhaled deeply, drawing the heat back through a tobacco filter and into your lungs. Along the way the heat released flavor from aluminum "flavor beads." Since the tobacco was warmed, not ignited, no smoke was produced. A four-page manual in each pack assured smokers they could master the art of smoking a Premier in less than a week. It also warned them to use only a butane lighter; the interaction with the chemicals in a match or conventional lighter would ruin a Premier's taste.

"You will know your Premier is out when it is no longer warm and you no longer get smoke," the manual said.

If this seemed like a lot of work just to smoke a cigarette, it was. After working up enough sucking power to get the heat flowing—at RJR, internal critics of the product jibed about "the hernia effect"—what you got for your exertions was a flavor more redolent of burning garbage than tobacco. RJR chairman Ross Johnson said it smelled "like a fart."

> **"I think there is a world market for about five computers."**
>
> —IBM chairman
> Thomas J. Watson (1943)

Of course the real reason smokers wrinkled their noses at Premier was that health concerns were of less concern to them than flavor. This was a lesson RJR should have learned several years earlier from the failure of Real, "the all-natural cigarette," noted Bryan Burrough and John Helyar in their book, *Barbarians at the Gate*. Nor could RJR play up the health angle in its advertising: to do so would imply that its other brands were *not* healthy. Four months after Premier's premiere, RJR stubbed it out. Its losses were more than $325 million.

Better footwear through chemistry.

Buried in landfills across America are thousands of shoes made from Corfam, a synthetic leather concocted by chemical giant E. P. Du Pont Nemours in the 1960s. And chances are, if you were to excavate a shoe and go over it with a damp cloth, it would look as new as the day it was bought.

That was the appeal of Corfam, or so the company's marketing wizards figured. "You used to worry about shoe grooming," said one ad. "No more. Not with Corfam . . . A mere wipe-off of normal soil or dust and your shoes are fine and fit again. Corfam repels water, resists most spots and stains."

"Every pint bottle should contain a quart."

—*Sir Boyle Roche, eighteenth century British parliamentarian*

Unfortunately, it also repelled customers. The reason: DuPont ignored the obvious fact that people *liked* leather. It smelled nice. It felt good. It molded itself around the shape of the foot. And it was natural: In those pre-p.c. days, the fact that it came from a cow and not a test tube was a big plus.

Even so DuPont might have established a foothold for Corfam by first using it in lower-priced shoes. But company chairman Lammot du Pont Copeland—the last du Pont, as it turned out, ever to head the company—was eager to establish the product's snob appeal, so he insisted on introducing it in top-of-the-line footwear. Few people took a shine to Corfam, and in 1971 the company was forced to dump it. The venture cost the company in excess of $150 million.

The life and death of Octagon City.

Long life, robust health, and tranquility are yours for the asking, Orson Squire Fowler promised his followers in the late 1800s. All you have to do is build yourself an eight-sided house.

Best known as the father of phrenology in the United States, Fowler was also the nation's most ardent champion of octagonal living. He built himself a great eight-sided mansion in Fishkill, New York, and went so far as to design an entire octagonal city, complete with an eight-sided Municipal Hall, jail, and public baths. "The octagon is a spiritually beautiful shape," he wrote. "The quality of living is much improved in rooms without right angles."

One Fowlerite, the Reverend Henry Stephen Clubb, took octagonism a step further. In 1856 he issued a brochure inviting settlement in Octagon City, his man-made community on the Neosho River in Kansas Territory. He described it as a true paradise of the plains—a planned city with an architecturally majestic Grand Octagon at the center, and several hundred smaller octagonal homes, each set on an octagonal lot.

"Experimental evidence is strongly in favor of my argument that the chemical purity of the air is of no importance."

—L. Erskine Hill, physiologist (1912)

More than sixty families took Fowler up on his offer. But when they arrived, there was nary an octagon to be found. Nor for that matter did they see a habitable structure of any shape—just endless flat acreage full of nothing. The settlers stuck it out for a few years, but it was tough sledding, what with tornadoes, searing heat waves, and devastating windstorms. In the early days the Reverend Clubb appeared occasionally to reassure his tenants and preach on Sundays; over time he was seen less and less, and finally disappeared altogether.

So did Octagon City.

Catmail.

In 1879 the city fathers of Liége, Belgium, attempted to train thirty-seven cats to deliver the mail between the town's central post office and outlying villages.

It didn't work.

"It won't be long before customers should be able to complete most of their banking transactions without any personal contact. This will enable banks to offer more personal contact."

—*Forecast in* Credit and Financial Management Magazine *(1976)*

In all fairness, the idea wasn't *altogether* crazy. Given the well-documented homing instincts of cats, delivering mail or even pizzas might seem a perfectly logical vocation for them. One theory popular among animal behaviorists holds that microscopic iron particles embedded in feline tissue endow cats with a kind of built-in compass that keeps them from getting lost.

Of course the balky independence of cats is even better-documented than their sense of direction—a fact that was evidently lost on the burghers of Liége: Just because a cat is capable of delivering letters doesn't mean it *will*. The cats of Liége wanted nothing to do with the mail, and the cat-courier project was quickly abandoned.

Patent nonsense II:

1. Invention: Tapeworm trap. *Patent No. 11,942. Date: 1854. Inventor: Alpheus Myers.* In Myers' day, the only relief tapeworm sufferers had was foul-tasting and possibly harmful patent medicines. In contrast, his device banished worms from the body mechanically. It consists of a small box attached to a string and baited with "any nutritious substance." The patient swallows the box, which works its way down the slippery slope of the alimentary canal as far as the tapeworm's head. When the worm reaches for the bait, a spring trap clamps down on its head. Feeling a tug the patient grabs the string protruding from his mouth and reels in his prey.

2. Invention: Wind Bag. *Patent No. 2,149,054. Date: 1939. Inventor: Thomas Lloyd Hollister.* Go on, have that second helping of kale: You're wearing The Hollister Wind Bag! This remarkable device traps offensive intestinal gases and stores them until they can be safely released. A rubber bulb receives the vapors directly via a perforated nipple, which fits snugly into "one end of the alimentary tract," in the graceful language of the patent application. Worn discreetly under one's clothes, the apparatus is held in place by a series of straps and fasteners.

3. Invention: Baby cry muffler. *Patent No. 4,792,013. Date: 1988. Inventor: Carter Boynton.* Just because your colicky three-month-old is having a bad day doesn't mean you have to. When the squalling starts, just strap the orange-shaped Boynton baby muffler around baby's head and go back to *Fear Factor*. An air vent directly over the infant's mouth allows unobstructed breathing while shunting even the most ear-piercing shrieks through a soundproof baffle. You won't hear a thing. "Some people ask me how I could imagine doing this to my baby," confessed Boynton, who invented the muffler after he almost went bananas when his own infant wouldn't cease and desist crying. "Others want to know how they can get one."

4. Invention: Power-driven skis. *Patent No. 2,625,229. Date: 1953. Inventor: Stanley Van Voorhees.* No need to fight the crowds waiting to ride the ski lift: With Van Voorhees' invention you can ski right up to the top of the highest slope. To make it work, the skier has to carry a gasoline engine strapped to his back, connected by a flexible drive shaft that turns a rubber belt on each ski, propelling him forward. Bristles on the belt provide traction. Optional accessory: a ten-gallon water tank and rubber hose, to be used in the event the skier crashes into a tree and ignites.

5. Invention: Cheese-flavored cigarette. *Patent No. 3,232,948. Date: 1966. Inventor: Stuart M. Stebbings.* It remains a mystery why Stebbings' invention never gained a foothold in the marketplace, coming as it did at a time when smoking was still respectable and cheese consumption was about to take off. Perhaps it was the specter of warning labels on every package: "The Surgeon General Has Determined That Smoking Velveeta Is Dangerous to Your Health."

Electroplating grandma.

Thinking of having baby's shoes bronzed? For a few bucks more, you can do the whole baby. Grandma and Uncle Phil, too.

The secret is an electroplating technique developed in the 1890s by a Paris surgeon named Varlot. The procedure involves dusting the body with silver nitrate and placing it in a vacuum chamber. There it is rendered conductive by exposing it to a solution of white phosphorus vapors dissolved in carbon disulphide. Grandma is then submerged in an electrolytic bath; a current is sent through the solution, coating her body with a thin layer of copper.

Varlot's process creates "a brilliant red copper finish of exceptional durability," reported one journal of the day. And it provides a far more stylish means of preserving the deceased than burial, cremation, or embalming.

The iceberg cometh.

With all that free ice drifting around in the Antarctic Circle, Prince Muhammad al-Faisal of Saudi Arabia decided there must be a way to bring some of it to his arid nation. In the late 1970s the prince bankrolled a new company, Iceberg Transport International (ITI), and charged it with finding a way to import icebergs to the Middle East.

According to ITI scientists, once a suitable berg was located via satellite, it could be swaddled in an 18-inch-thick blanket of plastic, trussed up like a Christmas goose, and harnessed to a fleet of powerful tugboats. Alternatively, huge propellers could be mounted directly on the iceberg's stern; in that case, the tugs could be dispensed with.

As it turned out, figuring out how to haul a one-hundred-million-ton chunk of ice was simpler than keeping it from melting along the way. Wrapping it in plastic would help; friction could also be minimized by slowing the tugboats to a glacial pace of, say, 1 to 2 knots. Even so, glaciologists calculated that on the 128-day trip from the Antarctic to the Red Sea port of Jidda, the berg would be pure liquid by day 104. One solution offered by ITI: forget about Saudi Arabia and aim for a closer destination, such as Australia. To date, however, no one has figured out how to tow an iceberg even that far.

A decade after the prince floated his proposal, consultant Terry Spragg proposed capturing an Antarctic iceberg and berthing it off the California coast. The venture offered two benefits, he claimed: It would eliminate the need for a costly desalinization plant by providing a new source of sorely needed fresh water. And it would be a major tourist attraction—for as long as it lasted, anyway.

The state legislature gave the plan a chilly reception.

The U.S. Camel Express.

After winning the Mexican War, the United States found itself with an extra half-million square miles of Mexican territory on its hands. The land was wide-open and arid, and not served by railways; transporting mail, people, and construction materials would be next to impossible. Then Jefferson Davis, secretary of war under President Pierce, came up with a near-brilliant solution: camels.

At Davis' urging, Congress appropriated $30,000 for the purchase of seventy-six single-humped camels from Turkey and Egypt. They arrived at Indianola, Texas, in 1856, and twenty-eight were shipped to the deserts of California and the southwest the following year.

Perhaps it wasn't an altogether crackbrained idea. Uniquely suited to desert life, the camel has a double row of eyelashes and can close its nostrils and ears against windblown sand; the male even has a rear-facing penis, so that he doesn't urinate into the wind. Capable of carrying 1,000-pound loads, traveling 40 miles a day, and going without water for a week at a time, the imported camels were used to cart road-building materials, do farm work, and deliver mail.

But the experiment was doomed. Horses freaked out whenever they saw the strange creatures; soldiers were afraid to ride them. Worse, the army hired a Turkish-born veterinarian as its camel expert, solely on the strength of his ancestry. Having no experience whatsoever with camels, he once tried to cure a sick animal by tickling its nose with a chameleon's tail.

Within a few years, the army gave up on the camels and sold them off to silver mines, zoos, and circuses. In the early 1860s, a German merchant named Otto Esche imported forty-five Mongolian camels to the United States with the hope of creating an east-west Camel Express. The project never materialized, and Esche sold his camels to a British mining company.

Dam foolishness.

Few public works projects have been undertaken with more hope and less foresight than Egypt's Aswan High Dam. Built from 1960 to 1970 with Soviet money and Egyptian manpower, the dam was supposed to tame the mighty Nile, preventing floods, generating hydroelectric energy, and increasing the amount of arable land in the delta.

It did all that, more or less—at a cost of $1.5 billion, not to mention the destruction of priceless archaeological treasures and the uprooting of 90,000 Egyptian and Sudanese settlers. It also created catastrophic health and environmental problems that vastly outweigh any benefits the dam may have rendered.

Before the dam was built, the Nile carried millions of tons of silt that fertilized the river valley, fortified the banks with new layers of topsoil, and prevented erosion by slowing the course of the river. Now the silt is largely gone from the Nile, once-ripe farmlands require massive infusions of fertilizer, and serious erosion has occurred; it may be only a matter of time before large chunks of the riverbank collapse and wash out to sea.

The dam has also robbed the river of nutrients that supported marine life—and a thriving fishing industry. Meanwhile, salt seepage, another by-product of the dam, is eating away at building foundations and turning millions of previously fertile acres into wasteland. As if that weren't enough, snails and blood flukes, never a problem in predam days, began to flourish in the irrigation channels, spreading schistosomiasis and other parasitic diseases.

Hailed upon its opening as the greatest architectural marvel since the Pyramids at Giza, the Aswan High Dam may be the worst scourge to be visited upon Egypt since the ten plagues.

Run your stereo on cow farts.

America's cows burp an estimated fifty million tons of hydrocarbons into the atmosphere each year. During the energy crisis of the 1970s, the Texas Department of Highways funded an investigation into the feasibility of trapping and recycling those precious burps and converting them into electricity. According to the researchers, the gross annual burp output of ten average-size Holsteins could adequately heat a small house and keep its stove working for a year.

In a separate study the federal Environmental Protection Administration awarded a $500,000 grant to Utah State University to fit rangeland cattle with a breathing apparatus that would collect and measure the volume of methane they expel through their mouths. The EPA also gave Washington State University $300,000 to measure and analyze the methane contained in bovine flatulence.

When Tommy Dorsey Played for the Apes

Bad Ideas in Flora and Fauna

The plant that ate Alabama.

Kudzu was the hit of the 1884 New Orleans Exposition. The Japanese had cultivated the broad-leafed vine for 2,000 years, weaving its fibers into cloth and boiling its roots to make everything from cookies to diarrhea remedies. But what turned on the fairgoers were its decorative possibilities.

In the 1880s southerners began planting kudzu around their homes for shade and beautification. Farmers also found it a rich source of hay and fodder.

In the 1930s the U.S. Department of Agriculture had a better idea: plant kudzu to prevent erosion. Growing as much as a foot a day, the vine would sink its roots deep into barren soil, enriching it with nitrogen and holding it fast against the ravages of time and weather.

Farmers grabbed up the free seed packets as fast as the government could hand them out. At times they were paid up to $8.00 an acre to plant. The region went kudzu-krazy. There were kudzu clubs and "Kudzu Queen" pageants. "Cotton isn't king anymore," wrote one enthusiast. "Kudzu is king!"

But there was a problem. The growth of the "miracle vine" went out of control. The hardiest of perennials, it lay dormant during the winter, then came back with a vengeance in the spring, growing over anything in its path, like a vegetative first cousin of "The Blob"—trees, small buildings, telephone poles, even abandoned cars. Kudzu strangled gardens and killed acres of timber trees by depriving them of sunlight. It had to be stopped.

The kudzu clubs were disbanded and planting ceased. There was talk of reversing the government subsidy—paying farmers *not* to plant. But getting rid of kudzu was not as easy as spreading it. People tried chopping, burning, and poisoning the vine, now reclassified a weed. Still it grew. In his poem "Kudzu," James Dickey called it "a vegetable form of cancer," and hinted that it killed animals and attacked people in their homes.

Kudzu covers seven million acres today, although some optimists claim they're making headway against further encroachments. New chemicals, such as Tordon 10K, which attacks the roots, are sending kudzu a message that it's not welcome. Meanwhile southerners can barely walk 3 feet without stepping into a clump of the stuff. It's everywhere, and there's no getting rid of it.

Kerr's Bees.

In the 1950s a geneticist named Warrick Kerr imported seventy lethal African bees to his laboratory in São Paulo, Brazil, with the intention of studying their habits and learning how they might be safely cross-bred with homegrown bees to beef up Brazil's honey reserves.

However, Kerr's bees had crossbreeding plans of their own. When twenty-six escaped from his labs in 1956, they immediately took to mating with the local talent, and within a few months there were several million offspring. Each one was every bit as aggressive and deadly as its progenitors.

Drifting northward en masse at a rate of 200 miles a year, the bees passed through Bolivia, Paraguay, Peru, and Venezuela, swarming down upon cattle and humans alike without the slightest provocation. Following the first recorded human fatality, in southern Brazil in 1966, Kerr's bees went on to disrupt weddings, garden parties, and even funeral processions. They once plagued inmates in a jail so relentlessly that the prisoners assumed they were being tortured by the authorities and screamed out their confessions.

When Australia gassed the Easter Bunny.

Australian immigration authorities would have been wise to post a NO EXPLOSIVES, FIREARMS, OR RABBITS sign at Melbourne harbor in the mid-1880s. Actually NO RABBITS would have been adequate; a shipload of bazookas couldn't have done as much damage to the country as the dozen Old World rabbits witlessly imported by English settlers in 1859.

The bunnies, installed in Melbourne's Barwan Park, had no trouble escaping. Fast, fertile, adaptable to a wide range of climates, and not at all picky about food, they traveled quickly and multiplied wildly. By 1900 eastern Australia was overrun with millions of rabbits; most were descendants of the original twelve. They made quick work of farms and grasslands and hogged the food meant for domesticated sheep. Inevitably the sheep-ranching industry, critical to the economy, rolled over and died.

The government tried building containment fences, pumping poison gas into rabbit warrens, and promoting the sale of rabbit pelts for use in the manufacture of hats. Nothing worked.

What finally did Australia's rabbits in was biological warfare. Beginning in 1950, crack antirabbit troops released swarms of mosquitoes bearing lethal doses of the myxomatosis virus in areas where rabbits congregated. Only then was the population brought under control.

Meanwhile Chilean hunters had introduced rabbits to their country, inexplicably confident that they could somehow avoid the catastrophe that befell Australia. Chile's experience was even more disastrous. By the 1930s the rabbits had overrun the country and begun crossing the Andes into Argentina. Even today enough remain to torment ranchers and farmers from Africa to Cape Horn.

The bat bombers.

At least two years before Hiroshima, the United States began work on a secret plan to bomb Japan into submission with live bats.

The idea for "Operation X-Ray" came from a Pennsylvania oral surgeon named Lytle S. Adams. In a letter to the War Department, Adams suggested that bats carrying timed incendiary devices could be sealed into lightweight canisters and dropped from planes over Osaka, where much of Japan's war matériel was manufactured. The canisters would spring open before hitting the ground, and the bats, partial to darkness and quiet, would head for the remotest corners of houses and buildings. The simultaneous explosion of thousands of undetected bombs would ignite the tinder-dry wooden structures and cause an inferno.

"Bears produce a formless fetus, giving birth to something like a bit of pulp, and this the mother-bear arranges into the proper legs and arms by licking it."

—The Book of Beasts
(Twelfth century A.D.)

The army liked the idea and in 1942 captured two million bats from caves in Texas and New Mexico and stored them, asleep, in giant freezers. Meanwhile a special one-ounce bomb was designed, small enough to be clipped to a bat yet powerful enough to flare for eight minutes with a 22-inch flame. When one accidentally went off at a New Mexico airfield, a large hangar and an automobile were incinerated.

The army spent $2 million on Operation X-Ray before scrapping the project in the fall of 1943. Not one bat was ever sent into battle.

Smelling out the enemy.

In a misguided, and undeniably racist initiative during World War II, the U.S. Army attempted to train dogs to recognize Japanese soldiers by their "characteristic" body smells.

In November 1942 about twenty-five men from the 100th Infantry Battalion, which consisted entirely of Japanese Americans, were shipped to Cat Island, in the Gulf of Mexico, along with about fifty dogs of various breeds. Each day the men were pressed into a bizarre game of hide-and-seek with the animals. They would walk into the jungle and conceal themselves in the dense foliage, doing their best to throw the dogs off their scent.

At first the men carried chunks of horsemeat, which the animals devoured hungrily when they found their prey; later, when the bait was eliminated, the dogs attacked the *men,* who wore padded clothing and face masks. If the dogs could be trained to smell the presence of Americans of Japanese ancestry on tropical, densely forested Cat Island, the army reasoned, they would fare just as well in the Pacific against native Japanese troops.

But the program, which had been approved by President Roosevelt, was a total failure. Later in the war the army did rely on dogs to sniff out enemy troops in the Pacific, but not by distinguishing Japanese from Americans. The Cat Island experiment produced absolutely no evidence that ethnic Japanese exuded a tell-tale odor.

Skin flicks in the ape house.

When the primate population of England's Chessington Zoo began to dwindle in the early 1970s, officials devised a revolutionary plan to perk up the apes' flagging sex life and get them to mate: show them pornographic movies.

The first step in the program, before the chimps would be graduated to hard-core porn, was to treat them to a BBC documentary film featuring scenes of amorous chimpanzees cuddling. "We tried it in three cages in the ape house," said zoo spokesman Andy Bowman. "The orangutans were only interested in the projector, and the gorillas became aggressive."

The second feature was never shown.

The dogs of war (airborne division).

In a 1980 project that was blessed by the Pentagon but condemned by humane societies and animal-rights lobbyists, the U.S. Army attempted to train forty German shepherds to be paratroopers.

After a ten-week training course at Lackland Air Force Base, Texas, the pooches were assigned to the Eighty-second Airborne Division at Fort Bragg, North Carolina, where they started off with easy jumps from an 8-foot tower; later, they leaped from the fantail of a Navy destroyer and took part in a beach assault in Virginia. Each dog was strapped to the back of a human paratrooper, who would lower the animal to the ground on a tether from 200 feet up. That way dog and man landed a few seconds apart, avoiding tangling and collisions.

"I wouldn't ask my dogs to do anything a man wouldn't do," Sgt. First Class Robert Meade, Kennel Master of the Sixteenth Military Police Group at Fort Bragg, told the Associated Press. "I can't think of anything a man could do that a dog can't, except drive a jeep or operate a radio." Although Meade claimed the animals enjoyed parachuting, injuries to canine and human jumpers as well as protests by the ASPCA ultimately convinced the Department of Defense to abort the program.

The dogs of war (naval division).

Not to be outdone by its army rivals, the U.S. Navy sponsored a project in the

1970s to teach dogs to swim underwater and attack enemy frogmen. The top-secret initiative was called Project Aquadog.

Around the same time, Navy scientists were also conducting experiments to establish the feasibility of using dolphins to retrieve spent torpedoes that had missed their mark.

The man in the monkey house.

Zoo cages are for animals, not people. But that didn't stop New York's Bronx Zoo from putting a man in a cage—to the amusement of zoogoers and the outrage of early civil-rights advocates.

On a 1904 trip to the Congo, explorer Samuel Verner rescued a group of pygmies from the clutches of cannibals and brought them back to America, where they were a smash hit at the St. Louis Exposition. When the fair was over, most of the Africans returned to their homes on the Kasai River. One got only as far as the Bronx.

Ota Benga made his Bronx Zoo debut on September 10, 1906; he was twenty-three. Huge crowds thronged the primate house, where the 4'11", 103-pound bushman shared a cage first with a chimpanzee and later with an orangutan and a parrot. Remarkably unself-conscious, Benga publicly slept, ate, defecated, and roughhoused with his cagemates and generally seemed to enjoy himself. The delighted crowds tossed peanuts to the monkeys and coins to the bushman.

But not everyone was amused. One prominent black cleric, the Reverend MacArthur of Calvary Baptist Church, decried the "degrading" spectacle and said, "instead of making a beast of this little fellow, he should be put in school." The Colored Ministers Conference likewise found the whole business distasteful in the extreme and futilely implored the mayor to step in and straighten out the zoo directors.

One minister tried to find Benga a place in a foster home; another offered to house him under his own roof. Meanwhile the crowds kept coming, and zoo director William Hornaday held his ground. Though the black community cried racism, Hornaday insisted he had installed Benga in the primate house only "because that was the most comfortable place we could find for him."

"Plants and trees arise directly out of the earth in the same manner that feathers and hair grow from the bodies of animals."

—Titus Lucretius Carus (first century B.C.)

By late September the zoo released Benga from his cage and gave him free rein around the zoo grounds. He was rarely without a small crowd as he wandered about in white duck trousers, chatting amiably and doing odd jobs. Occasionally, though, the crowds got a bit too aggressive; one time he fired his bow and arrow in defense and wounded a man.

Eventually Benga left the zoo and went south, where he was educated in local schools and cared for by a succession of sponsors; he later worked in a tobacco factory. Never happy in America but too poor to afford return passage to Africa, Benga committed suicide in 1916 in Lynchburg, Virginia.

When Tommy Dorsey played for the apes.

The Big-Band era was in full swing in 1940, and the Dorsey Brothers presumably had as much work as they could handle. So one can only guess what was on Tommy's mind when he installed eight members of his band in a cage at the Philadelphia Zoo that summer to play for the monkeys.

In point of fact, it was part of a grand experiment to see if simians appreciate music. Well, you ask, did they dig it?

"The monkeys couldn't stand it," noted a zookeeper interviewed by the musical journal *Etude*. "The band first played some violent jazz. The chimpanzees were scared to death." They scampered all over the place, desperately seeking the protection of their keepers and hiding under benches. One outraged chimp tried to pull the trombone out of Dorsey's hands.

The response to that number was so bad, in fact, that the band was forced to stop playing. One aging ape had such a wounded and resentful look on his face that the band members couldn't bear to continue.

In all fairness the Dorsey concert wasn't entirely a flop. When the band played their theme song, "I'm Getting Sentimental Over You," the animals calmed noticeably. They even sat quietly on their benches for a while, the zookeeper reported, showing none of their previous agitation and "watching the players with interest."

In a related story, animal behaviorists D. Porter and A. Neuringer played recordings of Bach flute sonatas and works for viola by the twentieth-century composer Paul Hindemith to an audience of pigeons. After repeated hearings the birds were able to distinguish one composer from the other four out of five times. The birds proved just as discerning in differentiating Stravinsky's *The Rite of Spring* from a Bach organ prelude.

Bringing starlings to America.

Starlings, to paraphrase Rambo, are your worst ecological nightmare. Screechy and aggressive, they gather in noisy flocks, showering the nation's byways with their excreta, decimating wheatfields, scaring off nicer birds, and spreading disease. The worst part is that America would be starling-free had it not been for one man's misguided obsession with the plays of Shakespeare.

On a spring day in 1890, a wealthy New Yorker named Eugene Scheifflin led several friends to Manhattan's Central Park, where they released forty pairs of starlings imported from Europe. No starling had ever entered U.S. airspace before; the launching of these eighty was part of Scheifflin's grand scheme to introduce specimens of every bird mentioned in Shakespeare. ("I'll have a starling that shall be taught to speak nothing but 'Mortimer'": *Henry IV, Part I*.)

> "A man could not be in two places at the same time unless he were a bird."
>
> —Sir Boyle Roche, eighteenth-century British parliamentarian

Luckily, most of the other Old World birds brought over by Scheifflin died out, but his starlings bred like bunnies. Sizable colonies were spotted as far away as Brooklyn by 1896, in Connecticut by 1898, and in Pennsylvania, Delaware, and upstate New York by 1910. By 1947 they had spread to the West Coast. Today they're everywhere.

And, like cockroaches and magazine blow-in cards, there's no getting rid of them. Starlings are dogged nesters who won't easily be displaced by other animals or seasonal changes. The U.S. Army has tried to downsize the starling population with blasts of Tergitol, a potent detergent that washes away the protective coating of oil that keeps the birds from freezing to death. But so far, Scheifflin's babies are doing just fine.

No pigs were harmed during the production of this musical instrument.

When King Louis XI (reigned 1461–1483) of France commanded the Abbot of Baigne to invent a new musical instrument to entertain His Majesty's friends, the abbot obliged by assembling a herd of hogs, ranging in size from nursing piglets to mature swine. Under a velvet tent, he lined them up by size in adjacent cages, with the basso profundo porkers on the left, the middle-range sows in the middle, and the soprano piglets on the right. Their tails protruded from one side of the cage, their snouts from the other.

Then the abbot modified an organ keyboard, attaching the keys to a complex apparatus terminating in a series of small spikes, one poised over the rump of each pig. The courtiers were gathered together and the abbot played his keyboard, causing the spikes to prick the pigs, who naturally let out a piercing squeal, each in its own particular voice range.

The tunes were actually recognizable, sort of, though the abbot's quirky entertainment outraged the sensibilities of the king and his guests, not to mention the pigs. Four centuries later, a now-forgotten inventor in Cincinnati introduced a similar contrivance. He called it the "Porco-Forte."

Yaks and cows together.

A Saskatchewan cattle breeder named Roy Carlson decided to cross a cow with a Tibetan yak. His hope was that the resultant offspring—presumably to be called either a yow or a cak—would combine the grace of a heifer with the durability of a yak, and provide leaner meat and richer milk to boot.

Carlson's first step was to purchase two male yaks from a local game farm. He placed them among his 120 cows and waited for That Special Spark. Nothing happened. The yaks, named Royal Yak I and Royal Yak II, and the cows wanted no part of each other.

Carlson then abandoned his role as matchmaker and turned his thoughts to artificial insemination. But the market for yak semen was bullish, and Carlson had to delay that plan until he could raise enough cash to artificially impregnate his cows. Meanwhile Royal II broke loose from the untended feedlot where he had been kept and rampaged through the surrounding countryside, killing a dog and demolishing a parked automobile. Finally he plunged into the South Saskatchewan River and swam to refuge on an uninhabited island. As of this writing, the fugitive yak was still at large.

Opera bufo.

To eradicate the cane beetles that were ravaging crops in Queensland in the 1930s, Australia imported large numbers of *bufo marinus,* a ravenous species of South American toad. The Aussies had misjudged the toads' voraciousness, however, because after the beetles were gone, the toads, now grown as large as house cats, reproduced wildly and took to devouring garbage, Ping-Pong balls, dogs, and cattle, attacking their prey with a poisonous glandular secretion.

By the early 1970s the bufo explosion had become a biological nightmare in Australia. The National Wildlife Department put a $30 bounty on each toad brought in; "Wanted" posters were everywhere. And, as a public service, at least one radio station was broadcasting tape-recorded mating calls of male bufos in an attempt to lure love-starved females to destruction.

Fleurs du mal (de tête):

1. There are some 125 species of goldenrod, or solidago—a bright yellow perennial that brings color to the countryside and the agonies of hell to millions of hay-fever sufferers. Goldenrod grows just about everywhere in the continental United States, but for some perverse reason, the Nebraska state legislature designated it the official state flower in 1895, and Kentucky followed suit in 1926. Neither state has yet taken the next logical step and made sneezing the official state sport.

2. In 1957, Indiana chose the peony as its state flower, despite the fact that

no peony has ever grown in that state. A large minority of lawmakers more sensibly favored the dogwood blossom, but some say a well-connected commercial peony grower may have influenced the vote.

3. After acquiring a sixty-pound bulb from Harvard University, T. H. Everett, assistant curator of the New York Botanical Gardens, spent five years nursing it to flowerhood. Finally on June 8, 1937, the giant Sumatran calla lily *(amorphophallus titanium)* was about to burst into blossom. The largest flower ever seen, the lily measured 8½ feet in height. It began to bloom at exactly 1:00 P.M.; hundreds of flower freaks crowded the garden hothouse, enduring 93 degree temperatures for a view of the historic unfolding, which took place at the leisurely rate of four inches per hour.

    They should have stayed home and watched it on radio. Fully opened, the flower was 4 feet in diameter and 12 feet in circumference, with an inflorescent stalk containing thousands of small flowers. But only those with severe head colds could enjoy it. In bloom the lily smelled like rotting fish. Since then the flower has been seen in its full glory only about fifteen times in the United States. The most recent blooming took place at the Quail Botanical Gardens in Encinitas, California, in 2002. "Eeeewwwww," said nine-year-old Todd Fritz, writhing on the ground in mock agony. "It's the worst thing I ever smelled." At least two other visitors, Ruth and Ken Mitzner, brought along a pair of respirators. "Just in case," they said.

4. Sir Stamford Raffles, who founded modern Singapore, also discovered a Brobdingnagian flower in the hills of Sumatra that was later named the Rafflesia in his honor. Some honor. In the same size class as the Sumatran calla lily, the Rafflesia measures up to 3 feet across, blossoms into a hideous bloodred flower covered with pimples, and stinks to high heaven. Appropriately, it is pollinated not by bees, but by flies.

Fawning over flora.

"When it comes down to it, there is not much an animal can do that a plant cannot do, except, perhaps, walk around," Malcolm Wilkins, who is Regis Professor of Botany at Glasgow University, told Great Britain's Association for Science Education in 2000. While some plants are less cognitively endowed than others—like humans—there are many that can smell, taste, differentiate colors, and tell the time, Wilkins said. Touch the sensory hairs of a Venus fly-trap once, he noted, and it will not react. "But touch it twice and it snaps shut. The plant is able to count from naught to one to two. The most complex computer can only count from zero to nine." At a conference at Loughborough University, Wilkins railed against vegetarians, "who don't like animals being killed" but have little compassion for defenseless produce. "You are perfectly happy to slice up a tomato or cucumber," he said. "Where is your logic?"

Lamebrained Crimes, Misdemeanors, and Legal Pronouncements

Evil wears a cunning face.

Eugene "Butch" Flenough Jr. wore a motorcycle helmet to conceal his face while allegedly holding up an Austin, Texas, restaurant in 1991. But employees were reportedly able to identify Flenough and lead the police to him without too much trouble because his name was painted on the front of the helmet.

Pulling up to the drive-in window of a bank in Lubbock, Texas, a man handed teller Penny Friend a note that said, "Give me $10,000 or I'll blow you up." Friend was prepared to comply when she noticed the robber's fake mustache beginning to slide off his lip. She began laughing hysterically. The driver left empty-handed.

Well, ex-c-u-u-u-se me!

FBI agent Melvin Purvis and sixteen of his men staked out Chicago's Biograph Theatre for two hours on July 24, 1934, waiting for the show to break and John Dillinger to emerge. When he did (after viewing *Manhattan Melodrama,* starring Clark Gable and William Powell), Purvis' men gunned him down. Acclaimed a national hero, the G-man later appeared on the Fleischmann's Yeast Hour, where he burped loudly into a live microphone.

The coast-to-coast eructation was heard by millions of listeners, grossed out executives at the J. Walter Thompson advertising agency, and earned Purvis a dressing-down from FBI boss J. Edgar Hoover. He was not invited back on the show.

The plot to kill Charlie Chaplin.

Nearly a decade before Pearl Harbor, Japanese terrorists thought they could provoke a war with the United States by assassinating Charlie Chaplin.

"Obviously, when you see someone go berserk and get a weapon and go in and murder people, of course, of course, it troubles me."

—George H. W. Bush, commenting on the shooting of twenty-three people by a gunman in a Texas cafeteria in 1991

While traveling in the Far East in 1932, Chaplin stopped off in Tokyo. On May 15, the day before he was to attend a tea reception hosted by Prime Minister Inukai Ki, six young military officers stormed the residence of the seventy-five-year-old leader and shot him to death in the presence of his daughter-in-law and grandchild.

The assassins were members of a fanatical band of ultranationalists with a string of political killings to their credit. At their trial, ringleader Seishi Koga revealed that they had originally planned to kill both Chaplin and the prime minister at the tea reception. "Chaplin is a popular figure in the United States and the darling of the capitalist class," Koga explained. "We believed that killing him would cause a war with America." They scrapped their plans when they realized the United States was not likely to go to war over the death of a movie star. And anyway, Chaplin was English, not American.

Throughout Japan, popular sentiment was behind the assassins. Their lawyer received 110,000 letters of support, many written in blood. In a more dramatic gesture of sympathy, nine men amputated their little fingers and sent them, preserved in alcohol, to the Japanese War Minister. In the end the assassins got off with light sentences.

Hoist by his own petard.

Architect Hugues Aubriot should have thought twice about designing the Bastille—even if it was at the request of King Charles V of France. He was one of the first people to be imprisoned in it.

To be sure, Aubriot designed the Bastille in 1370 not as a prison but, rather, as a moated fortress guarding a major entrance to Paris. After Charles' death, Aubriot got into hot water with the church and was accused of a range of crimes, from sodomy to neglecting to take holy communion on Easter. He was sentenced to a brief but unpleasant stay in the very fortress he built.

Have a nice execution.

Harris County (Texas) Court Judge Charles J. Hearn never let a hard day get him down. Whenever he signed his name, he would always include a perky "happy face"—the kind that graces "Have a nice day" bumper stickers. The logo added a nice touch to Christmas greetings and credit card receipts.

But in 1993 Hearn scribbled it on an order of execution issued to convicted murderer Robert Nelson Drew. Drew and his attorney, William Kunstler, were strangely unamused by the judge's artwork. They challenged the order and sought Judge Hearn's disqualification from the case. "It's like he's saying 'Have a nice death,'" Kunstler said.

But from where Judge Hearn sat, Drew and Kunstler were missing the point. "It's just a signature, like yours is or anyone else's is," he explained. "It's that simple. I'm a happy person. You've got to be a happy person. We've got too many people walking around this world with grim looks on their faces."

Terrorism by micturition.

In 1993, minutes after takeoff from Hollywood–Fort Lauderdale Airport, passenger Johann Peter Grzeganek had to use the bathroom. Although the seatbelt sign was still on, Grzeganek had been drinking heavily and couldn't wait. Unless he was given immediate leave to use the lavatory, he told a flight attendant in German, his bladder would explode "and the roof will fly."

It was the wrong metaphor—and the wrong place to use it.

Though the flight attendant spoke German, she missed the point and assumed Grzeganek was threatening to detonate a bomb, not his bladder. Crew members wrestled him to the floor, and the plane returned to the airport for an emergency landing. Grzeganek spent nine months in a federal prison before a judge sorted out the confusion and released him.

"Do you see anything that happened that couldn't have been remedied by letting this man go to the bathroom?" the judge railed at prosecutors.

A new life.

A prisoner serving a sentence for larceny at an Iowa correctional facility, escaped and eluded police for nearly a year. The law finally caught up with him when he appeared as a contestant on *The Dating Game*, and, later, *The Gong Show*.

Charged with drug possession in Jackson, Tennessee, Amanda Guild ran off to Saginaw, Michigan, where she made a new life for herself and joined a bowling league. After scoring 587 over three consecutive games, she was named "Bowler of the Week" and allowed her picture to appear in the local newspaper. An IRS man who remembered Guild from her Tennessee days tipped off the police, who arrested her the following week at bowling practice.

Patrick Quinn, or at least a man calling himself Patrick Quinn, appeared as a contestant on TV's *Super Password* in 1987 and bagged $58,600 on a single show, a record. When he showed up at the studio to collect his winnings, he was arrested by a Secret Service agent, who had seen him on TV. Quinn, whose name was actually Kerry Ketchum, had been on the run from authorities for some time and was wanted for mail fraud in three states.

Masters of deceit.

James Sanders of Baton Rouge, Louisiana, was charged with clipping the corners from a $20.00 bill, grafting them onto a $1.00 bill, and attempting to pass off the pastiche as a twenty. *The Arizona Republic* reported that sentencing judge John Parker of Federal District Court called Sanders "the most inept counterfeiter I ever heard of" and gave him five years' probation.

After failing his driving test, Ronald Sturkes complained loudly about it to employees at the State Motor Vehicles Bureau office in Hicksville, New York, according to the *Edmonton Journal*. Having made a lasting impression on the staff, a few days later he sent a friend to retake the written test in his place. Sturkes was twenty-seven years old and white; his stand-in was fifty-five and black. Both were arrested.

In 1984 the manager of a brokerage office in White Plains, New York, allegedly swiped a $51,000 check made out to Mellon Bank, at the time the nation's fifth-largest financial institution, and brought it to a local bank, where he opened an account under the name "Mellon Bank." As reported in Chuck Shepard's News of the Weird column, the man subsequently returned to the bank and wrote out a withdrawal slip for $3,850, identifying himself as "Mellon E. Bank." The teller quietly called the FBI, and then stalled the thief long enough for the feds to arrive and arrest him.

The plot to kidnap George Washington.

In June 1776, with the British due to attack New York City that summer, colonial governor William Tryon of New York bribed some 700 Americans into deserting to the British once the gunfire started. In addition, his plan called for surprising the American troops from behind with their own guns and, nerviest move of all, kidnapping their commander in chief, George Washington, who would then be either executed or handed over to the British.

Tryon's conspiracy never had a chance. For one thing, it relied more on petty criminals than on skilled insurrectionists. Even New York City mayor David Matthews, who was Tryon's principal agent, was described by a fellow Tory as "a person low in estimation as a lawyer, profligate, abandoned, and dissipated."

"The streets are safe in Philadelphia. It's only the people who make them unsafe."

—*Mayor Frank Rizzo of Philadelphia*

Moreover, leaks were everywhere. A jailed counterfeiter named Isaac Ketchum overheard some other prisoners discussing the conspiracy and tipped off the New York Provincial Congress; a waiter in the Sergeant's Arms Tavern also got wind of the plot and reported it to New York City officials. Before things got very far, forty of the ringleaders were rounded up and the treachery was quashed.

Surprisingly, of all those arrested, only one was court-martialed—

Washington's bodyguard, Thomas Hickey. The court heard charges that he had even gone so far as to poison a dish of peas meant for the general's table. Washington had turned them down, the story went, and they were instead fed to some chickens, which promptly died. Hickey was convicted of mutiny, sedition, and treachery, and on June 28 he was hanged in New York City before 20,000 people.

The nine-trillion-dollar bail.

In 1990 a Birmingham, Alabama, district court judge with a reputation for excessive leniency silenced his critics by setting bail for a theft suspect at $9 trillion.

According to Birmingham mayor Richard Arrington, Judge Jack Montgomery had frequently set ludicrously low bonds for repeat offenders. In the case of one theft suspect who had been arrested six times in as many months, the judge had never set a bond higher than $5,000. Given the man's history, the mayor argued, bail should have been much higher.

Judge Montgomery obliged. When the suspect came before him an eighth time on charges of theft, he set bail at $9 trillion—a bit less than triple the national debt at the time.

"This is so he doesn't get in any more trouble," he explained.

Near-perfect crimes.

Two car thieves working a Detroit parking lot jimmied open the door of a parked minivan and began poking around for valuables. Thus occupied, they failed to notice two plainclothesmen sitting in the front seat. The driver quietly put the car in gear and proceeded to the police station.

Armed with a gun, a man stole two canned hams from a Waterloo, Iowa, grocery store. He was arrested when he returned an hour later with one of the hams—with the date and store label still on it—and asked for a $45.58 refund.

In 1984 a man applied in person for check-cashing privileges at a Safeway supermarket in Long Beach, California. He left after completing the forms and returned twenty-five minutes later to rob the store, only to lose his nerve and flee empty-handed. He hid out at his home, where police had little trouble tracking him down since he'd provided his correct address when he applied for the check-cashing card.

After committing a burglary, an Opelousas, Louisiana man realized he'd left his wallet at the scene of the crime. He was arrested while reporting the loss at the local police station.

After thumbing a ride with a passing motorist, a man punched his benefactor in the face, stole his wallet, and fled. Later he discovered that the wallet had no cash. Worse, he'd left his own wallet on the front seat; it contained $70. He phoned his victim and suggested that they meet to swap wallets. The victim showed up with the police.

The Lazy Man's Guide to Riches.

Attempting to rob a Citibank branch in Queens, New York, an out-of-work shoe salesman handed the teller a note demanding "all your tens, twenties, and thirties." He was arrested fifteen minutes later by a bank officer who trailed him on foot to a motel a block away.

An Orlando, Florida, man purchased a Canon color copying machine for $19,000 and used it to print three million Polish zlotys, worth about $300. He was convicted of counterfeiting. Commented a U.S. Secret Service agent at the time of the 1990 case, "He could have printed a boxcar full of them and not have enough to buy an expensive suit."

Lazaros Alberis allegedly broke into a movie house in Athens, Greece, after hours and unsuccessfully attempted to pry open the cash register with a pair of scissors. Exhausted by the effort, he fell asleep on the spot. Police woke him up and arrested him the following morning.

Queen Victoria, floozie.

"Buffalo Bill" Cody's wife once sued him for divorce on the grounds that he had slept with Queen Victoria.

In 1886 the great cowboy-showman toured Europe with his popular "Wild West" show, and audiences went wild. More than a million people turned out for the spectacle during its five-month tour, including 83,000 on one record-breaking day at Earl's Court in London. Among the show's biggest fans was Queen Victoria, who evinced markedly un-Victorian excitement over the dancing cowgirls, whooping Indians, and heart-stopping displays of stunt riding and marksmanship. Cody gave a command performance before her and later met with her privately.

> **"Outside of the killings, [Washington, D.C.] has one of the lowest crime rates in the country."**
>
> —*Mayor Marion Barry of Washington*

"I found the Queen a most gracious and charming woman," Cody reported afterwards. For her part, Victoria described Cody as "the best-looking man" she had ever seen.

But back home Cody's wife, Louisa, fumed at his phenomenal popularity abroad—especially with the women. On his return she nagged him continually and flew into jealous rages. In 1904 she sued Cody for divorce.

At the trial a witness recalled Louisa's jealousy over Cody's flings with English women in 1886—especially Queen Victoria. It was pure fantasy. The plump and proper queen had been in her sixties back then and still in mourning for her late husband, Prince Albert. True, Cody had dallied with dozens of women during his European tour, but the Queen of England wasn't among them. The judge tossed the case out of court, and Cody and Louisa remained married till his death in 1917.

The man who put lobsters in his underwear.

Shoplifter Winston Treadway allegedly plucked two live lobsters from a tank in a Boston supermarket and hid them in his jockey shorts. He left the store undetected, but doubled up in pain outside when one of the crustaceans clamped down on his genitals. Police borrowed a pair of pliers to free the stricken thief; then they arrested him. Doctors later told Treadway he might never father children.

This is your brain. This is your brain on vacation.

While staying at a resort hotel in Marco Island, Florida, in 1983, a guest complained to the security staff that a thousand dollars' worth of cocaine had been stolen from his room. When the guards located the coke and brought it to his room, the complainant said, "It's mine, but a lot's missing." Local deputies asked him to sign a receipt for it, never believing he'd be dumb enough to comply. When he did, they arrested him. "That's the last time I'm going to trust a security officer," he said.

The good news is that they didn't leave fingerprints.

In Zurich, Switzerland, a burglar severed his thumb smashing the window of a jewelry store and then ran off without stealing a thing. Police retrieved the detached digit, matched it with the owner's fingerprints, and arrested him two hours later.

Thanks to Filbert Maestas, Denver has 1,200 fewer assholes.

Filbert Maestas allegedly broke into a Denver meat warehouse in 1977 and stole several thousand pounds of what he assumed was prime beef. Instead he had apparently lifted 1,200 beef rectums, which have no food value and are used only by dairies in the processing of cheese. "If I go to jail for stealing 1,200 beef assholes, I'm really going to be mad," he reportedly told police.

Fat men in chimneys.

In Jones, Oklahoma, police freed—and then jailed—a man who had attempted to sneak into the home of his ex-wife via the chimney and gotten stuck. By the time he was freed, he'd been trapped more than eleven hours; his lungs were so full of chimney ash that he couldn't speak and had to be treated for chest pains. "This is the first time I've ever worked with someone overdosing on soot," said Oklahoma County undersheriff Jerry Biggers.

A twenty-one-year-old thief spent the night lodged in the chimney of the Warwick, Rhode Island, public library. When police found him the following morning, he was not wearing pants.

In St. Petersburg, Florida, a patient returned to his doctor's office after hours and attempted to break in through the chimney. A secretary found him in the morning, hanging upside down. Police read him his rights before extricating him.

A prisoner tried to escape from a county jail in Houston by crawling through the air-conditioning duct. Along the way he crashed through a weak spot into a courtroom below.

Near-perfect crimes II.

In Tracy, California, in 1989, police arrested a twenty-one-year-old man after he brought in a 9-millimeter handgun for repairs to the store he'd stolen it from a few weeks before.

Undeterred by the fact that he was blind, a man tried to hold up a London bank. But he panicked at the sound of approaching police sirens, tried to leave, and ran into the door.

Five teenagers spray painted graffiti on the tomb of Abraham Lincoln in Springfield, Illinois, in 1987. Police had little difficulty breaking the case since what the vandals spray painted was their names.

Thieves sneaked into the attic of a supermarket in County Meath, Ireland, under cover of night and began drilling a hole in the floor. But the floor turned out to be made of concrete rather than wood, and their exertions took much longer than they expected. Completing the hole, they slipped through and dropped to the floor below to find themselves on the street. They had drilled in the wrong place.

After swiping a large quantity of change from a Red Wing, Minnesota, amusement park, a teenager leaped into the Mississippi River and started swimming across. But the coins weighed him down, and he was forced to struggle back to shore, where police were waiting for him.

Guns without holsters. Thieves without brains.

In the process of holding up a Pittsburgh gas station at gunpoint, a man accidentally fired his pistol into his pants when he slipped it under his belt. The gunman screamed and ran off; police later found a bullet lodged in the floor.

A man held up an adult bookstore in Dallas in 1990, helping himself to the contents of the cash register as well as to a handgun concealed behind the counter. When he jammed the gun into his waistband, it fired, and he staggered from the store with a bullet wound in his genitals—and without the money.

After robbing a Paris bank at gunpoint, the robber ordered the employees to stay put and keep their hands in the air. They watched in amazement as he stuffed the money *and* his gun into a bag and zippered it shut. They had no difficulty wrestling him to the ground and restraining him until the police arrived.

"Get the thing straight for once and for all. The policeman isn't there to create disorder. The policeman is there to preserve disorder."

—*Mayor Richard J. Daley of Chicago*

Driving on empty along the highway of good sense.

A gang of armed robbers held up a Los Angeles automobile shipping company, abducted the security guard, and drove off with nine cars. Had they bothered to check the fuel gauges, they would have seen that the gas tanks were almost empty. But they didn't, and all nine stalled out before they reached the freeway. One also had a flat tire.

Escape to San Quentin.

A man jailed on a driving-while-intoxicated charge in Winterset, Iowa, escaped and fled to his girlfriend's home, where he spent the night. His libido calmed, he tried to slip quietly back into jail the following morning, but tripped an alarm and was caught.

Three young men trying to steal a parked pickup truck in Larkspur, California, in 1989 were caught offguard by the owner, who called the police. Chased by a patrol car, the thieves climbed a fence and kept running, only to discover they were on the grounds of San Quentin State Penitentiary. "Nothing like this has ever happened here before," said Lieutenant Cal White. "People just don't break into prison every day."

Bank error in your favor. Collect $60,000 and go directly to jail, jerk.

James Duffy couldn't believe his luck: A $60,000 deposit earmarked for the Philadelphia Saving Fund Society was mistakenly credited to his account. Although he later insisted he'd tried to alert his bank to the error, his good intentions were not evident at his trial for theft. In the space of a few weeks, Duffy allegedly used the windfall to finance a Florida vacation, buy a new car, pay off a school loan, refurnish his sister's home and help her with mortgage payments, cater a party, and disburse thousands of dollars in gifts to friends and relatives. "There are a large number of people with a finders-keepers mentality," said prosecuting attorney Steven Kaplan. "That's okay for a children's verse, but it's not the law."

Blind driver. Enter crosswalk cautiously.

Three times George Lizarralde, of Brea, California, applied for a driver's license, and three times the California Department of Motor Vehicles turned him

down. But on his fourth attempt, in 1985, the department relented and pronounced him fit to drive.

They should have held their ground. The applicant was blind.

Inevitably, Lizarralde's disability caught up with him: Ploughing through
an intersection, he struck three pedestrians. A jury found the DMV at fault,
and awarded the victims $4.1 million.

Near-perfect crimes III.

A masked gunman attempted to rob the Park Motel in Louisiana in 1987.
However, he discovered too late that he'd neglected to cut eye slits in the
dark-green Hefty bag he used to conceal his identity. He stumbled about,
wildly clawing at the plastic to tear holes in it. Police arrived shortly to
assist him.

An experienced burglar slipped into a store in Barnsley, England, in
1979 and stole a large amount of merchandise. None of the store employees or customers saw him, but he was nailed at the door by eight detectives. They were attending a conference of store detectives taking place on
the premises.

An eighteen-year-old burglar swiped an expensive camera from a
home in Killington, Connecticut, in 1979 and sold it for $740—after tak-
ing several pictures of himself and forgetting to remove the film. He was
arraigned on charges of burglary and larceny.

Would-be robbers in Halloween masks burst into a supermarket in
Vancouver and began beating an employee. From several feet away,
another employee hurled a ten-pound frozen turkey at the attackers, striking one in the back. They fled from the store in a hail of frozen poultry.

Presumably it was worth it.

A man climaxed a 3-mile drive through the streets of Buffalo, New York, in
1990 by crashing into a telephone pole. Police arrested him on the spot.

He was blind.

The thirty-one-year-old man explained that he'd always wanted to drive a car, notwithstanding his visual impairment. Riding with him were his brother and a friend, who gave him directions. Said arresting officer Karen Czekalski, "This is one for the books."

Excuses, excuses.

"I snapped or something," Orvall Wyatt told Dallas police, who arrested him on murder charges. Wyatt said he'd mistaken his mother-in-law for a large raccoon, prompting him to hack her to death with an ax.

This is your plane. This is your plane's management. This is your plane's management on drugs. Any questions?

The head of a major U.S. airline was caught trying to carry 2.7 grams of marijuana onto a flight in 1994.

Gary Wilson, co-chairman of Northwest Airlines, was boarding a flight in Boise, Idaho, when airport security guards asked to examine his briefcase. They found the grass along with a small pipe.

Wilson could have been fined $1,000 and drawn a year in jail for each count. Prosecutors agreed to a $500 fine and no jail time. Wilson relinquished his duties while the Northwest board of directors looked into the matter.

World's worst hors d'oeuvres.

In a fit of before-dinner passion, Mrs. Stoyan Pandov of Bulgaria affectionately bit her husband on the ear. He went into shock and was rushed to a hospital, where he died of blood poisoning.

We've seen the future and it's Lorena Bobbitt.

1. Antonio Lama of Naples, Italy, awoke one fine summer's morning in 1975 to find his wife Amalia removing his nose with a pair of pliers. "She was jealous," he explained to hospital surgeons who stitched up the wound.

2. An enraged housewife in Thailand woke her slumbering spouse by scissoring off his penis and tossing it out the window, where a duck picked it up in its mouth and waddled away with it, according to the *Bangkok Post*.

3. Jealousy allegedly drove Vital da Silva to cut off his wife's ears with a 12-inch stiletto when he caught her flirting with another man in a bar in Maceió, Brazil, in 1975. He then reportedly tossed them idly on the floor and walked out the door.

> **"If crime went down 100 percent, it would still be fifty times higher than it should be."**
>
> —*Washington, D.C. councilman John Bowman*

The man who shot Capone.

Crime czar Al Capone once accidentally shot himself in the groin while playing golf.

In 1928 Capone was playing at Burnham Woods Golf Course, just south of Chicago. As usual the gangster had packed a loaded .45 revolver with the woods and irons, and as he reached into his golf bag to withdraw a club, he snagged the trigger. The gun fired, and the bullet tore through his right leg, narrowly missing his abdomen and lodging in his left foot.

Capone hopped wildly around the green, screaming in agony and cursing the heavens. He eventually calmed down enough for his bodyguards to drive him to St. Margaret's Hospital, in nearby Hammond, Indiana, where doctors treated him for flesh wounds in his legs and groin and sent him limping home the following day. Years later his caddy, Tim Sullivan, told an interviewer, "After that, the boys double-checked to make sure the safety catch was on before they deposited any gun in a golf bag."

Pulling a fast one on J. Edgar.

At the height of his career in crime, bank robber John Dillinger tried to outsmart the FBI by burning off his fingerprints with sulfuric acid. It was an excruciating ordeal and Dillinger afterwards suffered several days of intense pain.

When the burns had healed, he discovered that his prints were totally unchanged and as distinct as ever.

It must have been a scatter rug.

As a matter of policy, most illegal aliens agree it's wise to avoid casual contact with immigration officers. But in Las Vegas in 1994, four undocumented Mexicans presented themselves at the home of the local director of the Immigration and Naturalization Service to install carpeting.

They were deported before they could finish the job.

"Out of 900,000 people in Las Vegas, they picked my house," said the official, Arthur Strapp. "It was the wrong house."

Strapp was at the office when his wife telephoned him to say that the men, employed by a local flooring company, had arrived as scheduled to lay carpet, and that she thought they might be illegal aliens. An agent went to Strapp's house, where the workers admitted having entered the country without proper documentation. They were returned to Mexico the following day.

The Strapps' carpet installation was completed by properly documented workers the day after.

They should have counted to ten first:

1. When a fellow student at San Francisco State University declined to put out her cigarette in an elevator, a man drew a knife and stabbed her in the chest. He claimed self-defense. "She attacked me and forced me to defend myself," he told police. "She thought she had a right to pollute my air."

2. A hungry Vladimir Zhirinovsky, firebrand legislator of the Russian Parliament, cut into the buffet line at the Parliament cafeteria in 1994, loudly demanding to be served at once. Eager waitresses leaped to his side, whereupon Mark L. Goryachev, a fellow legislator from St. Petersburg, protested that he'd been waiting longer. When Zhirinovsky told his colleague to "shut up," Goryachev responded by punching him in the face. On another day— actually in the course of a single afternoon—Zhirinovsky got into a fistfight with a fellow Parliament member and shouted at another, "I'll tear your beard out hair by hair!"

   "When the president does it, that means it is not illegal."

   —Richard Nixon

3. Agence-France Presse reported in 1975 that a man in Gummersbach, Germany, was stabbed to death by his wife when she found him wiping his hands on the sheets after eating strawberries in bed.

4. On the floor of the U.S. House of Representatives in 1798, Rep. Roger Griswold of Connecticut said some unkind things about Vermont Rep. Matthew Lyon's war record. Lyon answered by spitting in Griswold's face. Two weeks later Griswold marched into the House chamber and attacked Lyon with a heavy cane; Lyon fought back with a pair of fireplace tongs. Their colleagues had to wrestle them apart.

5. In a blistering abolitionist tirade entitled "The Crime Against Kansas," Sen. Charles Sumner of Massachusetts aimed some savage barbs at Sen. Andrew Butler of South Carolina. Butler wasn't present, but his nephew, Rep. Preston Brooks, got wind of it and decided the family honor had been attacked. Showing up unannounced in the Senate chamber, he clubbed Sumner unconscious with a gutta-percha cane. Sumner's injuries kept him out of work for three years.

6. Unable to locate the show *Desert Island* on his radio, a retired vicar in London became so frustrated that he clubbed his eighty-five-year-old wife to death with a variety of household objects. "I am mad, bad, and I have murdered my wife who I loved dearly," the repentant cleric said at his trial. "She has gone to heaven and I will never see her again because I will go to hell."

7. Enraged by the constant din from a supermarket construction project in Ashiya, Japan, tavernkeeper Yotsuo Seo fatally shot the supermarket owner's sister, wounded two others, and then committed suicide by biting off his tongue.

8. Police arrested a Bensalem, Pennsylvania, man on charges of having fatally shot his friend with a bow and arrow. The two had been playing Monopoly and gotten into an argument when, according to the Bucks County district attorney, "The defendant decided he wanted to be the car [game token] rather than the thimble or hat."

9. In New York City, police arrested Albert Simon on charges of shooting his car. The vehicle had stalled out on a busy street, and while his passenger tinkered under the hood, Simon allegedly drew a gun and fired four rounds into the windshield.

10. An anesthesiologist and surgeon were each fined $10,000 by the Massachusetts State Board of Registration for fighting with each other in an operating room, while their patient lay anesthetized. In its report the board said the surgeon swore at the anesthesiologist just as the operation was about to begin. The anesthesiologist retaliated by hurling a prep stick at the surgeon, and then the two came to blows, scuffling briefly on the floor. During the fistfight a nurse monitored the elderly female patient. After the fight the two doctors attended to the patient, performing a successful operation.

Will the epidemic of violence against America's road-paving industry never end?

An intoxicated man stole a steamroller parked on a Los Angeles street in 1988. He careened into several parked cars and led police on a hair-raising 5-mile-per-hour chase before one patrolman jumped aboard and brought the vehicle to a halt. The man told officers he'd stolen the steamroller because he was "tired of walking."

If an apple a day keeps the doctor away, what does a whole pair of Fruit of the Looms get me?

Under no circumstances is it a good idea to eat your underwear. Nevertheless, that is precisely what an eighteen-year-old motorist in Stettler, Alberta, did in 1985, according to the *San Jose Mercury News.* Suspected of driving while intoxicated, the young man was pulled over to the side of the road by police and given a Breathalyzer test. While waiting in the back seat for the apparatus to be readied, he ripped out the crotch from his undershorts and ate it.

At his trial the driver testified that he had hoped the cotton would absorb the alcohol in his blood. Several spectators were so utterly convulsed with laughter that they had to be removed from the courtroom.

"ATTICA PRISON TO BE

CONVICT'S PARADISE"

—**New York Times** *headline,*
August 2, 1931

Light on his feet.

Even though it was nighttime, Charles City, Virginia, lawmen had no trouble staying with a suspected drug dealer who led them on a wild chase through the woods. The fugitive was wearing L. A. Gear Light Gear Sneakers, which are equipped with battery-powered lights that twinkle brightly whenever the foot hits the ground.

"Every time he took a step, we knew exactly where he was," one deputy said.

A photo op with hizzoner.

In Chicago's Bohemia Cemetery, two eighteen-year-olds were caught trying to dig up the body of Anton Cermak, the Chicago mayor who was shot in 1933 by a crazed vagrant. They told police they wanted to pose with the mayor for photographs.

Happy new year, Mr. President.

Two years after the close of World War I, a U.S. Army officer led a half-baked attempt to kidnap Kaiser Wilhelm and deliver him to President Wilson as a New Year's gift.

With Germany's defeat, the kaiser and his family took refuge at Amerogen, a castle in Holland owned by their friends the Betincks. Col. Luke Lea, stationed in nearby Luxembourg, enlisted seven other officers and drove across the border one night to pay the kaiser a visit. Arriving after the kaiser's bedtime, they slipped past the guards and got as far as the castle library. There they were received by Count Charles von Betinck, who politely interrogated the officers as to their intention. Just as politely, Colonel Lea explained that they'd come to confiscate the kaiser.

The count summoned the mayor of Amerogen, who brought along

several police and military guards. The Americans were scolded for their frat-house behavior and escorted to the border with a warning not to come back. The kaiser slept through the whole thing.

Later the Dutch authorities reported the offense to Gen. John J. Pershing, who had Lea and his cohorts shipped home and briefly jailed. Outwardly, Pershing expressed deep annoyance and threatened to have the officers court-martialed. But he confided to aides that he would gladly forfeit "a year's pay" to have been part of the escapade.

"I don't need bodyguards."

—Jimmy Hoffa, one week before he disappeared in 1975

The old coot would have been touched.

A name-the-new-high-school contest in Agua Dulce, California, yielded such likely entries as Magic Johnson and John Wayne. In the end the school was named for Tiburcio Velazquez, a career robber and cattle thief who was hanged in 1875 for the murder of three unarmed men.

The New York Bullet Exchange.

New York businessman Fernando Mateo scored a symbolic victory in the war against guns in 1993 by sponsoring a "Toys for Guns" exchange program. For every weapon turned in, participants received a Toys R Us gift certificate—no questions asked.

Mateo's success prompted the Federation of New York State Rifle and Pistol Clubs to launch an exchange program of its own—this one involving *bullets* for guns. Anyone owning an unregistered gun could bring it in and, with the federation's help, apply for a license. Then he would receive 1,000 free bullets.

Would the program unwittingly aid felons? No, no, insisted federation president Gerald Preiser. The idea was to supply ammunition to *good* gun owners, not bad ones. That way, "we can raise the body count of criminals," he explained.

This is your hat. This is your hat on drugs.

When his car was impounded, a Wichita Falls, Texas, man appeared at police headquarters to reclaim it. Directed to the precinct captain, he courteously removed his hat and two concealed packages of marijuana fell off his head. He was booked on the spot.

The End

Death As the Ultimate Bad Idea

Guilty — with an explanation.

Distraught over her husband's infidelities, Vera Czermak of Prague threw herself from the window of her third-floor apartment.

Her fall was broken when she landed on her husband, who was entering the building. He died instantly. She survived.

The patron saint of unsightly and embarrassing facial hair.

As a child, St. Wilgefortis was converted to Christianity and took a vow of chastity. Nonetheless, her father, the heathen King of Portugal, married her off to the King of Sicily. Wilgefortis prayed fervently for deliverance from the lascivious king, and miraculously, on her wedding day, she sprouted a full black beard and mustache.

That may have not been as good an idea as she'd hoped. While her fiancé lost interest, her father, in a rage, had her crucified.

In England, St. Wilgefortis is known as St. Uncumber, and in France she is Liberata, the patron saint of women who wish to be rid of beastly husbands. These days most hagiographers believe she never existed—that medieval clerics mistook a popular representation of Jesus Christ in a gown for a woman and created the Wilgefortis story to go with it.

An aversion to facial hair on females—especially when it sprouts suddenly—is not confined to humans. As part of a 1936 study of the courtship practices of the flicker (an American woodpecker), ornithologist G. K. Noble pasted a fake mustache on the face of a female flicker. Her mate, unable to recognize her, took her for a male challenger and attacked her.

Swimming with Brian.

A plastics firm created an inflatable, life-size replica of Brian Jones, deceased member of the Rolling Stones. The giant pool toy was designed to float facedown in the water, simulating the guitarist's suicide.

Slow-moving mourners, keep to the right.

The sting of grief is painful to bear. It should not be made sharper by the lack of adequate parking.

That's what prompted Hirschel Thompson of Atlanta to open the world's first drive-in funeral home in 1968.

The idea was simple: install the deceased behind a glass partition and allow the bereaved to file by and pay their last respects without having to leave their cars. Over the next few years, others copied the idea, according to the trade journal *Mortuary Management*. Perhaps the most successful was the Point Coupee Funeral Home, operated by Alvin and Irma Jean Verrette in New Road, Louisiana. For the convenience of time-pressed mourners, the deceased was displayed before a 5-foot by 7-foot picture window, the casket marked with a cross and framed in blue neon light. Friends and relatives could drive up to the window, pay their last respects, sign the registry, and depart—and still make it home in time for *Wheel of Fortune*.

For those with more traditional tastes, the Verrettes also offered proper sit-down funerals with all the amenities. In fact the appointments within were so tasteful that Future Young Women of America rented the place for a wine-and-cheese party.

Dear Frank: Sorry about the accident, neighbor. It's not the same without you. PS: You never returned my hedge clippers.

In the early 1980s, a California firm hired dying people as couriers to deliver memos to the dead.

Headquartered in Granada Hills, a Los Angeles suburb, the firm, Heavens Union, recruited terminally ill people to convey personal messages from this world to the next. Customers were provided with Western Union–type blank forms labeled "Heavens Union—Messages to the Hereafter." Proprietor Gabe Gabor then brought the missive to one of his stable of couriers, who would commit it to memory and agree to convey it to the addressee as soon as practical after arriving in Heaven. The price: $60 for one hundred words, $125 for priority service (whereby the message is delivered by three separate messengers to increase the likelihood of its being delivered). The courier's fee was $10 per delivery—payable to the survivor of his or her choice.

"People send messages wishing happy birthday, or saying how much they miss them, or hoping for eternal peace," Gabor told the *Washington*

Post. "We've had a number of messages to John F. Kennedy, John Lennon, and Rudolph Valentino." No deliveries to Hell or to departed pets.

"That would be making a farce of this," Gabor said.

Slander by gravestone.

Bernard Gladsky didn't consider his sister a model daughter to their father, and when the old man died, he had his feelings engraved on the gravestone:

"Death: It is what we must all come to if only we live long enough."

—David Garrick, eighteenth-century British actor and playwright

"Stanley J. Gladsky, 1895–1977, abused, robbed and starved by his beloved daughter."

His sister, Gloria Kovatch, wasn't amused. She sued her brother for libel, asking for $500,000.

Brother Bernard agreed that he might have chosen less inflammatory language, but pointed out to the court that his sister had once sent their ailing father to the hospital on a bus. Another time, doctors had told him that the elder Gladsky suffered from malnutrition and dehydration.

Maryland Superior Court awarded Mrs. Kovatch $2,000 in damages from her brother, and an additional $3,000 from the stone mason who inscribed the stone.

Eating the Bible.

When his health declined late in life, Emperor Menelik II of Ethiopia decided that noshing on a few pages torn from the Old Testament would perk him up. In December 1913, incapacitated from a stroke, he attempted to eat the entire Book of Kings, a page at a time. Poisoned by the dyes in the colored illustrations, he died in mid-meal.

He should have stayed in bed.

In the summer of 1914, Europe was a war waiting to happen when the assassination of Archduke Franz Ferdinand of Austria provided the spark that ignited the hostilities. It didn't have to happen that way, though. The archduke could have helped prolong the peace—and saved his own skin in the bargain—if only he'd had the good sense to cancel a June 28 state visit to Sarajevo, the Bosnian capital.

To make matters worse, he was dressed altogether wrong for the occasion.

Hardly a popular figure in Austrian-held Bosnia, where separatist passions ran high, Ferdinand had been urged by advisors to steer clear of Sarajevo. But

"Your medical assistance is cancelled beginning 9/24/84 because of your death."

—Letter sent by the Iowa State Department of Human Services

he and his wife, Sophie, had been there before on shopping trips and never had a moment's trouble. He saw no reasons to change his plans.

As Ferdinand's motorcade car proceeded down Appel Quay, at least six assassins lurked in the crowds. Four lost their nerve, but a fifth managed to lob a bomb onto the hood of the archduke's open touring car. Ferdinand himself flicked it off in disgust. It exploded, injuring several spectators.

Rather than heed this clear signal, Ferdinand ordered the motorcade to proceed. At a ceremony on the steps of Town Hall, he made some testy unscripted remarks about local hospitality—"We have come to Sarajevo on a visit and have had a bomb thrown at us!"—but then dropped the matter. A local official pooh-poohed Sophie's fears, assuring her that "we have not more than one murderer in Sarajevo." The motorcade continued.

The route was changed, however—but without notification to the lead driver. When he turned off Appel Quay, the archduke's driver followed, then braked and backed up onto the quay again. Gavril Prinzip, the sixth assassin, had already given up trying to nail the archduke and gone for coffee instead. Given a second chance, he fired at Ferdinand and Sophie.

Struck in the neck, there is no way the archduke could have survived. But his obsessive fastidiousness didn't help his cause: All the buttonholes of his starched military uniform had been sewn shut for a neat, wrinkle-free appearance. By the time doctors could loosen his clothes to treat him, he had bled to death.

Puppy chow.

In 1971, Reuters reported, Hans and Erna W., a Swiss couple vacationing in Hong Kong, stopped to eat at a restaurant and asked the headwaiter to take their poodle into the kitchen and feed her. But the waiter misunderstood their request and returned some time later bearing a round-bottom frying pan in which the animal had been deep fried, bathed in sweet-and-sour sauce, and garnished with bamboo shoots and snow peas. The meal was left uneaten, and the W.'s were treated for shock.

Death by public relations.

On the night of January 20, 1936, King George V lay near death at Sandringham, the royal residence. His wife, his heir, the Archbishop of Canterbury, and his personal physician, Sir Bertrand Dawson, were at his side.

Around 11:00 P.M., Dawson injected the seventy-year-old monarch with morphine and cocaine. Death came fifty-five minutes later.

Euthanasia was illegal in Great Britain at the time; it still is. Small wonder that Dawson, who died in 1945, carried his secret to his grave. His actions, recorded in his diary, were first disclosed in a 1986 article in the journal

History Today. "It was evident that the last stage might endure for many hours," he wrote. "I therefore decided to determine the end."

However, what he did wasn't really euthanasia but savvy public relations—and, some say, murder. Dawson, ever the loyal retainer, could not abide the thought that the first accounts of his master's demise would appear in London's lurid evening tabloids. So he timed the king's death to give the more respectable morning papers a scoop.

> **"LUCKY MAN SEES PALS DIE."**
>
> —*Headline in the* **Baltimore News American**

Indeed, just after dispatching George, Dawson telephoned the editor of the *Times* of London to stand by for an announcement. The headline in the next morning's edition was "A PEACEFUL ENDING AT MIDNIGHT."

For many years afterwards, George was reported to have looked up at his physician moments before the end and said, "How stands the Empire?" A nice exit line—but, according to Dawson, the king said nothing of the sort. His final words, just before the syringe pierced his jugular vein, were, "Goddamn you."

George's final hours might have passed a bit more comfortably for him but for a foolish fancy of his father and predecessor, Edward VII. An ardent huntsman, Edward had all the clocks at Sandringham—there were hundreds—permanently set half an hour ahead in order to gain extra hunting time in the morning, and to trick his guests into rising early.

No one bothered to set the clocks back after he died, or until the night of George's death, when the discrepancy resulted in some minor mismanagement of his medication. When the Prince of Wales—soon to become Edward VIII—realized the reason for the mistake, he flew into a rage. Screaming, "I'll fix those bloody clocks," he ordered the chief clockmaker to restore every last clock to real time at once. It took him until dawn.

Death by enema.

The death of King Charles II of England in 1685 is commonly attributed to a cerebral hemorrhage. But in all probability it was the treatment for the malady that finished the monarch off. Instead of summoning the royal physicians, Charles would have been better off brewing himself a pot of Earl Grey tea and gutting it out.

Upon arrival in the royal chambers, the physicians—actually, a committee of twelve—immediately began an exhaustive treatment to flush all impurities from the king's body. First they drained off nearly a quart of blood; next they fed him massive doses of emetics to make him vomit up the toxins, along with everything else in his digestive tract. Just to be sure, they purged his intestines with a jolting fourteen-ingredient enema. Still, the king did not improve.

> "It is deplorable to think of a parish where there are 30,000 people living without a Christian burial."
>
> —*Anonymous British clergyman (nineteenth century)*

Over the next few days, the doctors shaved Charles' scalp and singed it with irons, forced vile substances up his nose to induce sneezing, blanketed him with hot mustard plasters that they then tore off, and administered another series of potent enemas, one of which bore fruit sixteen times in the night. Otherwise, no improvement. When the patient complained of a sore throat and suffered cold sweats, the medics daubed his feet with an emollient of resin and pigeon feces.

Meanwhile Charles continued to sink. Frantically, the doctors bled him, drilled holes in his skull, and pumped him full of purgatives, cathartics, and rock-shivering enemas. On the fifth day, apologizing for taking so long to die, Charles expired. He was fifty-four.

Death of a peacemaker.

Alexander became king at age twenty-four in 1917 when his father, King Constantine, was forced by the Allies to abdicate to permit Greece's entry into World War I. Alas, he ruled only three years. At Tatoi Palace in October 1920, the king was bitten on his royal nose while rashly attempting to break up a fight between his pet dog and monkey. He died of blood poisoning three weeks later. Rumors that the monkey had been secretly injected with rabies toxin by the king's enemies were never substantiated.

If it works for Folgers and Ted Williams, why not for house pets?

When her cat, Felix, was squashed by an eighteen-wheel tractor trailer, Mrs. Ormae Lewis of Bedford, Ohio, saw no reason to bury, burn, or otherwise dispose of the remains. Instead, she had him freeze-dried with a machine formerly owned by a coffee processor.

Mrs. Lewis was delighted with the result, according to the *Washington Post*. "He's just like he was in real life except he's a little flatter in the middle," she said. Dr. Marshall Pettibone, who rendered the service, reflected on the benefits of freeze-drying for animals.

"There's no sense in getting a new cat every ten years or so," he said, "when you can have the same one for fifty or sixty years."

Rank idiocy.

In a 2002 opinion poll conducted by U.K. History Channel, Britons ranked the death of Princess Diana in 1997 as the most significant event in British history during the preceding century. The start of World War II placed second; the end of World War I came in fifth.

The book that made suicide fashionable.

After being spurned by one young woman too many, the poet Johann Wolfgang von Goethe worked out his grief by writing *The Sorrows of Young Werther*, a novel about an unrequited young lover who kills himself. Goethe, who was twenty-five, would have been better off getting stinking drunk or writing a few reams of bad poetry. The book inspired an unprecedented rash of suicides all over Europe.

Actually the suicides were only the most lurid of the *Werther* spinoffs. The most popular cult novel ever, the 1774 work was translated into every European language including Icelandic and Catalan, and gave rise to snuff boxes, lacquered vases, dinnerware, and sundry tchotchkes depicting scenes from the book. *Werther* spoofs, knockoffs, songs, critiques, and sequels became a small but immensely profitable industry. And young men took to dressing like Werther in blue frock coats and beige vests, starving themselves into anorectic gauntness, and staging their own deaths with grand Wertherian flourishes. One Werther freak donned fresh clothes, shaved, braided his hair into a Wertherlike pigtail, and opened his copy of *Werther* to the page where the hero takes his life. He stepped outside his front door, waited for a small crowd to form, and shot himself in the eye.

> **"Well, that kind of puts a damper on even a Yankee win."**
>
> —*New York Yankee announcer Phil Rizzuto on the news that Pope Paul VI had died*

Clerics and teachers denounced the book, and several cities banned its sale. Roman Catholic clerics in Milan bought up every copy of the book they could find in Italian translation and destroyed them. One politician commented, "A fellow who shoots himself for the sake of a girl he cannot sleep with is a fool, and one fool, more or less, in the world is of no consequence." But the *Werther* craze lasted more than a decade, and considerably more than one fool died along the way. Said an unrepentant Goethe, "If my life were at stake, I would not suppress *Werther.*"

A popular but unrelentingly depressing ballad entitled "Gloomy Sunday," better known as "The Hungarian Suicide Song," is said to have inspired eighteen young people to take their lives in Budapest in 1936. In 1968 the composer of the song, Rezo Seress, leaped to his death from his apartment window.

Death as a theme park.

The ancient Egyptians had the right idea: Instead of deep-sixing the dead, warehouse them aboveground in giant pyramids. Not only does this method prevent annoying underground seepage and leave more room to dispose of toxic waste, it makes a nifty tourist attraction.

In 1994 a company called Pyramids Unlimited attempted to do in Florida what the pharaohs did in Giza: construct twin 495-foot-high pyramidal burial vaults, each big enough to hold 300,000 bodies. The $200-million complex would include a visitor center, meditation room, and glassed-in funeral chapels with a panoramic view.

"We're not talking some tacky mall here," insisted Pyramid Unlimited executive Ben Everidge. But the zoning board of at least one central Florida town—Bushnell—declined the honor of providing the site of the state's first mausoleum-theme park. Area sightseers will have to detour to Disneyworld, about an hour away.

The Timisis Deathclock.

Ever wonder about how much time you've got left before the fat person sings? Well, stop wondering and invest $99.95 in the Timisis Lifeclock. "Enter your name, gender and age," says the catalog from Amertel Corp. "This microcomputer clock then counts down the actual hours, minutes and seconds remaining in your lifetime."

Do the folks at Amertel know something you don't—like the exact moment you're fated to ski off the edge of the beginner's slope at Gstaad or succumb to some as-yet-undiscovered disease? Hardly. The time allotment indicated by the Lifeclock is based on the average life expectancy of a person the same age and sex as you. Which would imply that if you outlive the countdown, your money should be cheerfully refunded to you—or to your estate, should you expire prematurely.

About the Author

Bruce Felton has written for numerous magazines, contributed to *The People's Almanac* and *The Book of Lists,* served as a Peace Corps volunteer in Borneo, and placed 24,926th in the 1992 NYC Marathon. He is the author of four other books, including *Famous Americans You Never Knew Existed* and *One of a Kind: A Compendium of Unique People, Places, and Things.* He lives in New York City.

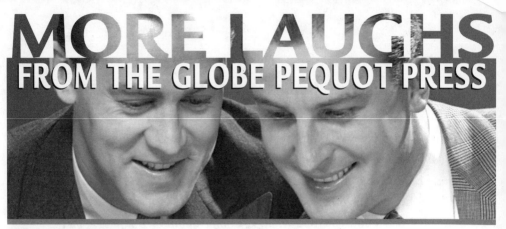

MORE LAUGHS
FROM THE GLOBE PEQUOT PRESS

THE WOLF FILES
Strange News from a Strange Planet
By Buck Wolf
ISBN 0-7627-2853-1 · $14.95

Laugh along with humor columnist Buck Wolf as he comments on weird news and the outer fringe of pop culture. As featured on abcnews.com.

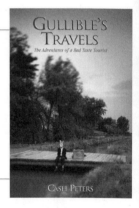

GULLIBLE'S TRAVELS
The Adventures of a Bad Taste Tourist
By Cash Peters
ISBN 0-7627-2714-4 · $16.95

Fans of Cash Peters' "Bad Taste Tours" on public radio hail this outrageously funny collection of essays about his experiences traveling to and reporting on the most bizarre and tacky tourist attractions across the United States.

THE CURIOSITIES SERIES
Quirky Characters, Roadside Oddities, and Other Offbeat Stuff

In this sassy series of more than twenty state-almanacs-gone-astray, prominent humor writers, columnists, and media personalities comb their home states for the most wacky and outrageous people, places, and things. Discover places overlooked on school field trips, people with odd and amazing talents, history left out of the books—a wealth of weird wonders most residents never dreamed existed!

Available from your favorite bookseller or at www.GlobePequot.com